PUBLIC SCHOOL EDUCATION IN NORTH CAROLINA

BY

EDGAR W. KNIGHT, Ph.D.

NEGRO UNIVERSITIES PRESS
NEW YORK

Originally published in 1916
by Houghton Mifflin Co., Boston

Reprinted 1969 by
Negro Universities Press
A DIVISION OF GREENWOOD PUBLISHING CORP.
NEW YORK

SBN 8371-1846-8

PRINTED IN UNITED STATES OF AMERICA

TO
MY MOTHER AND MY FATHER

PREFACE

THAT the history of education, as a subject which contributes to the professional training and equipment of teachers, has been on trial for its life, no serious student of the subject will undertake to deny. Some of the charges made against it have been grave enough to cause the real services of the subject to be honestly questioned by many of its ardent students and supporters. In fact, the conviction has grown in recent years, even among those engaged in the professional preparation of teachers, that the history of educational theory and practice needed to justify itself. As a result, its place in the curriculum of institutions devoted to the training of teachers has been challenged by subjects of a character more popularly accepted as utilitarian and immediately useful as pedagogical tools.

But the critics have served a useful purpose, and their charges against the history of education have tended to strengthen its cause and to increase its champions. In this respect its career bears a striking likeness to that of general history, which likewise tardily found a place in the curriculum. The more remote its interests and the more encyclopædic its completeness, the more worthy history was once esteemed, not so much for its practical value in interpreting present-day conditions and tendencies as for its alluring and fascinating character. For generations the results were far from wholesome and safe. To-day, however, the historical point of view is becoming more and more rationalized, narrowness and provincialism are decreasing, and a keener and more lively interest in human affairs is steadily developing.

A similar reform has been demanded of the history of education. In this subject a student might become an able expositor of the educational theories of Plato, Aristotle, Rabelais, Herbart, and Spencer, and discuss creditably the principal features of ancient school systems, without being able to recognize tendencies in modern education, detect an educational fad, or explain the manner of raising school finances or of electing local school officers. Gradually, therefore, it has become necessary to present the subject so as to impel a more complete analysis of modern educational problems and a clearer and more rational understanding of those practices with which the teachers themselves are constantly concerned.

In this conception of the value of the subject may be found the chief purpose of this book. The author believes that a study of the educational conditions of the past, which are often in striking contrast to present conditions, will help teachers and educational administrators to a more satisfactory understanding of the present situation, and assist in breaking up a complacent acceptance of those practices which are more traditional than rational. This report of public educational progress in North Carolina has been prepared in the hope that it may be of real service to teachers, on whom the burden of educational advancement so largely rests, and to whom every possible encouragement, inspiration, and support should be given in their work of disseminating intelligence.

The author has undertaken to include in the book

PREFACE

historical material sufficient to aid the reader and student to draw correct conclusions concerning the subject. An effort has also been made to make clear the relation between social and economic forces and educational development; to show how the ideals of a people are reflected in their school system; and to suggest relations between present educational problems and current educational practices so many of which have been traditionally received. There would be less excuse for such a book if there were already accessible to teachers and the general reader any complete story of public education in the State. Parts of two chapters were first published in the *South Atlantic Quarterly* and in the *North Carolina Booklet* and are here included through the courtesy of the editors of those publications. In order that the entire work may later be relieved of its inaccuracies the author will welcome any criticisms concerning it.

To my colleagues and former teachers, Professor Eugene C. Brooks, of the Department of Education, and Professor William K. Boyd, of the Department of History, in Trinity College, I am especially indebted; to the former for first stimulating my interest in educational history, and to the latter for arousing my interest in North Carolina and Southern history, and to both for constant encouragement and advice and for sympathetic interest and assistance in the present work. I also acknowledge my indebtedness to my former teacher, Professor Paul Monroe, of Columbia University, whose scholarly advice has all along encouraged my historical and educational studies. To Dr. James Y. Joyner, state superintendent of public instruction, I am indebted for the concluding chapter and for his kindly interest in the entire book. I am also indebted to Professor N. W.

Walker, state inspector of high schools and Professor of Secondary Education in the University of North Carolina, for suggestions concerning, and assistance in the treatment of, secondary education, in Chapter XVI, and for reading a part of the proof; to Mr. E. E. Sams, state supervisor of teacher-training, Professor L. A. Williams, of the University of North Carolina, Professor C. W. Wilson, of the East Carolina Teachers' Training School, and Superintendent Samuel B. Underwood, of the Pitt County Schools, I am indebted for examining the manuscript and for making helpful suggestions. To my wife, Annie Turner Knight, I am indebted for assistance in reading the proof and in the preparation of the index.

EDGAR W. KNIGHT.

Trinity College
Durham, North Carolina
August, 1916

CONTENTS

I. Under the Lords Proprietors	1
II. The Apprenticeship System	14
III. Under Royal Rule	32
IV. The Academy Movement	44
V. The Early Agitation (1776–1825)	63
VI. The Literary Fund	84
VII. Growth of Educational Sentiment (1825–1837)	113
VIII. The Beginnings of Public Education (1838–1852)	138
IX. The Educational Revival under Wiley (1853–1865)	158
X. Ante-Bellum Educational Practice	192
XI. The Beginnings of Reconstruction	212
XII. Education during Reconstruction	238
XIII. The Work and Influence of the Peabody Fund	271
XIV. Attempts at Readjustment (1877–1900)	294
XV. Aycock and the Revival (1900–1910)	329
XVI. The Present System: Its Tasks and Tendencies	345
XVII. What of the Future?	368
Index	375

PUBLIC SCHOOL EDUCATION IN NORTH CAROLINA

CHAPTER I

UNDER THE LORDS PROPRIETORS

ALTHOUGH North Carolina developed before 1860 the most creditable system of public education to be found in any of the States which seceded from the Union, her intellectual and educational growth was very slow during the colonial period. This slowness was due to the conditions under which the colony was settled — conditions which naturally lent themselves very sparingly to educational enterprises. Especially is this true of the period from 1663, when settlements first began to be made in the region around Albemarle Sound, to 1728, when the transfer from proprietary to royal ownership of the colony was made.

The earliest settlers in North Carolina migrated from the northern colony of Virginia from 1650 to 1675, not as religious refugees, but principally for economic advantage. After 1663, however, when the intolerant and illegal government of Berkeley in Virginia was resisted by Bacon's rebellion, some came for political reasons, and North Carolina soon found herself accommodating "rogues, runaways, and rebels" who refused to tolerate Berkeley and his tyranny. But the colony grew exceedingly slowly, although in 1670 immigrants were encouraged by the promise of the Assembly of exemption from taxation for one year and protection for five years from suits for debts made before coming into the colony. Even these attractions, however, induced but few. When William Drummond was appointed the first "governor of Albemarle," in 1663, his commission extended over sixteen hundred square miles of territory which was so sparsely settled that there were perhaps not more than fifteen hundred people in the entire settlement. In 1675 there were probably four thousand people in the colony, less than three to a square mile. In 1728 the entire population was not more than ten thousand. Immigration before 1728, therefore, must have been very slight.[1]

This slow growth of population is but one explanation of the colony's slow educational development. From the beginning of the colony the tendency was necessarily toward rural rather than urban communities, the mild climate and the fertile soil both contributing to a stimulation of rural life. The earliest settlers took up large tracts of land on the water-courses, which furnished practically the only means of communication, and agriculture soon became the most promising pursuit of the colonists. The dangerous coasts and poor harbors made the colony difficult of access and retarded the commercial interests of the people. Moreover, there were frequent complaints against the unsatisfactory government, and conflicts between the inhabitants and the proprietors, or their representatives, "who reckoned the lives of the colonists only in quitrents and taxes." Occasional religious dissensions and a scarcity of teachers

[1] Weeks, *Libraries and Literature in North Carolina in the Eighteenth Century*, in House Documents, vol. 62.

may also be noted as other conditions unfavorable to educational and intellectual activity.

Likewise, the need for schools and education was not keenly felt by those in authority. The educational philosophy of seventeenth-century England, "that the great body of the people were to obey and not to govern, and that the social status of unborn generations was already fixed," was now, as at a later time, widespread and persistent. This was the philosophy, not only for the colonies, but for the mother country as well. As late as the beginning of the nineteenth century it was held by many that the surest way to serve the public welfare was by keeping great numbers of the people "ignorant as well as poor. Knowledge both enlarges and multiplies our desires, and the few things man wishes for, the more easily his necessity may be supplied." [1] This is an argument which has been frequently used to defeat universal public education.[2]

A few teachers gradually found their way into the colony, however. The first of these were the lay readers appointed in the churches built by the early settlers. In the charter which granted Carolina to Robert Heath in 1629, provisions were made for the establishment of a State Church, and these provisions were continued in the charters to the lords proprietors in 1663 and 1665. The first practical effort to build up a State Church in the colony came with the Vestry Act of 1701. The first preacher of the English Church arrived about 1703 and the first churches were built a few years later. By the Vestry Act of 1715 the colony was divided into nine parishes and vestrymen were appointed in each. Provi-

[1] See p. 68, note.
[2] Adams, *History of the Elementary School Contest in England*, p. 46.

sion was made for the purchase of glebe lands, for the employment and support of ministers, and for general church organization.

Brickell, writing of North Carolina in the early eighteenth century, said: —

> The religion by law established is the Protestant, as it is professed in England, and though they seldom have orthodox clergymen among them, yet there are not only glebe lands laid out for that use commodious to each town, but likewise for building churches. The want of these Protestant clergy is generally supplied by some schoolmasters who read the Liturgy, and then a sermon out of Dr. Tillotson or some good practical divine every Sunday. These are the most numerous and are dispersed through the whole province.[1]

But this establishment of the English Church was not altogether an advantage to education, even though perhaps many if not all of the schoolmasters in the colony were its missionaries, ministers, or lay readers. Dissenters, especially Baptists and Quakers, were numerous in the colony and sternly opposed the regulations of the establishment. The troubles which naturally arose resulted in a lack of union in educational ideals and practices. After the transfer to royal control in 1729, the instructions to the governors, beginning with George Burrington in 1730 and continuing for many years, proved retarding to educational development. By these instructions North Carolina, already under the ecclesiastical control of the English Church, was seriously hampered in the case of school-teachers: —

> And we do further direct that no Schoolmaster be henceforth permitted to come from the Kingdom and to keep school in that our said Province without the license of the Lord

---

[1] *Natural History of North Carolina*, p. 35.

Bishop of London, and that no other person now there or that shall come from other parts shall be admitted to keep school in North Carolina without your license first obtained.[1]

These instructions to Burrington practically reproduced that tyrannical measure known as the English Schism Act of 1714, which deprived dissenters of the means of providing educational facilities for their own children. By it no one was allowed to teach in a public or private school or to give instruction in any form without first securing the privilege from the Bishop of London. This reproduced Schism Act seems to have been enforced in the colony at least three times after it was repealed in England, in a school at Newbern in 1766, at Edenton in 1768, and in the case of Queen's Museum, at Charlotte, in 1773. The repeal of the act in England only makes its reënactment for the colony the more exasperating. School-teachers were few enough in North Carolina during the whole period of its colonial existence. Of those who did appear, some, no doubt, were dissenters; but with fiendish atrocity the English Government closes to them the avenue to greater usefulness. This is the greeting which the royal government sends out to the daughter rejoicing in her recent escape from the rule of the proprietors. This was the precious heritage with which the first royal governor comes out to meet the subjects who had thrown off the rule of the proprietors and claimed the king's protection. It seemed that the new government was to be worse than the old, for the royal government now took the lead in ecclesiastical legislation and had, unfortunately, a large following in the colony.[2]

In spite of the ecclesiastical evils which followed the establishment of the English Church in North Carolina, however, the intellectual and educational life of the col-

[1] *Col. Rec.*, vol. III, pp. 110, 111.
[2] Weeks, *Church and State in North Carolina*, pp. 24, 25.

ony was somewhat encouraged and assisted by it. Almost simultaneously with its establishment, the Society for the Propagation of the Gospel in Foreign Parts began its educational labors in the colony. This organization was one of the most prominent of the charitable and religious agencies which assisted education in most of the English colonies. It was formed in London by royal charter in 1701 to aid the Established Church in its colonial possessions, in supplying better-trained ministers, in establishing and reviving churches, and in training children in church doctrine as well as in other subjects. The membership of the organization was made up largely of prelates, the clergy, and the more influential laity. Funds for its maintenance and work were secured by subscriptions, bequests, donations, royal benefactions, and frequent church contributions. From 1701 to 1780 the Society spent more than £230,000 in its work in the colonies of America. Of the Southern colonies, South Carolina received the greatest attention.

The missionaries of the Society "brought with them the first parish or public libraries and its lay readers were the first teachers." Charles Griffin, who in 1705 came from the West Indies and settled in Pasquotank, is said to have been the first professional teacher in the colony. Here he taught school three years and with such success that even the Quakers patronized him. In 1708 his school was transferred to a missionary of the Society for the Propagation of the Gospel in Foreign Parts, the Reverend James Adams, who had settled in that community. Griffin later went to Chowan, where he became reader of the vestry, and conducted a school for one year. In 1709 he became a Quaker. Ten years later he probably taught a school for Indians in Christina, Virginia, and later still he probably became a professor in William and Mary College.[1]

A few others were also engaged in teaching in the colony during the proprietary period. One of these, Mashburn by name, had a school at Sarum near the Virginia border in 1712, and his work was so well thought of that he deserved compensation by the Society. "What children he has under his care can both write and read very distinctly," wrote the Reverend Giles Rainsford, "and gave before me such an account of the grounds and principles of the Christian religion that it strangely surprised me to hear it." Rainsford believed that Mashburn's work should be encouraged.

Not only did the Society furnish teachers, but its missionaries gave books for the use of the pupils and also established parish or public libraries. The first of these public libraries was made possible by the Reverend Thomas Bray, founder and one of the leaders of the Society, and later the Bishop of London's commissary in Maryland. He came to America in March, 1700. The establishment of libraries soon became a part of his larger scheme of educational and religious activity in the colonies, and during his work here he helped to establish thirty-nine or more, many of them with more than one thousand volumes.

The only library which Dr. Bray gave to North Carolina was established in Bath, which was made a township about 1705. Here it seems not to have been properly cared for and used, and in 1712 the Reverend Giles Rainsford said that the books were lost "by those wretches that do not consider the benefit of so valuable

[1] Weeks, *Libraries and Literature in North Carolina*, in House Documents, vol. 62, p. 175, note.

a gift"; and two years later John Urmstone, that quarrelsome, haughty, and notoriously wicked clergyman of the English Church whose career in the colony was a constant reproach, stated that the "famous library sent in by Dr. Bray's directions is, in a great measure, destroyed. I am told the books are all unbound and have served for some time as waste paper."

Urmstone's statements are probably incorrect, however, because in 1715 there was passed the only act during the proprietary period which looked to an encouragement of literature, and this looked to the preservation of the library. This law is very similar to one passed on the same subject in South Carolina in 1700, concerning which Dr. Weeks says: "Is it not possible that a draft of the act was sent over with the books, filled out in the province, and passed in each near the same time? I am inclined to think that the North Carolina act was several years old in 1715." [1]

Fear that the books of the library "will quickly be embezzled, damaged, or lost" led to the passage of the law "for the more effectual preservation of the same." By this act provision was made for the appointment of a librarian who was to become responsible for the books, and be "bound and obliged to keep and preserve the several and respective books therein, from waste, damage, embezzlement, and all other destruction," and to give for them two receipts, one to the library commissioners and one to the church wardens. The library was not to be moved from Bath. Books could be borrowed by giving a receipt for them, "with a promise to return the said book or books, if a folio, in four months' time;

[1] *Libraries and Literature in North Carolina*, in House Documents, vol. 62, pp. 179, 180, and note.

if a quarto, in two months' time; if an octavo, or under, in one month's time; upon penalty of paying three times the value of the said book or books so borrowed, in case of failure in returning the same." Catalogues of all the books were to be made, and the commissioners every Easter Monday were to examine the catalogues to see that no books were lost.

What the library contained, who the librarians were, how extensively the books were used, and what disposition was finally made of them are questions about which little or nothing is known. With the exception of the law of 1715 there is no further record of the library. One view held is that the books finally came into the hands of Edward Moseley and were the same as those he gave to Edenton eight years later.[1]

There were a few other parish libraries in the colony before 1729, the end of proprietary control. All the missionaries of the Society for the Propagation of the Gospel had books which were not only of service to them, but were perhaps intended for a limited use among the people in educating them in the orthodox faith. Most of these books were religious and doctrinal. Among these missionaries whose supply of books was more or less adequate were the Reverends James Adams, Giles Rainsford, John Urmstone, Ebenezer Taylor, and William Gordon. Through some of these men tracts were distributed and frequently "some books for the use of scholars." The missionaries occasionally received new supplies of books from the Society. Only a few books were sent over, however, during the closing years of proprietary control and but few during the early years of royal rule. During the middle and latter part of royal

[1] See p. 10.

rule, however, new interest was taken in this phase of the work of the Society and many books were received in the colony. This part of the Society's activity must be highly praised, for through it opportunity was given to cultivate a taste for books and to foster an educational sentiment which was beginning to show slight growth.

The establishment of a library in Edenton by Edward Moseley, for nearly half a century the leading figure in the life of the colony, is one of the few notable efforts of the period to encourage education. In 1720 he sent some money to the secretary of the Society for the Propagation of the Gospel with the instruction that it be spent for some useful books for use in Chowan, but the Society seems to have taken no notice of his request and the books were never received. Three years later he sent to the secretary a list of books which he had collected in America with the request that the Society accept them as the nucleus of a provincial library to be established in Edenton. The books, which were worth several hundred dollars, were mostly religious and scholastic and largely in Latin, Greek, or Hebrew. There were listed twenty-six folio volumes, twelve quarto volumes, and thirty-eight octavo volumes. There is no evidence that the Society ever accepted Moseley's gift, and the books probably remained in his private collection, which at his death in 1749 numbered four hundred volumes. Many of these were folios and bound in sheep.

Perhaps the most complete and representative colonial library of North Carolina was the collection of Samuel Johnston (1733–1816), the beginning of which was made by Governor Eden (1673–1722), whose daughter, Penelope, married Governor Gabriel Johnston. At the death of Governor Johnston in 1752 the library passed to his nephew, Samuel. The collection, as made by Eden, Gabriel Johnston, and Samuel Johnston, consisted of history and politics, biography, travels, philosophy, the classics, science and medicine, law, domestic affairs and agriculture, theology and sermons, essays and miscellaneous literature, encyclopædias, grammars, poetry and the drama — in all perhaps more than five hundred volumes.

In the eastern part of the colony there were many other less important private libraries which are evidence of a degree of culture not often believed to have existed in North Carolina in the eighteenth century. This section of the colony was the first part to be settled and was more or less representative of English culture. The libraries of James Innes, of John Hodgson, James Iredell, William Hooper, Archibald Maclaine, Joseph Gantier, Willie Jones, of Halifax County, John Burgwin, William Cathcart, and others were more or less important, however, as reflecting educational conditions in the eastern and older section of the colony which was settled largely by the English. In the western section, where many Scotch and Scotch-Irish emigrated after 1746, there was evidence also of intellectual activity. Libraries existed here as in the eastern section, and many of the settlers were educated and cultured. The influence of Princeton College, to be noted later, from which many preachers and teachers came, soon came to be extensive and powerful. Among those of this region who had valuable collections of books may be mentioned, Waightstill Avery, the Reverend David Caldwell, the Reverend James Hall, the Reverend John Barr, the founder of the Thyatira Circulating Library, Joseph

Graham, the Reverend Henry Patillo, and others. Circulating libraries were founded in some of the counties and seem to have been extensively used.[1]

In the eastern section especially, the Established Church doubtless assisted somewhat in furnishing the few teachers who were at work before 1729. Through it and its adjunct organization, the Society for the Propagation of the Gospel in Foreign Parts, books and tracts were distributed among the parishioners and furnished to the children. But the work of the Society was slight in North Carolina as compared with its achievements in the colony of South Carolina. More could perhaps have been accomplished in North Carolina if the reproduced Schism Act had not been applied and if the dissenters had not been unfortunately alienated. Little common religion resulted in lack of union in educational matters. Moreover, the people were not homogeneous and a long time was required to fuse the many diverse elements of the population. The well-to-do were provided for by a form of tutorial instruction, but schools and the means of education for the less fortunate classes were few. However, in spite of the conditions which retarded public schools for the masses, local efforts were occasionally made for a form of education which was more or less popular for many years. The chief of these efforts was that of the poor law and apprenticeship system, the operation of which will be considered in the following chapter.

[1] Weeks, *Libraries and Literature in North Carolina*.

REFERENCES

The Colonial Records of North Carolina; Brickell, *A Natural History of North Carolina;* Weeks, *Church and State in North Carolina, Libraries and Literature in North Carolina in the Eighteenth Century, The Religious Development in the Province of North Carolina,* and *Calvin Henderson Wiley and the Organization of the Common Schools of North Carolina;* Smith, *History of Education in North Carolina;* Kemp, *The Support of Schools in Colonial New York by the S. P. G.;* Lecky, *History of England in the Eighteenth Century,* vol. I; Hawks, *History of North Carolina;* Foote, *Sketches of North Carolina; Cyclopedia of Education,* edited by Paul Monroe, vol. II, article, "Colonial Period in American Education."

SUGGESTIONS FOR FURTHER STUDY

1. What were some of the natural obstacles in the way of educational development in North Carolina during the early history of the colony?
2. Compare the economic and social conditions of North Carolina with those of the New England colonies.
3. Compare the early settlers of North Carolina with those of the other American colonies with respect to origin, religious and economic conditions.
4. What was the condition of education in England when settlements began to be made in America?
5. How did this condition affect the educational ideals and practices of the colonists?
6. In what way did the Established Church aid education in North Carolina? In what way did it retard educational progress?
7. What was the purpose of the Society for the Propagation of the Gospel in Foreign Parts?
8. Illustrate by the early history of North Carolina how educational conditions are the result of social and economic forces.
9. How are the ideals of a people reflected in their educational practices?

CHAPTER II

THE APPRENTICESHIP SYSTEM

JUST as our modern public-school system cannot be adequately understood except in the light of colonial conditions, so also must colonial custom and practice be explained in view of European antecedents. This applies to education in all the English colonies, and especially in Virginia and the Carolinas, where the general mental attitude toward education in colonial days was similar to that of the mother country. Here the English spirit was everywhere in evidence. The dominating influences were here, as in England, more or less aristocratic; and these produced a tardiness and indifference to so-called popular education. In actual practice the tutor or the small school, or, as in not a few cases, education in England, was the rule of the well-to-do. The less prosperous classes were cared for educationally through poor-relief and apprenticeship laws after the manner of the mother country. A brief consideration of this practice is now in order.

The poor-law and the apprenticeship system not only had their foundations in similar laws and practices in England, but in many cases the legislation was directly taken over, certainly adapted, from the principles found in the famous series of poor-relief and apprenticeship statutes which developed in England during the second half of the sixteenth century.[1] Legislation of this kind

[1] "Be it therefore enacted by the authoritie of this Grand Assembly, according to the aforesayd laudable custom in the Kingdom of Eng-

THE APPRENTICESHIP SYSTEM

seemed necessary in order to take care of the gradually increasing dependent class, a group made up of journeymen, apprentices, vagrants, "thieves and sturdy beggars," whose wages, employment, or migration was in almost every case determined by some one of the upper classes of English population. Caring for this dependent element was an immense task. The suppression of English monasteries by Henry VIII and Edward VI, on the alleged ground of negligence and certain forms of irreligion and immorality, destroyed many facilities and important agencies for poor relief and elementary education.[1] Elizabeth undertook to make amends for these acts of destruction to monasteries and guilds, by a series of poor-relief and apprenticeship enactments which culminated in the oft-cited law of 1601, which remained in force in England until the early part of the nineteenth century.[2] The execution and enforcement of these acts, however, were placed in the hands of local justices of the peace, who were country gentlemen. It should be noted at this point that many of the early colonists were of this class and were trained in the interpretation and

land . . ." is now and then a part of the preamble of some of the early Virginia acts on which similar acts in the colony of North Carolina were based. The influence of the legislation in Virginia, based on the laws in England, is seen in North Carolina throughout the colonial period.

[1] Leach, *English Schools at the Reformation*. It is said that as many as one thousand foundations were destroyed — about ten million dollars in the present valuation. By the law of 1536 (27 Henry VIII, c. 28) all monasteries were to be "given to the King, which have not lands above 200*l*. by the year." By the law of 1546 (37 Henry VIII, c. 4) "all colleges, chantries, free chapels, etc., shall be in the King's Majesty's disposition." By the law of 1547 (1 Edward VI, c. 14) the statute of 37 Henry VIII was somewhat revised and redracted. See *English Statutes at Large*, vols. 4 and 5.

[2] 43 Elizabeth, c. 2. *English Statutes at Large*, vol. 7, pp. 30–37. This is the real statutory foundation of the poor law system.

administration of these laws. This was especially true of Virginia, and the influence of that colony on North Carolina was far-reaching in the matter of the poor and apprenticeship system.[1]

By the law of 1601 the church wardens of every parish, and two, three, or four "substantial householders there," depending on the size of the parish, were to be nominated annually, at Easter or one month thereafter, by the justices of the peace, to be called "overseers of the poor." These officers were to give attention to

setting to work the children of all such whose parents shall not ... be thought able to maintain their children, ... and also to raise weekly or otherwise (by taxation of every inhabitant, parson, vicar, and other, and of every occupier of lands, houses, tithes impropriate, propriations of tithes, coal mines, or saleable underwoods in the said parish, in such competent sum or sums of money as they shall see fit) a convenient stock of flax, hemp, wool, thread, iron, and necessary ware and stuff, to set the poor to work: and also competent sums of money for ... putting out of such children as apprentices, to be gathered out of the same parish, according to the ability of the same parish. ...

These overseers were to meet monthly on Sunday afternoon, after divine service, "to consider some good course to be taken." They were to give a true and perfect account of all moneys received by them, or of all stock, and of "all the things concerning their said office." A penalty of twenty shillings was prescribed for every case of negligence or default on the part of the overseers, and imprisonment was prescribed for the overseers who refused "to account." Whenever the justices of the peace found that the inhabitants of any parish were

[1] An illuminating discussion of the English system of poor and apprenticeship laws may be had in Sir George Nicholls's *A History of the English Poor-Law*.

unable to relieve their poor, the justices were to "tax, rate, and assess as aforesaid," any other parishes in "the hundred where the said parish is." In case the hundred was not regarded as able to bear the tax, the justices, at their quarter sessions, were to rate and assess other parishes "within the said county" for the purpose of the law. Those people who refused to pay their assessment saw their property sold for the rate.

Other duties of the church wardens and overseers of the poor were to bind as apprentices the children affected by this act, the males until they were twenty-four years of age, and the females until they were twenty-one, or until the time of their marriage; and to have houses built on "any waste or common" in the parish at the "general charges of the parish" as habitations for the poor. Powers similar to those given to justices of the peace were given to officers of towns and corporations. Justices in the county and officers in the towns who failed regularly to nominate the overseers of the poor were to "lose and forfeit for every such default five pounds."

The system of poor-relief and apprenticeship thus built up in England was inherited in Virginia where it became very popular. One of the first pieces of similar legislation in Virginia which had a public educational aspect was passed in March, 1643: —

And all overseers and guardians of such orphans are enjoyned by the authoritie aforesayd [the county courts] to educate and instruct them according to their best endeavors in Christian religion and in rudiments of learning and to provide for them necessaries according to the competence of their estates. . . .[1]

---

[1] 18 Charles I. Hening, *Statutes*, vol. I, p. 261.

The custom soon became more or less popular in North Carolina also, though in that colony the system seems not to have been so extensive as in Virginia, which was more nearly like the mother country. In Virginia the practice was so widely extended that the *ante-bellum* educational system of that State seems a gradual evolution from it.[1]

As an attempt to foster a form of education with emphasis on a minimum of formal intellectual training, this poor-law and apprenticeship system forms a unique educational scheme. But in order to understand the popular mental attitude to the class of dependents entrusted to its care — an attitude which the system itself reflects — it is necessary to consider that "education" is a term of varying meaning. The term now generally means an expansion of the mental faculties through a specific organized course of a more or less literary nature. For the more prosperous part of society a "certain tincture of letters" has, in the popular mind, always been regarded as essential, but this particular form of a literary training has not been held in high esteem for the poorer classes. The popular view has been that formal intellectual and literary training was not necessary for the poor youth of the community. And parents or guardians often appeared more concerned about the practical training of their children or wards in the occupations and crafts through which they were later to maintain themselves than they were interested in "book learning."

It is through the apprenticeship system that one form of local educational effort may be seen in North Carolina during the colonial period, and evidence that the legislation in Virginia influenced the practice in North Caro-

---

[1] See Knight, "The Evolution of Public Education in Virginia," in the *Sewanee Review*, January, 1916.

THE APPRENTICESHIP SYSTEM 19

lina is not wanting. We have seen that the first law in Virginia which had an educational aspect in the formal sense was passed in 1643. It was some years before legislation on the subject was enacted in North Carolina, but that the system was in operation here at an early date may be seen from the following records of February, 1695, and of April, 1698: —

Upon ye Peticon of Hon^{ell} Thomas Harvey esq^r Ordered y^t W^m ye son of Timothy Pead late of the County of Albemarle Dec^d being left destitute be bound unto ye s^d Thomas Harvey esq^r and Sarah his wife untill he be at ye age of twenty one years and the said Thomas Harvey to teach him to read.[1]

Three years later, in April, 1698, the records of Perquimans Precinct Court show that Elizabeth Gardner,

ye Rellock William Gardner desesed p^{r}sented his selfe before ye Court to bind hir Son William Gardner to ye Hon^{bl} Govener Thomas Harvi or his Heires Thay Ingagen to Learn him to Reed Which In or to Was doon till he comes to ye Age of Twenty on yeares he being five years ould now a fortnite before Crismas.[2]

Four years later, at the January, 1699, term of the same court, the following orders appeared: —

Jonathan Taylor And William Taylor Orfens Being Left destressed ordered that they be Bound to William Long and Sarah His Wife Till they Come of Age.

Thomas Tailer Orfen Being Left destressed ordered that He be bound to John Lawrence And Hannah his Wife till he Comes of age.

Mare Tayler Orfen being Left destressed ordered that Shee be bound to Mr Caleb Galleway And Elisabeth his Wife till Shee Comes of Age.

Thomas Hallom Orfen being Left destressed ordered that he be bound to ffrancis ffoster And Hannah his Wife till he Comes of Age.[3]

---

[1] *Col. Rec.*, vol. I, p. 448. [2] *Ibid.*, p. 495. [3] *Ibid.*, p. 522.

These examples are the bare court records and nothing is said about the maintenance and education of the children who were bound. Indentures covering each case were likely signed later by the guardian and the court which appointed him. Ordinarily these indentures called for the education and maintenance, according to his "rank and degree," of the orphan bound or apprenticed. This meant to feed, clothe, lodge, and to provide "accommodations fit and necessary" for the child, and to teach or cause him to be taught to read and write, as well as a suitable trade. This was the customary agreement made with the courts. The absence of these features in the cases above is hardly proof that they were here neglected. The indentures were likely formally signed later, as appears to have been the case in the following agreement made in March, 1703, in the same court: —

Upon a petition of Gabriell Newby for two orphants left him by Mary Hancock the late wife of Thom^s Hancocke and proveing the same by the oathes of Eliz. Steward and her daughter the Court doe agree to bind them unto him he Ingagen & promising before the Court to doe his endeavours to learne the boy the trade of a wheelwright and likewise give him at the expiration of his time one year old heifer and to ye girle at her freedome one Cow and Calfe besides the Custome of the Country and has promised to ye next orphans Court to Sign Indentures for that effect.[1]

At the October, 1704, term of the same court, Nathan Sutton petitioned to be appointed guardian for Richard Sutton, the orphan son of George Sutton, who was probably Nathan's relative, but the petition was rejected. A year later, however, he was appointed guardian for the boy. The same court which appointed him guardian

[1] *Col. Rec.*, vol. I, p. 577.

THE APPRENTICESHIP SYSTEM 21

heard complaints made by the "orphans of George Sutton deced That Abraham Warren their guardian hath given Imoderate Correccon & deprived them of Competent Sustenance." The result was that the court appointed Dennis Macclendon the guardian of Elizabeth and Deborah Sutton and Nathan Sutton guardian for Richard.[1]

Other examples will throw further light on the operation of the system in North Carolina: —

Upon petition of George Bell setting forth that he had two serv^{ts} bound to him by the precinct Court of Craven in ye month of July 17 12/13 namely Charles Coggdaile and George Coggdaile as by Indenture may appeare. And further that ye Court af^{sd} have pretended to sett ye said Servt at Liberty as he is informed by reason that they could not perfectly read and write when as the time of their servitude is not half expired And he further claimes that during the time they were with him they were well used and much time allowed them to perfect them in their reading and writeing and that he intended to instruct them in ye building of Vessells Therefore prays that in regard there is no other allegation made appeare ag^t him they may remain with him till ye time of the Indenture Specifyed be expired &c. . . .

It was ordered that the servants remain with their master in accordance with their former indentures.[2]

The records of Chowan Precinct Court for August, 1716, show another feature of the general practice of apprenticing in North Carolina which is of interest here: —

Upon Petition of John Avery Shewing that sometime in August 1713 ye said Avery being in Prince George's County in Virginia met with one John Fox aged ab^t fifteen years who being Desireous to live in North Carolina to learn to be a Ship Carpenter bound himselfe an apprentice to ye said John Avery

---

[1] *Col. Rec.*, vol. I, pp. 613, 626.   [2] *Ibid.*, vol. II, p. 172.

22 THE PUBLIC SCHOOL IN NORTH CAROLINA

for Six years before one Stith Bolling Gent one of her Maj[ties] Justices of y[e] said County as is practiable in y[e] Governm[t] of Virginia whereupon y[e] said Avery brought y[e] said Fox into North Carolina with him and Caused the sd John his said Apprentice to be Taught and Instructed to read and write and was at other Charges and Expenses concerning him and haveing now made him serviceable and usefull to him in y[e] Occupation of a Shipp Carpenter to y[e] Great Content and Seeming Satisfaction of the said Foxes Mother and Father in Law one Cary Godby of Chowan Precinct But y[e] Said Cary intending to proffitt and advantage himselfe by the Labour and usefullness of y[e] said John Fox hath advised the said Fox to withdraw himselfe from yo[r] petition[rs] service and to bring along his Indentures of apprenticeship & is now Entertained and harboured by the said Cary Godby and therefore prayes that the s[d] Fox may be apprehended and brought before this Board their to be dealt with according to law.

Fox was ordered to return to his master.[1]

A record of November, 1716, in Chowan Precinct Court, shows that the practice applied to girls as well as to boys: —

Upon the Peticon of John Swain praying that Elizabeth Swain his sister an Orphane Girle bound by the Precinct Court of Chowan to John Worley Esq[r] May in the time of her service be taught to read by her said Master Ordered, that she be taught to read.[2]

These examples are sufficient to indicate the early operation of the practice in North Carolina. If the records were more complete considerably earlier examples would doubtless appear. By the practice, poor children were bound to masters and guardians were appointed for orphans, the masters or guardians agreeing with the local court, which had charge of this dependent class, to teach the wards a trade or occupation and also to read

[1] *Col. Rec.*, vol. II, p. 241.   [2] *Ibid.*, p. 266.

and write. When an orphan had an estate the master was entitled to receive remuneration for administering it; but if his estate yielded no profit the master ordinarily agreed to bind the orphan for his services. Under these conditions the child likely took his place in the household on an equality with the other children, and perhaps received the same educational advantages afforded them.

Although the practice of apprenticing and binding orphans and poor children under the conditions described was more or less extensive in the colony at an early date, no legislation seems to have been enacted on the subject until 1715. In that year a law was passed by which no children were allowed to be bound except by the precinct court, which was empowered to "grant letters of tuition or guardianship to such persons as they shall think proper," for caring for the "education of all orphans & for taking care of their estates...." The law required that

all Orphans shall be Educated & provided for according to their Rank & degree out of the Income or Interest of their Estate & Stock if the same will be sufficient Otherwise such Orphans shall be bound Apprentice to some Handycraft Trade (the Master or Mistress of such Orphan not being of the Profession called Quakers) till they shall come of Age unless some kin to such Orphan will undertake to maintain & Educate him or them for the interest or income of his or her Estate without Diminution of the Principal whether the same be great or small....[1]

The principal features of this legislation are similar to the features of a law on the same subject in Virginia. Close contact with that colony, from which many of the early settlers of North Carolina came and in which

[1] *Col. Rec.*, vol. XXIII, pp. 70–71.

the poor and apprenticeship laws formed practically the only educational system for the poorer classes, may have influenced the gradual introduction of apprenticeship practices into North Carolina. In Virginia, one of the first pieces of apprenticeship legislation which has a public educational aspect was that of March, 1643, when the county courts enjoined the overseers of the poor and guardians of orphans

to educate and instruct them according to their best endeavors in Christian religion and in the rudiments of learning and to provide for them necessaries according to the competence of their estates. . . .[1]

By an act of 1705, it was ordered that when the estate of any orphan was so small

that no person will maintain him for the profits thereof, then such orphan shall be bound apprentice to some handicraft trade, or mariner, until he shall attain to the age of one and twenty. And the master of each of such orphan shall be obliged to teach him to read and write: and at the expiration of his servitude, to pay and allow him in like manner as is appointed for servants, by indenture or custom.[2]

Another example will serve to make clearer the similarity of legislation on this subject in the two colonies and the probable influence of the law of Virginia on the law of North Carolina. In 1748 it was enacted in the former colony that whenever the profits of an orphan's estate were insufficient to maintain him, such an orphan was to be bound apprentice,

every male to some tradesman, merchant, mariner, or other person approved by the court, until he shall attain the age of one and twenty years, and every female to some suitable trade

---

[1] 18 Charles I. Hening, *Statutes*, vol. I, p. 261
[2] 4 Anne. Hening, *Statutes*, vol. III, p. 375.

or employment, till her age of eighteen years; and the master or mistress of every such servant shall find and provide for him or her, diet, clothes, lodgings and accommodations fit and necessary, and shall teach, or cause him or her to be taught to read and write, and at the expiration of his or her apprenticeship, shall pay every such servant, the like allowance as is by law appointed for servants by indenture or custom. . . .[1]

Seven years later, in September, 1755, there was enacted in North Carolina a law regulating the estates of orphans and their guardians. The preamble of this law explained the need for further legislation on this subject: —

Whereas, for want of proper laws for regulating guardians, and the management of orphans, their interests and estates have been greatly abused and their education very much neglected; for prevention whereof for the future, be it enacted. . . .

By this law the church wardens of every parish were to furnish to the justices of the orphans' court, at its annual session, the names of all children without guardians. Failure to perform this duty was punishable by a fine of "ten pounds proclamation money each." The court was to appoint guardians for all such children and these guardians were to make reports to the court of their wards and apprentices. When the court "shall know or be informed that any guardian or guardians by them respectfully appointed, do waste or convert the money or estate of any orphan to his or her own use, or do in any manner mismanage the same . . . or neglects to educate or maintain any orphan according to his or her degree and circumstances," the court was then empowered to establish other rules and regulations for the better management of such estate and "for the better

[1] 22 George II. Hening, *Statutes*, vol. v, pp. 449 *ff*.

educating and maintaining such orphans." When the profits of any orphan's estate "shall be more than sufficient to maintain and educate him," the surplus was to be invested on good and sufficient security. But if the estate

shall be of so small value that no person will educate or maintain him or her for the profits thereof, such orphan shall by the direction of the court be bound apprentice, every male to some tradesman, merchant, mariner, or other person approved by the court, until he shall attain the age of twenty-one years, and every female to some suitable employment till her age of eighteen years, and the master or mistress of every such servant shall find and provide for him or her diet, clothes, lodging, and accommodations fit and necessary, and shall teach, or cause him or her to be taught, to read and write, and at the expiration of his or her apprenticeship shall pay every such servant the like allowance as is by law appointed for servants by indenture or custom, and on refusal shall be compelled thereto in like manner. . . .

The act was to remain in force for five years from passage.

In April, 1760, a law similar to the law of 1755 was enacted, and two years later we find further legislation on the subject of the maintenance and education of orphans. Additional legislation was justified, according to the preamble, by the "experience that the court of each respective county, exercising the power of regulating the education of orphans, and the management of their estates, have proved of singular service to them." This differed from previous legislation in one essential point. Formerly the church wardens of every parish were required to report to the court the names of orphans and poor children without guardians or masters. By this act that duty was transferred to the grand jury of every county. Provision was further made for an orphans' court to be held by the justices of every inferior court of pleas and quarter sessions. This court was to be held once a year when accounts of guardians were to be exhibited and complaints heard.

The educational features of the act have a certain interest. The guardian of any orphan whose estate furnished the orphan an economic competency was to supervise his education and maintenance. When the estate was of such small value that "no person will educate and maintain him or her for the profits thereof," the orphan was to be bound apprentice by the court,

every male to some tradesman, merchant, mariner, or other person approved by the court, until he shall attain to the age of twenty-one years; and every female to some suitable employment, till her age of eighteen years; and also such court may, in like manner, bind apprentice all free base born children; and every such female child being a mulatto or mustee, until she shall attain the age of twenty-one years; and the master or mistress of every such apprentice, shall find and provide for him or her diet, clothes, lodging, accommodations, fit and necessary; and shall teach or cause him or her to be taught, to read and write; and at the expiration of his or her apprenticeship, shall pay every such apprentice the like allowance as is by law appointed, for servants by indenture or custom; and on refusal, shall be compelled thereto, in like manner; and if on complaint made to the inferior court of pleas and quarter sessions, it shall appear that any such apprentice is ill-used, or not taught the trade, profession or employment to which he or she is bound, it shall be lawful for such court to remove and bind him or her to such other person or persons as they shall think fit.

With the exception of certain vestry acts this remained until the national period practically the only legislation governing apprentices and the poor in the colony of North Carolina. The chief of these acts was passed in January, 1764, and described the duties of vestrymen in making provision for the clergy and the poor. By this act the vestrymen of each parish were "directed and required," annually between Easter and November, "to lay a poll tax on the taxable persons in their parish, not exceeding ten shillings, for building churches and chapels, paying the ministers' salary, purchasing a glebe . . . encouraging schools, maintaining the poor, paying clerks and readers, etc." [1] No important changes were made in this legislation until 1777 when an act was passed transferring to "overseers of the poor" certain powers and duties which hitherto had devolved on the vestrymen.[2]

Here may be seen an important change in the conception of educational control. By the act of 1762, already described, the duty of reporting to the justices of the local court the names of orphans and poor children without guardians or masters was transferred from the church wardens to the county grand jury. By the Vestry Act of 1777 similar authority was transferred from the vestrymen to the "overseers of the poor." The educational significance of these changes is important: now the authority for controlling the maintenance and education of the poor is transferred from the Church to the State. From this change is gradually developed the idea that caring for and "educating" the poor of the community is a state function. This general change is also clearly marked in the legislation dealing with the poor in Virginia.[3]

In the main, the foregoing describes the practice in

[1] *Col. Rec.*, vol. XXIII, p. 601.   [2] *Ibid.*, vol. XXIV, p. 93.
[3] See Knight, "The Evolution of Public Education in Virginia," in the *Sewanee Review*, January, 1916.

North Carolina of apprenticing poor children and orphans whose economic competency was insufficient to maintain and educate them. The custom was not so extensive and popular as in Virginia which was more directly influenced by conditions and practices in England. Scarcity of evidence on the subject in North Carolina may be accounted for by the fact that children apprenticed by the court probably took their places in the homes of their guardians or masters on conditions of maintenance and education usually allowed other members of the household. The master was probably required to give his apprentice practically the same care and attention given to his own children; for when it appeared that the apprentice was ill-used, not properly provided with "accommodations fit and necessary," or not properly taught as agreed to in the indentures, he was removed and re-apprenticed to some other master approved by the court. This important feature of the apprenticeship practice seems to have been a regular requirement.

A study of the system in North Carolina is not only suggestive, but leads to certain interesting conclusions. From it we may see that as early as 1695 the practice required provision for teaching the apprentice to read and write, and that the court released apprentices when "they could not perfectly read and write." It is probable that this requirement was universal in the colony, though abundant evidence on the extent of the custom of apprenticing is unfortunately not accessible. We have also seen that the apprenticeship legislation in the colony of Virginia influenced similar legislation in North Carolina, as the act of 1748 in the former, and of 1755 in the latter, colony give evidence. It also appeared that the practice in North Carolina applied to orphans, poor children, free illegitimate children, to girls as well as to boys, and to female mulattoes and mustees. Moreover, by the act of 1715, requiring that "all Orphans shall be Educated & provided for according to their Rank and degree," the existence of schools or other means of intellectual training is implied. The language of the law of 1755, "neglects to educate or maintain an orphan according to his or her degree and circumstances," and that of the law of 1762, "regulating the education of orphans, and the management of their estates, have proved of singular service to them," and "educate and maintain," may be considered additional evidence that certain educational facilities, however meager they may have been, were available for this dependent class.[1]

[1] The law of 1762 remained strictly in force for many years. As late as February, 1827, a bill "to repeal so much of an act passed in 1762 as requires the master or mistress to teach or cause to be taught colored apprentices to read and write" failed in the Legislature. See *House Journal*, 1826–27, pp. 202, 207.

REFERENCES

The Colonial Records of North Carolina; Davis's *Revisal* (1773); Hening, *Statutes of Virginia;* Bruce, *Institutional History of Virginia in the Seventeenth Century;* Clews, *Educational Legislation and Administration of the Colonial Governments;* Nicholls, *A History of the English Poor-Law;* Leach, *English Schools at the Reformation; Cyclopedia of Education,* edited by Paul Monroe, vol. v, article, "Poor-Laws and Education"; Knight, "The Evolution of Public Education in Virginia," in the *Sewanee Review,* January, 1916.

SUGGESTIONS FOR FURTHER STUDY

1. How did the poor-laws and the apprenticeship practices form an educational system?
2. Show how the system grew up in Europe and how it was transferred to this country.
3. Show how the practice in Virginia probably influenced the custom in North Carolina.
4. What were the educational advantages of such a system? What were the disadvantages?
5. Compare the aim of education under this system with the aim of education to-day.
6. Point out other relations between this form of education and our present public-school system.
7. In what respect is our present system of education a development from the apprenticeship system?
8. Examine the court records of your county for examples of the educational features of the apprenticeship system.
9. Why is the apprenticeship practice less extensive than formerly? How extensive is the custom in North Carolina to-day?
10. Examine the agreements by which children are bound out by the court to-day and note any educational features which they contain.

CHAPTER III

UNDER ROYAL RULE

IT was pointed out in Chapter I that but little was accomplished for educational improvement under the lords proprietors. For nearly a quarter of a century after the transfer of the colony to royal control, in 1729, practically the same conditions prevailed as before. In 1729 the white population of the colony was estimated at not more than thirteen thousand, and the inhabitants were sparsely distributed. Conditions still continued unfavorable to intellectual and educational development. As late as 1736 the colony had no printing-press, no printed collection of its laws, and perhaps only a few regularly settled schoolmasters. The first printing-press came into the colony in 1749 and the laws were first published two years later. For a long time no governmental provision was made for schools, but "there were many highly educated citizens scattered throughout the province, who lived with considerable style and refinement. Sturdy, honest, and hospitable agriculturists gathered around themselves elements of large future development, and their premises showed wealth, industry, and care." Later on many of these well-to-do families of the Cape Fear region sent their sons to Harvard, those of the northeast section sent theirs to England for education, and the Presbyterians of the interior region educated their sons at Princeton. Some local provision was also made for education, though the poorer classes of the population were neglected and more or less ignorant.

Occasional attempts were made, however, for educational improvement of the masses. The first notable example of such efforts was in 1736, when, in his message to the Assembly, Governor Gabriel Johnston said, after "observing the deplorable and almost total want of divine worship throughout the Province" of North Carolina: —

> In all civilized Societys of men, it has always been looked upon as a matter of the greatest consequence to their Peace and happiness, to polish the minds of Young Persons with some degree of learning, and early to instill into them the Principles of Virtue and religion, and that the Legislature has never yet taken the least care to erect one school, which deserves the name in this wide extended country, must in the judgement of all thinking men, be reckoned one of our greatest misfortunes. To what purpose Gentlemen is all your toil and labour, all your pains and endeavours for the advantage and enriching your families and Posterity, if within ourselves you cannot afford them such an education as may qualify them to be usefull to their Country and to enjoy what you leave them with decency ... and now Gentlemen represent all this to yourselves at one view; consider a country where there has never yet any Provision been made for Keeping up the sense and awe of a Deity on the minds of People; where no care has been taken to inspire the youth with generous sentiments, worthy Principles, or the least tincture of literature; where the Laws are dispersed up and down in different Places on loose Papers, some of them contradictory, others unintelligible.... Then consider yourselves as the Representatives of this Country, who have not only the power and means, but are earnestly pressed and desired to remedy these calamities, to supply these defects; and when you have done all this, lay your hands upon your hearts and consider how you can answer it to God and your own consciences, how you can answer it to your Country or your Posterity, if you either neglect this oppor-

tunity of pursuing such valuable ends, or are diverted from it by the trifling arts of designing men.[1]

Three days later the Assembly replied sympathetically to the governor's message: —

> We lament very much the want of Divine Public worship (a crying scandal in any, but more especially in a Christian Community;) as well as the general neglect in point of education, the main sources of all disorders and Corruptions, which we should rejoice to see removed and remedeyed, and are ready to do our parts, towards the reformation of such flagrant and prolifick Evils.

The Assembly then assured the governor "that no insinuations, no artifices of any party or sett of men whatsoever, can alter our sentiments or change these our views."

In October the committee on grievances in the lower House presented a list of grievances which included the collection of quitrents and other matters. The governor, discussing the report, regretted that the committee had "been so remiss in their duty as to present so few grievances and those so little material. In any other country besides this, I am satisfied they would have taken notice of the want of divine worship, the neglect of the education of youth, the bad state of your laws and the impossibility to execute them. . . ." The next year the governor again called attention, in his message to the Assembly, to the need for making "provision for the education of youth."

Nothing was done for education, however, until 1745, when an act was passed empowering the town commissioners of Edenton to build a schoolhouse, the expense of which was to be defrayed by money arising from the

[1] *Col. Rec.*, vol. IV, pp. 227, 228.

sale of town lots and by donations and subscriptions which the commissioners were authorized to receive. There is no evidence that the house was ever built. Again in 1749 a bill was introduced looking to the establishment of a free school, but it was never enacted into law. In 1752 effort was again made to erect schools, and the lower House of the Assembly promised the governor to take measures to promote the "virtuous education of our youth," but this failed also. Two years later, in 1754, the sum of £6000 was appropriated by the Assembly for the purpose of building a school. Later "a reasonable tax on each negro" in the colony was promised to supplement a liberal offer of George Vaughan, an English merchant, who agreed to give "one thousand pounds yearly forever" to promote education among the Indians of the province, but this tax was agreed to on condition that Vaughan would allow his donation to "extend as an academy or seminary of religion and learning to all His Majesty's subjects in North Carolina." After legal provision was made for the school, however, the funds appropriated were used for war and other purposes with the result that the Vaughan plan never materialized.

Governor Dobbs, who succeeded Governor Johnston, was, like his predecessor, solicitous for the encouragement and promotion of education, and continually urged the establishment of "proper schools in the province, for the education of youth...." In November, 1758, the lower House of the Assembly assured the governor "that nothing shall be wanting to promote a work of such interesting consequences, though at present we are somewhat at a loss in what manner to accomplish it..."; and the upper House declared that it had "at

heart nothing more than the defences of the country, the promoting true religion, the education of our youth in the reformed Protestant religion and moral virtues. . . ."
In 1759, and again in 1764, the governor petitioned the Board of Trade to permit a reissue in bills of the money originally intended for education, but this was refused, as was also the request that the colony's share of the reimbursement for war purposes be applied to schools.

In November, 1760, Dobbs again urged the Assembly to "seriously consider of giving encouragement for schools," and as usual the Assembly promised coöperation. In December, 1762, the Reverend James Reed preached before the Assembly a sermon on the importance of education and this sermon was printed at public expense and distributed in the colony. Dr. Weeks says that this was probably the first public expenditure for education in the province.

Only a few other efforts were made during the colonial period to promote education, and fewer still were successful. In January, 1764, Thomas Tomlinson opened a private school in Newbern and the Reverend James Reed reported that subscriptions in notes amounting to £110 sterling had been secured for the purpose of building a house. Later he and numerous residents of the town petitioned Governor Tryon to solicit the Society for the Propagation of the Gospel to settle a salary on Tomlinson. This the governor did, and the Society responded favorably. The school had at that time about thirty pupils. In 1766 further provision was made for establishing a schoolhouse in the town of Newbern. In order that the benefits of the school "may be as extensive as possible, and that the poor who may be unable to educate their children may enjoy the benefits thereof," an import tax of one penny a gallon was levied on all rum and other liquors brought into the Neuse River for seven years, and with this revenue ten poor children were to be educated. This was the first school or academy incorporated in North Carolina and this was the first law of any great importance passed in the colony on the subject of education. In 1767 and 1768 efforts were made to establish a school in the town of Edenton, but attempted legislation on the subject failed temporarily when the Assembly opposed the enforcement of the terms of the Schism Act which required all teachers to be members of the Established Church. Later, however, the school was chartered as the Edenton Academy and under terms similar to those of the charter of the school at Newbern. Under the terms of the reproduced Schism Act, no person could teach in either of these schools except members of the Established Church. This requirement, which proved so exasperating to the colonists, permitted no one, under penalty of imprisonment for three months, to keep a private or public school or to act as tutor or usher, unless he first obtained license from the Bishop of London and conformed to the Anglican liturgy. Such a requirement was attended by many evils and prevented the dissenters in the colony from providing educational facilities for their children.

Notable educational advancement through private incorporated academies began before the close of the colonial period, however, and continued through the first quarter of the nineteenth century and later. One of the factors influencing this development was the immigration as early as 1740 of the Scotch and Scotch-Irish into the colony. Thousands of these people, disabled in consequence of their religion, sought homes in America, and many of them came to North Carolina and settled in the Piedmont section of the State. In every community where they came a schoolhouse and church sprang up simultaneously with the settlement; "almost invariably as soon as a neighborhood was settled preparations were made for the preaching of the gospel by a regular stated pastor, and wherever a pastor was located, in that congregation there was a classical school. . . ." Before 1750 the New York and Pennsylvania Presbyterian synods began to send missionaries into North Carolina, and these helped to stimulate educational activity. Moreover, Princeton College proved an educational impulse to the State. Scores of graduates of that institution, some natives of North Carolina who went there for their training, and many from other States, cast their lot here and for half a century had a predominating influence in the religious and educational life of the State. One of the first of these was the Reverend Hugh McAden, a graduate of the class of 1733 and one of the founders of the Presbyterian Church in the South.

The German element, migrating from Pennsylvania, proved another educational influence. The migration of these people began as early as 1745, and by 1785 there were as many as fifteen thousand of them in the State. Like the Scotch-Irish, they established churches and schools as soon as they had made a settlement, and if there was a scarcity of teachers among them the needed supply was brought in from Germany. The coming of the Pennsylvania Quakers between 1743 and 1785 also added a certain educational and moral strength to the colony.

The first classical school established in the colony

under the Presbyterian influence was Tate's Academy, founded in Wilmington in 1760, by the Reverend James Tate and continued by him until 1778. In the same year that this school was founded, Crowfield Academy was opened in Mecklenburg County, near the present location of Davidson College. This school had an extensive influence and furnished a classical training to many young men who later became prominent in the life of the State. It was from this academy that Davidson College is said to have grown.

Perhaps the most illustrious educator of this period was Dr. David Caldwell, whose celebrated "log college," which was located near Greensboro, served for so many years in the capacity of academy, college, and theological seminary. The school was founded in 1767 and in a short time became the most important institution of learning in North Carolina and one of the most influential in the entire South. Thoroughness rather than an extensive curriculum was its chief feature. The average annual enrollment in the school was between fifty and sixty, and it is said that more men entered the learned professions from its student body than from any other school in the South. Five of Dr. Caldwell's students became governors of States, several went to Congress, and many became prominent as jurists, physicians, and preachers. But for a temporary interruption by the British in 1781 the institution had an unbroken career of success until 1822, when old age compelled its brilliant leader to retire from active service.

Clio's Nursery and Science Hall was a school conducted in Iredell County by Dr. James Hall, of the class of 1774 of Princeton, a man of considerable ability as teacher and preacher. The school was opened about the beginning of the Revolution. The "academy of sciences" in which Dr. Hall was the only instructor was conducted in connection with the Nursery and was perhaps the first scientific course in the State. Many young men who later became prominent in public life were students of Dr. Hall.

Zion Parnassus, another Presbyterian school of considerable influence, was established at Thyatira, near Salisbury, in 1785, by the Reverend Samuel C. McCorkle, a graduate of Princeton of the class of 1772, and a man of force and ability. This school is best known for its normal department, which was the first attempt at teacher training in the State and one of the first in this country, and for its assistance of tuition and books to worthy students. The school maintained a high order of scholarship and had an extensive influence. Six of the seven members of the first graduating class of the state university received their college preparation in this school. After Dr. McCorkle's death in 1811 the institution was suspended, but it was later opened in Salisbury where for many years it was conducted as the Salisbury High School.

Queen's College, also known as Queen's Museum, was another Presbyterian school and the most important institution for higher education in the colony, though its career was brief and beset with numerous obstacles. This was the last institution to seek incorporation from the king and the first to receive a charter from the new State. The school had its beginning in the work of the Reverend Joseph Alexander, a graduate of Princeton of the class of 1760, who, with a Mr. Benedict, established a small classical school at the Sugar Creek Presbyterian Church in a prosperous and intelligent community near

Charlotte, in 1767. In December, 1770, it was chartered by the Assembly as Queen's Museum, but the charter was repealed by the king and council. Later a second charter was secured only to meet the same fate. The chartering of this school furnished the first clear example of the operation of the reproduced Schism Act in the colony. The organizers of the institution were willing to allow a member of the Established Church to serve as president, but insisted that its trustees and instructors should be free from the requirement of the Schism Act. Fear that the school would become a great and permanent advantage to the dissenters and a "fountain of republicanism" led to a repeal of its charter. In spite of royal disfavor, however, the institution flourished without a charter. The house was used for debating and literary clubs and accommodated the meeting which formulated the Mecklenburg Declaration of Independence. In 1775 the name was changed to Liberty Hall Academy, and two years later it received a charter from the new State Government. The institution soon came directly under the control of the Presbyterians. The curriculum was advanced for the time, though no degrees were ever awarded; diplomas and certificates of attendance were given, however. The school continued until 1780 when it was suspended, never to be reopened.

Providence Academy, near Charlotte, established by the Reverend James Wallis in 1792, Poplar Tent Academy in Cabarrus County, established by the Reverend Robert Archibald in 1778, and a school established in Fayetteville by the Reverend David Ker in 1791, were other schools of influence and usefulness founded and promoted by the Presbyterians of North Carolina in the eighteenth century.

REFERENCES

Swann's *Revisal* (1752); Davis's *Revisal* (1773); *The Colonial Records of North Carolina;* Weeks, *Libraries and Literature in North Carolina in the Eighteenth Century, The Press in North Carolina in the Eighteenth Century, Church and State in North Carolina, The Religious Development in the Province of North Carolina,* and *Calvin Henderson Wiley and the Organization of the Common Schools of North Carolina;* Raper, *The Church and Private Schools in North Carolina;* Cheshire, *Sketches of Church History in North Carolina;* McRee, *The Life and Correspondence of James Iredell;* Hawks, *History of North Carolina;* Waddell, *A Colonial Officer and His Times;* Foote, *Sketches of North Carolina;* Smith, *History of Education in North Carolina;* Brickell, *A Natural History of North Carolina; Cyclopedia of Education,* edited by Paul Monroe, vol. II, article, "Colonial Period in American Education."

SUGGESTIONS FOR FURTHER STUDY

1. Why was the colony of North Carolina transferred from proprietary to royal management?
2. What political and social changes, if any, took place as a result of the transfer?
3. Were conditions as favorable for education after the transfer as under the lords proprietors?
4. What were some of the obstacles in the way of educational development in the colony between 1729 and the Revolutionary period?
5. What was the attitude of the mother country toward education in the colonies during this time?
6. What attempts were made for the education of the masses during these years?
7. How did England's attitude toward the education of the masses reflect itself in her policy toward the colonies in the eighteenth century?
8. What was being done for education in the other colonies between 1700 and 1775?

9. Make a study of immigration to North Carolina in the eighteenth century and point out its educational influence.
10. Study the educational influence of the religious denominations in North Carolina before 1800.
11. What was the actual educational influence of the Schism Act in North Carolina?

CHAPTER IV

THE ACADEMY MOVEMENT

WITH the American Revolution and the beginning of the national period, a new type of institution began to develop in the United States and to provide more or less extensive educational facilities. This new school was the academy, the forerunner of the modern public high school, and from the Revolutionary period until near the middle of the nineteenth century the academy was recognized as the leader in secondary education in this country. Its development was demanded by the changed conditions of the time. During colonial days the Latin Grammar School, which was largely reproduced from the English type, was narrow in its curriculum, the classics occupying chief place, and its primary purpose was to prepare for college. This institution was therefore naturally exclusive in character. After the Revolution, however, the tendency toward religious diversity and the gradual growth of the democratic spirit demanded a type of institution which would furnish a training to the majority who would not go to college and one more nearly suited to the demands of the changed conditions.

This new type of school was usually private, but in most cases was recognized by the State, and in a few States, especially in New York and Georgia, it was given state support. Tuition charges were always made. No degrees were given, but diplomas and certificates

THE ACADEMY MOVEMENT 45

were awarded. The institution flourished until about 1850 when it began to decline, and later it was generally deposed by the public high school which began to develop after the Civil War.

With the granting of a charter to Liberty Hall Academy in 1777,[1] North Carolina began to recognize academies, which for half a century or more had an extensive growth in the State.[2] Science Hall, at Hillsboro, was the next to secure a charter, in 1779, and was given the same privileges as were given Liberty Hall, that of a corporation, of naming its own trustees, and of awarding diplomas and certificates of study. In 1784 Science Hall was given the privilege of raising money by lottery, perhaps "the first instance in the history of the free State in which the aid of the Government to schools extended beyond the mere formal granting of charters."

Granville Hall, in Granville County, was chartered in October, 1779, with Richard Caswell, Governor, and Abner Nash and Thomas Benbury, President of the Senate and Speaker of the House, respectively, the leading trustees. Considerable money seems to have been subscribed for the school and the trustees were authorized to purchase five hundred acres of land and to erect buildings. The Reverend Henry Pattillo, another Princeton man, a prominent early teacher of the State

[1] See p. 41.
[2] Jedidiah Morse, in his *American Universal Geography*, which first appeared in 1793, says of North Carolina: "There is a good academy at Warrenton, another at Williamsborough in Granville, and three or four others in the State, of considerable note." The identical statement, it is interesting to observe, also appeared in W. Winterbotham's *An Historical, Geographical, Commercial, and Philosophical View of the American United States, and of the European Settlements in America and the West Indies*, a work in four volumes which was published in London in 1795.

and an author of some note, was principal of this school.[1]

Smith Academy, in Edenton, chartered by the Assembly in 1782, was the gift of Robert Smith, a lawyer-merchant of that town. The following year the Assembly chartered Innes Academy in Wilmington, a school founded by a gift made by the following portion of the will of Colonel James Innes, made in 1754: —

I also give and bequeth att the Death of my Loving Wife Jean Innes my Plantation Called Point Pleasant and the Opposite mash Land over the River for which ther is a Seperate Patent, Two Negero Young Woomen One Negero young Man and there Increase, all the Stock of Cattle and Hogs, halfe the Stock of Horses belonging at the time to that Plantation With all my Books, and One Hundred Pounds Sterling or the Equivalent thereunto in the Currency of the Country For the Use of a Free School for the benefite of the Youth of North Carolina. And to see that this part of my Will is dewly executed att the time, I appoint the Colonell of the New Hanover Regement, the Parson of Wilmington Church and the Vestrey for the time being, or the Majority of them as they shall from time to time be choised or appointed. . . .

The act of incorporation provided that

the rector, professors, and tutors of this academy, and all other academies and public schools in this state established by law, shall be exempt from military duty during their continuance in those offices, provided the number of teachers in any of the said academies or public schools shall not exceed three; provided, also, that all scholars and students entering into said academy, or any other public school and being of the age of fifteen years or under at the time of entering, shall, during their continuance thereat, be exempt from all military duties.

---

[1] Weeks, *Calvin Henderson Wiley and the Organization of the Common Schools of North Carolina.*

THE ACADEMY MOVEMENT 47

Of the life and work of Innes Academy little is known. A building was begun soon after the charter was granted, but in 1803 the school seemed to be in unfortunate circumstances, and the hope of the donor was probably never realized.

The only other example of similar individual interest in education during the Colonial period was the will of James Winwright, of Carteret County, which was made in 1744: —

> I will and appoint that the yearly Rents and profits of all the Town land and Houses in Beaufort Town Belonging unto me with the other Land adjoining thereto (which I purchased of John Pindar) after the Decease of my wife Ann to be applyed to the Uses hereinafter Mentioned for Ever (to wit) for The encouragement of a Sober discreet Quallifyed Man to teach a School at least Reading Writing Vulgar and Decimal Arithmetick in the aforesd. town of Beaufort, wch said Man Shall be Chosen and appointed by the Chair Man (or the Next in Commission) of Carteret County Court and one of Church Wardens of St. John parish in the aforesd. County and Their Successors for Ever, also I give and Bequeath the Summ of Fifty pounds Sterling (provided that my estate Shall be Worth so much after my Just Debts and other Legacys are paid and Discharged) to be applyed for the Building and finishing of a Creditable House for a School and Dwelling house for the Master to be Erected and Built on Some part of my Land Near the White house Which I bought of the aforesaid Pindar, and my True Intent and Meaning is that all the yearly profits and advantages arising by the aforesd. Town Lotts and Lands thereunto adjoining as aforesd. with the Use of the sd Land for Making and Improving a plantation for the planting and Raising of Corn, etc. (if the aforesd. Master or teacher of sd. School Shall think proper to plant and Improve the same) be entirely for the use and Benefitt of ye sd. Master and his Successors During his and their Good Behaviour, — Also that the sd. Master Shall not be obliged to teach or take under his Care any Shoolar or Schoolars Imposed on him by the Trustees

herein Mentioned or their successors or by any other person, But shall have free Liberty to teach and take under his care Such and so many Schoolars as he shall think Convenient and to Receive his Reward for the Teaching of them as he and the persons tendering them shall agree.

There is no record that a school was ever established on this foundation.

In April 1783, the Assembly incorporated Martin Academy, in what is now Washington County, Tennessee, with the same powers as were granted Liberty Hall Academy in Charlotte. This school, which is said to be the first educational institution established in the Mississippi Valley, became Washington College in 1795. In 1785 Davidson Academy, at Nashville, was chartered by the Assembly of North Carolina. In 1806 this school was rechartered as Cumberland College, and in 1826 as the University of Nashville, which had a long and useful career. In 1875 an arrangement was made between this institution and the trustees of the Peabody Fund by which the Peabody Normal School developed and later absorbed the University of Nashville.

From 1785 until 1825 or later, various other schools and academies were chartered by authority of the General Assembly, though little is known of the career of many of them subsequent to their incorporation. The privileges accorded these schools were usually the same. Certificates could be granted, but degrees were not allowed. The pupils and teachers were occasionally exempted from military duty, now and then the school property was exempted from taxation, and occasionally permission was given to raise funds by lottery. In most cases the trustees selected the teachers and had general control over the school. The number of schools thus chartered during these years, from 1785 to 1825, may be seen from the following summary: [1]

In 1785: Dobbs Academy at Kinston, and Grove Academy in Duplin County.

In 1786: Franklin Academy at Louisburg, Pittsboro Academy in Chatham County, Pitt Academy at Greenville, and Warrenton Academy in Warren County.

In 1789: Richmond Academy in Richmond County, and the Currituck Seminary of Learning in Currituck County.

In 1791: Onslow Academy in Onslow County, and Stokes Seminary at Wadesboro.

In 1793: Tarboro Academy in Edgecombe County and Lumberton Academy and Raft-Swamp Academy in Robeson County.

In 1797: Murfreesboro Academy in Hertford County, Montgomery Seminary in Montgomery County, and Bladen Academy at Elizabethtown.

In 1798: Unity Academy in Randolph County, Adams Creek Academy in Craven County, Smithville Academy in Brunswick County, Salisbury Academy in Rowan County, and an academy in Guilford County.

In 1799: Fayetteville Seminary in Cumberland County, Peasley Academy in Moore County, and Williamsboro Franklin Library Society in Granville County.

In 1800: Sneedsboro Academy in Anson County, and Edenton Academy at Edenton.

In 1801: Union Meeting House Academy in Duplin County, Clio Montana Seminary in Rockingham County, and Raleigh Academy at Raleigh.

In 1802: Franklin Academy in Franklin County,

[1] See Weeks, *Calvin Henderson Wiley and the Organization of the Common Schools of North Carolina.*

Wadesboro Academy in Anson County, Caswell Academy at Yanceyville and Spring Hill Seminary in Lenoir County.

In 1804: Cedar Grove Academy in Richmond County, Wilmington Academy at Wilmington and Nixonton Academy in Pasquotank County.

In 1805: Philomathia Academy in Wilkes County, Hico Academy in Caswell County, Solemn Grove Academy in Moore County, Green Academy (later changed to Hookerton Academy) in Green County, and Union Hill Academy in Buncombe County.

In 1806: Oxford Academy in Rowan County, Windsor Academy in Bertie County, Mount Clio Academy in Robeson County, Rutherford Academy in Rutherford County, and Union Hall School in Perquimans County.

In 1807: Trenton Academy in Jones County, Portsmouth Academy in Carteret County, Indian Woods Academy in Bertie County, and Elizabeth City Academy in Pasquotank County.

In 1808: Washington Academy in Beaufort County, and Zion Parnassus Academy in Robeson County.

In 1809: Onslow Academy in Onslow County, Thisbe Academy in Guilford County, Hertford Academy in Hertford County, Green Hill Academy in Haywood County, Laurel Hill Academy in Richmond County, Mount Parnassus Academy in Moore County, Fayetteville Academy in Cumberland County, Newland Academy in Pasquotank County, Vine Hill Academy in Halifax County, and Germantown Academy in Stokes County.

In 1810: Carteret Academy in Carteret County, Jonesboro Academy in Camden County, Wilkesboro Academy in Wilkes County, Swansboro Academy in

THE ACADEMY MOVEMENT

Onslow County, Springfield Academy in Halifax County, Poplar Tent Academy in Cabarrus County, Elizabethtown Academy in Bladen County, Plymouth Academy in Washington County, Montpelier Academy in Granville County, Nutbush Mineral Springs Academy in Granville County, and the Waynesboro Academy.

In 1811: Euphronean Academy in Moore County, Oxford Academy at Oxford, and New Providence Academy in Mecklenburg County.

In 1812: Snow Hill Academy in Greene County, Philadelphus Academy in Robeson County, Rocky River Academy in Cabarrus County, and the Newbern Female Charitable Seminary at Newbern.

In 1813: Greene Academy in Greene County, Goshen Academy in Duplin County, Tarboro Academy in Edgecombe County, Williamsboro Academy in Granville County, Pleasant Retreat Academy in Lincoln County, Female Orphan Asylum Society at Fayetteville, Military and Literary Society of Lenoir County, Free School in Wayne County, and the North Carolina Bible Society.

In 1814: Union Academy in Halifax County, Greenville Academy in Pitt County, Hillsboro Academy at Hillsboro, Rush Academy in Hyde County, Louisburg Female Academy at Louisburg, Free School in Duplin County, and Clio Academy in Iredell County. The name of this last institution was changed to Statesville Academy in 1815. It had been in existence many years prior to its chartering.

In 1816: Williamston Academy in Martin County, Pleasant Grove Academy in Perquimans County, and Greensboro Academy at Greensboro.

52 THE PUBLIC SCHOOL IN NORTH CAROLINA

In 1817: Fairfield School in Lenoir County, New Prospect Academy in Perquimans County, Blakely Academy at Pittsboro, and the Female Benevolent Society at Wilmington.

In 1818: Milton Female Academy in Caswell County, Wayne Academy in Wayne County, Jonesville Academy in Surry County, Haywood Academy in Chatham County, Asheville Academy at Asheville, Lawrenceville Academy in Montgomery County, Hilliardston Academy in Nash County, Forest Hill Academy in Wake County, Trenton Academy in Jones County, and Female Academy in Orange County.

In 1819: Enfield Academy in Halifax County, Camden Academy in Camden County, Wilkesboro Academy in Wilkes County, Smithfield Academy in Johnston County, Madison Academy in Rockingham County, Lumberton Academy in Tyrrell County, New Salem Library Society in Randolph County, and the Leaksville Female Academy.

In 1820: Spring Hill Academy in Gates County, Concord Academy in Perquimans County, Shocco Female Academy in Warren County, Elizabeth City Academy in Pasquotank County, Farnewell Grove Academy in Halifax County, and Carraway Library Society in Randolph County.

In 1821: Lincolnton Female Academy at Lincolnton, Sardis Academy in Johnston County, Clinton Academy in Sampson County, Midway Academy in Franklin County, Union Library Society in Iredell County, Spring Grove Academy in Anson County, Halifax Academy at Halifax, Raleigh Female Benevolent Society at Raleigh, Liberty Male Academy at Charlotte, and Charlotte Female Academy at Charlotte.

THE ACADEMY MOVEMENT

In 1822: Ebenezer Academy in Iredell County, Culpeper Academy in Anson County, Franklin Library Society at Hillsboro, Miltonsville Academy in Anson County, Hopewell Academy in Edgecombe County, Durham's Creek Academy in Beaufort County, Richland Creek Library Society in Guilford County, and the Shady Grove Male and Female Academy in Warren County.

In 1823: Bertie Union Academy in Bertie County, Lumberton Academy in Robeson County, Milton Male Academy in Carteret County, Friendship Academy in Edgecombe County, Town Creek Academy in Edgecombe County, Sandy Creek Library Society in Davidson County, Morganton Academy at Morganton, and the New Providence Library Company in Mecklenburg County.

In 1824: Swansboro Academy in Onslow County, Wake Union Academy in Wake County, Clinton Library Society in Stokes County, New Hope Academy in Randolph County, Davidson Academy in Montgomery County, Hillsboro Female Academy in Orange County, Mount Prospect Academy in Edgecombe County, and Harmony Grove Academy in Edgecombe County.

In 1825: Line Academy in Sampson County, Colerain Academy in Bertie County, Williams Academy in Duplin County, Oak Grove Academy in Greene County, Pleasant Grove Academy in Edgecombe County, Lexington Academy at Lexington, Shady Grove Academy in Rockingham County, The Greensboro Library Society at Greensboro, The Farmers' Library Society of Northampton County, and the Abbott's Creek Library Society in Davidson County.

Similar new institutions continued to be chartered, or the charters of old academies were revised, from 1825 until after the middle of the century or somewhat later. After 1850 the academy movement began to decline, and following the war a new type of school, the public high school, began to take its place.

Several interesting features of the academy, such as the course of study, material equipment, methods of support, qualifications and salaries of teachers, and methods of teaching, at once suggest themselves. A brief discussion of these features will serve to show the institution as it actually operated in North Carolina.[1]

The curricula or courses of study offered in these schools show a wide range of subjects. Reading, writing, English grammar, geography, mathematics, and Latin and Greek were taught in an academy at Pittsboro in 1800; the same subjects and bookkeeping were given in a school at Hillsboro in 1801; Latin, Greek, geography, arithmetic, natural and moral philosophy, astronomy, and reading and writing were taught in the Caswell Academy in 1802; the following year the boys in the Fayetteville Academy were studying reading, spelling, ciphering, English grammar, Nepos, Cæsar, Sallust, and Virgil; and the girls were taught spelling, reading, English grammar, geography, letter-writing, copy-writing, ciphering, Dresden work, tambour work, and embroidery.

In 1805 the Pittsboro Academy had classes in history, astronomy, and moral philosophy, and the same year the principal of the school at Louisburg, with the aid of

[1] For further interesting material on these subjects see Coon, *North Carolina Schools and Academies, 1790–1840, A Documentary History*, from which much of the present discussion is largely taken.

one assistant, "advertised to teach belles-lettres, rhetoric, ethics, metaphysics, Hebrew, French, Italian, algebra, geometry, trigonometry, conic sections, surveying, natural philosophy, astronomy, navigation, mensuration, altimetry, longimetry, Latin, and Greek, in addition to reading, writing, arithmetic, geography, and English grammar."

The Salisbury Academy in 1807 had classes in Virgil's *Eclogues*, Nepos, Erasmus, geography, reading, parsing, catechism, arithmetic, writing, and composition. Reading, writing, and spelling were required subjects, and Latin, French, music, painting, and needle-work were electives, for the girls in the Raleigh Academy in 1811. The course offered for the boys in the same school in that year "possibly required more time and work to complete than is now required to complete our elementary and high-school courses. The Latin course included grammar, Corderii, Cæsar, Ovid, Virgil, Odes of Horace, and Cicero. The Greek course embraced the grammar and Greek Testament. In mathematics, Euclid, arithmetic, and surveying were required. In English, grammar, parsing, and geography were taught."

In 1818 the principal of the Salisbury Academy offered to "teach all the branches of English, classical, mathematical and philosophical literature which are taught in universities, together with the French language, if required." The same year Miss Rachel Prendergast advertised that the "following sciences" would be taught at "A Female Seminary" in Caswell County: "Orthography, reading, writing, arithmetic, English grammar, needlework, drawing, painting, embroidery, geography and the use of the maps, also scanning poetry." In 1822, grammar and parsing, belles-lettres, geography, chemistry, botany, natural philosophy, astronomy, Latin, Greek, music, dancing, drawing, and painting, as well as the rudiments of learning, were taught in the Oxford Female Seminary.

The physical equipment of most of these schools was far from modern and adequate, though creditable buildings were now and then found. During this period the State was very sparsely settled, and agriculture was the principal pursuit of the population. Urban communities, therefore, developed slowly. As a rule the school buildings were of wood, though occasionally in the larger towns a brick building could be found. Blackboards were very rare and modern school furniture was also practically unknown. Maps were frequently reported as in use and occasionally a school could be found using a globe and "some geometrical apparatus." In 1826, the Salem Boys' School had "received a chemical and philosophical apparatus and mineralogical cabinet." In 1835, the Leasburg Classical School was "furnished with globes, maps, pianos, a collection of geographical specimens, and a chemical apparatus." Two years later the Northampton Academy advertised "an entirely new mathematical and philosophical apparatus." Libraries in the schools were slow in developing.

The schools were supported by tuition charges based, usually, on the age of the pupils or the subjects taught. The salaries of the teachers also varied. Franklin Academy, at Louisburg, illustrates both the tuition charged the pupils and the salary paid the teacher. In 1805 the trustees of that institution advertised that

each student shall pay to the treasurer of the academy ten dollars per annum, for instruction in reading, writing, arithmetic, English grammar, geography, belles lettres, and rhetoric; and sixteen dollars for instruction in ethics and metaphysics, the Latin, Greek, Hebrew, French and Italian languages, and the higher branches of metaphysics and philosophy, viz. algebra, geometry, trigonometry, conic sections, altimetry, longimetry, mensuration of superficies and solids, surveying, navigation, natural philosophy, and astronomy.

According to a diary of the time, Matthew Dickinson, a Yale man, who became principal of the school in 1805, was taken care of and prospered on his salary and a judicious management of his income: —

Mr. D. has acquired a very decent little estate since he first came here 4 years ago. He thinks himself worth between six and seven thousand dollars. The first year he had about seven hundred dollars — the next, the avails of his school 1000 Dlls. — the next they amounted to 1500 and the last year to 1200. Besides this too he pays an Usher (Mayhew from Wms. Col.) 300 Dlls. But he has improved opportunities to speculate by lending say 600 Dlls. cash to a young Sportsman and taking a Bond for 1000. Till lately he owned a house and farm of more than three hundred acres, six slaves, and a quantity of stock, as horses, sheep and cattle. Lately he sold his land for 4000 Dlls. which was one thousand more than it cost him. He now keeps a Gig, two horses and a servant or two and designs in the spring to visit Conn. *in this style.* Dickinson says literature is much respected in these parts and literary men reverenced. The first year he came when he had no property and nothing to recommend him but his books and education, he received flattering testimonials of respect and was treated with equal civility as at present.[1]

This remuneration was perhaps somewhat higher than many of the teachers received, however. David Ker received four hundred dollars for teaching and an additional four hundred dollars for preaching while he was principal of the Fayetteville Academy, in 1794. In

[1] Coon, *op. cit.*, pp. 84, 89, 90.

1826, a principal was sought for the Raleigh Academy to succeed the Reverend Doctor McPheeters, who was retiring after sixteen years' service. The salary offered was eight hundred dollars and a house and garden rent free. In the same year, Miss Mariah Allen received a salary of five hundred dollars as principal of a female academy at Lincolnton.[1]

The teachers in these academies and schools were in the main well trained and ably equipped, though few, if any, had received professional training for teaching. The influence of the graduates of the state university is early seen in the schools. The first graduating class of that institution in 1798 numbered seven, and as early as 1801 Andrew Flinn, an A.B. graduate of the college, became principal of the Hillsboro Academy; many other graduates had charge of schools and academies in the State throughout the period under discussion. The influence of Presbyterian ministers and Princeton graduates was also more or less extensive. There were also graduates of several other Northern and Eastern colleges and of European institutions engaged in teaching in these schools during the early decades of the nineteenth century.[2]

Advanced methods of teaching were not generally practiced in these institutions, though the few glimpses which we get of their conduct occasionally indicate more or less creditable and thorough teaching with emphasis now on one thing and now on another. In the Salisbury Academy in 1807 particular attention was "paid to the grammatical construction of the English language, to reading and spelling it correctly, and to writing a fair hand." In 1810 in a school in Warrenton,

[1] Coon, *op. cit.*, pp. 483, 206.   [2] *Ibid.*, Introduction.

kept by Jacob Mordecai with the assistance of his son and daughters, "the beauties of such authors as Addison and Pope are unfolded to the pupils in so interesting and engaging a manner that the taste is generally chastened and refined to the standard of classic purity. The mind is elevated superior to the enjoyment of silly novels, which but too often deprave the taste, corrupt the heart, and enfeeble the understanding." The students here were also taught both to read and compose music. In many of the schools memorizing the rules of English grammar and of arithmetic seems to have been a popular method of teaching these subjects. Some girls in a female academy at Charlotte "who began to memorize grammar since the commencement of the session, parsed blank verse with uncommon ease and propriety" in an examination in 1822. Classes in the schools at Lincolnton in 1827 were examined on "memorizing English grammar" and on "reciting the rules of arithmetic." Considerable attention seems to have been given to Latin and Greek prosody, and scanning English poetry was considered helpful to the students. So prevalent was the practice of emphasizing syntax and etymology in a study of the classics that Judge Archibald D. Murphey, celebrated in the educational history of the State for his efforts to promote popular education, severely criticized the custom in 1827. Geography seems to have been taught largely by memorizing names of places: "questions were asked rapidly, passing from one section of the globe to the other," is the description of an examination in one school.

References to the early use of blackboards are very few in the documents dealing with these schools. In 1835, however, "a visitor admired the facility with which ten- and twelve-year-old boys solved problems in interest and the rule of three on the blackboard" in the Raleigh Academy. Another reference is in a criticism of a teacher in a school for girls at Asheboro in 1839 for not using "the blackboard in teaching arithmetic. If a small school like Asheboro had blackboards in 1839, it is more than likely that blackboards were in common use in the schools of this State before 1840."[1] In spite of this criticism, however, it appears that the teacher, a Miss Rea, from Boston, was a successful instructor. Her methods are interesting. Her pupils were

taught the four principal divisions in arithmetic *orally* before they make use of a slate. . . . I understand that great pains is taken by the tutoress to make the pupils understand the *principles* and *reasons* of their operations. They are not permitted to pore over a question they can't understand, for an hour or two together . . . she is equally careful that they thoroughly understand everything they pass over. She is not content that a pupil can answer a question in the *identical words* of the book: by oral illustration and conversation she satisfies herself that the pupil understands *the principles* correctly.[2]

A few schools had features of the Lancaster system of instruction. The first Lancaster school established in the State was at Fayetteville in 1814, and the same year another was begun in Wake County to which children unable to pay for the instruction were admitted free of charge. In February of the following year a Lancaster school was opened in Raleigh where poor children were taught free of tuition charges. By November the enrollment was more than one hundred pupils. Many of these who, before entering the school, "did not know a letter in the book," were in a short time able to "read, write, have some knowledge of figures, and can repeat by

---

[1] Coon, *op. cit.*, Introduction.   [2] *Ibid.*, pp. 339, 340.

THE ACADEMY MOVEMENT

heart a number of moral verses. Some, indeed, have obtained a considerable knowledge of English grammar and geography." In 1822 there was a Lancaster school near Charlotte, which was also training teachers on this system of teaching, and one in Iredell County. The Newbern Academy seems to have had a department conducted on this system of education in 1822.[1]

REFERENCES

Brown, E. E., *The Making of Our Middle Schools;* Dexter, *History of Education in the United States;* Brown, J. F., *The American High School;* Coon, *North Carolina Schools and Academies, 1790–1840, A Documentary History;* Cyclopedia of Education, edited by Paul Monroe, vol. I, article, "Academies"; Weeks, *Calvin Henderson Wiley and the Organization of the Common Schools of North Carolina;* Raper, *The Church and Private Schools in North Carolina;* Smith, *History of Education in North Carolina.*

SUGGESTIONS FOR FURTHER STUDY

1. What conditions gave rise to the academy in England?
2. What influence did the Act of Uniformity, as renewed in 1662, have on the development of education in England?
3. What conditions gave rise to the academy in the United States?
4. How did the early American academy resemble the academy which developed in England in the seventeenth century?
5. How did the early American academy resemble the Latin Grammar School of colonial days?
6. In what respects was it similar to our modern public high school?
7. Why is the American public high school frequently spoken of as the "people's college"?

[1] Coon, *op. cit.*, Introduction.

8. How does the American high school reflect American character?
9. Make a study of any academies established in your county, noting their management, equipment, curriculum, qualifications of their teachers, and methods of teaching, and compare these features with similar features of any high schools in your county at the present time.
10. How late did academies flourish in your county? What caused their decline? In what instances were they absorbed by public high schools?
11. How do the courses of study offered in many of the academies in North Carolina (see pages 54–56) compare with the curriculum of the high schools of your county to-day?
12. Is there any evidence that the so-called modern subjects, such as domestic science and domestic art, manual training, and other practical subjects, were being taught in academies in North Carolina before the Civil War?
13. How sound do you consider the methods of teaching in use in the girls' school at Asheboro in 1839, described on page 60?

CHAPTER V

THE EARLY AGITATION (1776–1825)

NORTH CAROLINA was not only the first of the States adopting secession to work out prior to the war a creditable system of primary schools, but it developed the best system to be found in the entire South in 1860. This educational achievement was early recognized. Just before the war Superintendent Calvin H. Wiley said in commenting on the success and influence of the schools: —

> The educational system of North Carolina is now attracting the favorable attention of the States south, west, and north of us. . . . All modern statistical publications give us a rank far in advance of the position which we occupied in such works a few years ago; and without referring to numerous other facts equally significant, our moral influence may be illustrated by the fact that the superintendent of common schools was pressingly invited to visit, free of expense, the legislature of the most powerful State south of us [Georgia], to aid in preparing a system of public instruction similar to ours. He receives constant inquiries from abroad in regard to our plan; and beyond all doubt our schools, including those of all grades, are now the greatest temporal interest of the State. . . . North Carolina has the start of all her Southern sisters in educational matters. . . . If, then, she is true to herself, and justly comprehends the plain logic of the facts of her situation, she will now . . . prudently and courageously advance in the direction which leads alike to safety, to peace, and to prosperity. . . . Such action is not merely important as likely to lead to future greatness; it is also a defensive and imperative necessity of the present. If the Union remains, no one will deny the importance, to our peace as well as honor, of having a strong and

prosperous State, able to command the respect of her confederates; if the Union is dissolved, then North Carolina is our only country for the present, and our present security and future hopes will depend on her power to stand alone or honorably to compete with rivals in a new confederacy.

Later it was said of North Carolina's *ante-bellum* educational success: —

As it was, during the half-century under consideration — 1790–1840 — this State did make an educational record, if not in some respects so brilliant as Virginia, yet beyond the Old Dominion, more decided at first, more steady in the upbuilding of secondary education, and, at the close, 1835–1840, was able to place on the ground, beyond dispute, the best system of public instruction in the fourteen Southern States east of the Mississippi previous to the outbreak of the Civil War.[1]

The development of the ideal of public education in the State was slow, though it began early and grew steadily. The first significant step in the growth of this ideal was the adoption in 1776 of a constitutional provision for legislative establishment of schools and for a university. This provision of the constitution, which was adopted in December of that year and which was practically a literal copy of a section of the constitution of Pennsylvania, adopted three months earlier, was: —

That a school or schools shall be established by the Legislature for the convenient instruction of youth, with such salaries to the masters, paid by the public, as may enable them to instruct at low prices; and all useful learning shall be duly encouraged and promoted in one or more universities.

This provision was continued in the revised constitution of 1835.

The university was chartered in 1789 and organized

[1] *Report of the United States Commissioner of Education*, 1895–96, p. 282.

six years later, graduating its first class in 1798. With this exception, however, no legislation was enacted for public education until 1825 when an act was passed creating a literary fund. And with the exception of this action it was nearly fifty years from the organization of the university to the passage of the first public-school law of the State, in January, 1839.

There were many conditions which prevented an earlier obedience to the educational mandate of the constitution. Leaders in the State believed in the civilizing influences of schools and colleges and embodied that conviction in as substantial and effective activity as conditions would allow. But the terms of the constitution itself were more or less uncertain and variously interpreted by those who really had an earnest interest in promoting the cause of public schools. To some the constitutional provision meant that the Legislature should establish public free schools and provide for their maintenance by state taxation, while others believed that it was intended to give authority for legislative aid to private schools and academies. This latter interpretation was so general that frequent petitions were presented to the Assembly for aid of such schools, but they were invariably refused; and in 1803 a bill for establishing an academy in each district, to be maintained by the public, was also defeated. Another condition which hindered legislative action was the fear of taxation, inherited perhaps from colonial days. Taxation, it was argued, was designed in a republican form of government to defray its legitimate and necessary expenses, and the less the tax, the more ideal the government. Such a theory naturally stifled the proper conception of education in a democracy. Moreover, the intrusion of the State into the parental obligation was considered by some as dangerous and agrarian. To others, the element of charity read into a public-school system seemed humiliating — an attitude which cooled local pride and community patriotism. Besides, lack of communication between the eastern and the western counties produced sectional jealousies which unhappily prevented the development of a common educational interest. The entire absence of proper qualifications and a resulting lack of professional spirit among the teachers of the State also delayed the beginnings of a movement for popular education. Compared with many other pursuits, teaching was popularly considered contemptible.[1]

Agitation of a movement to establish a common-school system, however, began early after the opening of the national period. Many public-spirited men looked beyond the narrownesses, delusions, and jealousies which prevailed in the State and considered the larger interests of the whole people. Lack of educational facilities for the masses made a keen appeal to such leaders, who believed that legislative action should be sought to improve the pathetic condition. As early as 1802 Governor Williams recommended to the Legislature a provision, "through adequate and suitable means, for a general diffusion of learning and science throughout the State" so that the people could duly "appreciate and properly understand and defend, their natural, civil, and political rights." In 1803 Governor Turner urged "the establishment of schools in every part of the State. Education is the mortal enemy to arbitrary governments, and the surest basis of liberty and equal right." The following

[1] Coon, *Public Education in North Carolina, 1790-1840, A Documentary History*, vol. I, p. 560.

year he desired to see "a plan of education introduced, which will extend itself to every corner of the State," to be maintained by public taxation, which "every citizen will be willing and desirous to contribute toward an expense so well applied." In 1805 he again urged a general and effective legislative plan of educational action. Schools and the means of education were sorely needed and they could not prosper if left to individual effort, he argued.

Governor Alexander likewise, in his message in 1806 and again in 1807, made similar recommendations, which were urged by Governor Williams in 1808 and by Governor Stone in 1809 and in 1810. Governor Stone's enumeration of some advantages to be derived from the establishment of a judicious plan of education in the State is interesting. Among other advantages such a plan would "relieve parents from much of the anxiety and uneasiness of distant separation from their children," and would "save a considerable amount of our circulating medium among strangers." Moreover, it would

> prevent the impression upon the minds of our youth, of unreasonable predilections in favor of alien institutions and manners, as well as of prejudices against those of our own State, and against the condition of society, of which their interest and duty require them to become members. . . . Attach the respect, gratitude, and reverence of our own youth to persons and places within our own limits, as being their guides to science and virtue. . . .

He advocated the education of both boys and girls: —

> I trust we shall never consider our task as finished, until preparation shall be made, and opportunity afforded for the most obscure members of society to procure such a portion of

instruction for their offspring, as shall enable them satisfactorily to discharge the most important duties of society.

Governor Benjamin Smith, in his message in 1811, said: —

Too much attention cannot be paid to the all-important subject of education. In despotic governments, where the supreme power is in possession of a tyrant or divided among an hereditary aristocracy (generally corrupt and wicked), the ignorance of the people is a security to their rulers;[1] but in a free government, where the offices and honors of the State are open to all, the superiority of their political privileges should be infused into every citizen from their earliest infancy, so as to produce an enthusiastic attachment to their own country, and insure a jealous support of their own constitution, laws, and government. A certain degree of education should be placed within the reach of every child of the State; and I am persuaded a plan may be formed upon economical principles that would extend this down to the poor of every neighborhood, at an expense trifling beyond expectation, when compared with the incalculable benefits from such a philanthropic and politic system. . . .

Governor William Hawkins in 1812 and Governor Miller in 1815 recommended legislative establishment of schools. "It is under the hand of legislative patronage alone that the temple of science can be thrown open to all," declared Governor Miller. However, beyond refer-

[1] In this connection it is interesting to recall the type of argument advanced early in the nineteenth century against governmental aid to education in England: "In a free nation where slaves are not allowed of, the surest wealth consists in a multitude of laborious poor; for besides that they are the never-failing nursery of fleets and armies, without them there could be no enjoyment, and no product of any country would be valuable. To make the society happy and people easy under the meanest circumstances, it is requisite that great numbers should be ignorant as well as poor. Knowledge both enlarges and multiplies our desires, and the fewer things man wishes for, the more easily his necessity may be supplied." (See Adams, *History of the Elementary School Contest in England*, p. 46.)

ring the recommendation to a joint committee of both houses, the first Committee on Education appointed in the Legislature, no action was taken by the Assembly. The following year Governor Miller again called attention to the same subject and urged the adoption of some plan by which educational facilities could be afforded to all the youth of the State. At the same time he proposed the establishment of a fund for school support: "The example set in a neighboring State, in establishing funds for the advancement of literature and internal improvements, seems well worthy of imitation."[1]

That part of the message which related to education was referred to a committee of which Archibald D. Murphey, Senator from Orange County, whose work in promoting public education in the State won for him the name of "father of the common schools," was made chairman. The result was an interesting report, written by Murphey, in which the democratic theory of popular education was thoroughly elaborated. The report pointed out that the education of the youth of the State was then left to chance, and that thousands of children were growing up in ignorance. The strength of the State resided in its people, who should be educated at public expense without distinction of class. The Legislature, the report continued, was then able to appropriate half a million dollars for maintaining a general system of public instruction. In concluding, Murphey recommended the appointment of a legislative committee of three to digest a system of education based on the general principles of the report, to be submitted at the next session.

Two reports were presented at this session: one,

[1] Virginia established a literary fund in 1810.

dated December 6, 1817, and presented December 8, was signed by John M. Walker, a member of the committee, who had been "unable to communicate with the other members"; and another, dated November 27, 1817, and presented two days later, was signed by Murphey. Walker's report recommended that provision be made for training a sufficient number of teachers to reduce by competition charges of tuition so that education could be put within reach of all the children of the State. The education of the poor, the report declared, was of first importance.

The elaborate report by Murphey was more significant, however, in that it marked the dawn of a new educational era in North Carolina, and became the basis of the system of public instruction finally established in 1839. The report was presented after a careful study of the best systems of education in this country and in Europe and embodied the best of the practicable features revealed by the investigation. It outlined a general plan of public instruction which included, a literary fund. Provision was also made for a state board of education to manage the fund and to superintend the school system; for the state university, for academies, and primary schools, and their organization and course of study; and provision for the education of the poor and for an asylum for the deaf and dumb. The primary schools were considered of first importance in the plan, and one or more of these was to be established in each township. Since it is this degree of education which is of most interest here, that part of the plan may be given in full: —

That each county in this State be divided into two or more townships; and that one or more primary schools be established in each township, provided a lot of ground not less than four acres and a sufficient house erected thereon, be provided and vested in the board of public instruction. And that every incorporated town in the State, containing more than one hundred families, shall be divided into wards. Such town containing less than one hundred families shall be considered as forming only one ward. Each ward, upon conveying to the board of public instruction a lot of ground of the value of two hundred and fifty dollars, shall be entitled to the benefits and privileges of a primary school.

The court of pleas and quarter sessions shall annually elect for each township, in their respective counties, five persons as trustees of the primary schools to be established in such county, who shall have power to fix the sites of the primary schools to be established thereon, superintend and manage the same, make rules for their government, appoint trustees, appoint teachers, and remove them at pleasure. They shall select such children residing in their township, whose parents are unable to pay for their schooling, who shall be taught at the said schools for three years without charge. They shall report to the board of public instruction, the rules which they may adopt for the government of said schools, and shall annually report to the said board the state of the schools, the number and conduct of the pupils educated at the public expense, such books, stationery, and other implements for learning as may be necessary.

The teacher of each primary school shall receive a salary of one hundred dollars, to be paid out of the fund for public instruction.

This plan for establishing primary schools is simple, and can easily be carried into execution. It divides the expenses of these schools between the public and those individuals for whose immediate benefit they are established; it secures a regular stipend to the teachers, and yet holds out inducements to them to be active and faithful in their calling; and it enables every neighborhood, whether the number of its inhabitants be few or many, to have a primary school, at the cheap price of a small lot of ground, and a house erected thereon, sufficient for the purpose of the school. Were these schools in full operation in every section of the State, even in the present state of our population, more than fifteen thousand children would annually be taught in them. These schools would be to the rich a convenience, and to the poor, a blessing.

The plan provided for the following course of study in the primary schools: —

In the primary schools should be taught reading, writing, and arithmetic. A judicious selection of books should from time to time be made by the board of public instruction for the use of small children; books which shall excite their curiosity and improve their moral dispositions. And the board should be empowered to compile and have printed, for the use of primary schools, such books as they may think will best subserve the purposes of intellectual and moral instruction. In these books should be contained many of the historical parts of the Old and New Testaments, that children may early be made acquainted with the books which contain the word of truth, and the doctrines of eternal life.

It is interesting to note the method of teaching which was also recommended : —

The great object of education is intellectual and moral improvement; and that mode of instruction is to be preferred which best serves to effect this object. That mode is to be found only in a correct knowledge of the human mind, its habits, passions, and manner of operation. The philosophy of the mind, which in ages preceding has been cultivated only in its detached branches has of late years received form and system in the schools of Scotland. This new science promises the happiest results. It has sapped the foundation of skepticism by establishing the authority of those primitive truths and intuitive principles which form the basis of all demonstration; it has taught to man the extent of his intellectual powers, and marking the line which separates truth from hypothetical conjecture, has pointed out to his view the boundaries which Providence has prescribed to inquiries. It has determined the laws of the various faculties of the mind, and furnished a system of philosophic logic for conducting our inquiries in every branch of knowledge.

This new science has given birth to new methods of instruction; methods which, being founded upon a correct knowledge of the faculties of the mind, have eminently facilitated their development. Pestalozzi, of Switzerland, and Joseph Lancaster, of England, seem to have been most successful in the application of new methods to the instruction of the children. Their methods are different, but each is founded upon a profound knowledge of the human mind. The basis of each method is, *the excitement of the curiosity of children;* thereby awakening their minds and preparing them to receive instruction. The success which has attended the application of their methods, particularly that of Lancaster, has been astonishing. Although but very few years have elapsed since Lancastrian [sic] schools were first established, they have spread over the British Empire, extended into the continent of Europe, the Island of St. Domingo, and the United States. Various improvements in the details of his plan have been suggested by experience and adopted; and it is probable that in time, his will become the universal mode of instruction for children. The Lancastrian [sic] plan is equally distinguished by its simplicity, its facility of application, the rapid intellectual improvement which it gives, and the exact discipline which it enforces. The moral effects of the plan are also astonishing; exact and correct habits are the surest safeguards of morals; and it has often been remarked, that out of the immense number of children and grown persons instructed in Lancaster's schools, few, very few have ever been prosecuted in a court of justice for any offense. Your committee do, therefore, recommend that, whenever it be practicable, the Lancastrian [sic] mode of instruction may be successfully introduced into the primary schools. The general principles of this method may be successfully introduced into the academies and university; and your committee indulge the hope that the board of public instruction, and the professors and teachers in these respective institutions, will use their best endeavors to adopt and enforce the best methods of instruction which the present state of knowledge will enable them to devise.

The plan which the report recommended for the education of poor children is also of interest: —

One of the strongest reasons which we can have for establishing a general plan of public instruction, is the condition of the poor children of our country. Such has always been and probably always will be the allotment of human life, that the poor will form a large portion of every community; and it is the duty of those who manage the affairs of a State to extend relief to this unfortunate part of our species in every way in their power.

Providence, in the impartial distribution of its favors, whilst it has denied to the poor many of the comforts of life, has generally bestowed upon them the blessing of intelligent children. Poverty is the school of genius; it is a school in which the active powers of man are developed and disciplined, and in which that moral courage has acquired, which enables him to toil with difficulties, privations, and want. From this school generally come forth those men who act the principal parts upon the theater of life; men who impress a character upon the age in which forms grow up in it. The State should take this school under her special care, and nurturing the genius which there grows in rich luxuriance, give to it an honorable and profitable direction. Poor children are the peculiar property of the State, and by proper cultivation they will constitute a fund of intellectual and moral worth which will greatly subserve the public interest. Your committee have therefore endeavored to provide for the education of all poor children in the primary schools; they have also provided for the advancement into the academies and university of such of those children as are most distinguished for genius and give the best assurance of future usefulness. For three years they are to be educated in the primary schools free of charge; the portion of them who shall be selected for further advancement shall, during the whole course of their future education, be clothed, fed, and taught at the public expense. The number of children who are to be thus advanced, will depend upon the state of the fund set apart for public instruction, and your committee think it will be most advisable to leave the number to the discretion of the board, who shall have charge of the fund; and also to leave to them the providing of some just and particular mode of advancing this number from the primary schools to the academies, and from the academies to the university.

The scheme as outlined met the hearty support of the Assembly, and a bill, based on the report, was accordingly prepared and presented. The proposed legislation passed its first reading in both houses and then disappeared from the records. The impracticable feature of attempting to maintain as well as to educate the children of the poor, and the burdens of the war debt of 1812, were among the factors combining to defeat the scheme which "embraced the profoundest and most comprehensive educational wisdom ever presented for the consideration of a North Carolina Legislature." The friends of the proposed plan were unwilling to eliminate the impracticable features and legislative enactment of the bill proved an impossibility.

There is a certain interesting similarity between the general plan of education proposed in North Carolina at this time and the plan offered by the literary board to the Legislature of Virginia in 1817, which comprehended a university, colleges, academies, and primary schools. By that plan the counties were to be divided into townships in each of which a primary school was to be established. The teacher, selected by local trustees, could receive pupils, other than those to be educated free of charge, at rates to be decided on by the trustees. The privilege was given of using "the new mode of teaching, invented by Lancaster." A bill conformable to the recommendations of this plan was presented to the Assembly and passed in the House of Delegates by a vote of 66 to 49. But it was defeated in the Senate, the vote standing 7 to 7. This was in February, 1817. This plan and the bill based on it had been "diligently examined" by and had obviously influenced the Murphey committee. Both reports and the bills based on them finally met practically the same fate.

Although this attempt to establish schools failed, agitation of the subject did not cease. Governor Branch, in his message to the Legislature in 1818, referred especially to the "solemn injunction" of the constitution, and reminded that body that "by this chart we are bound, as the servants of the people under the solemnities of an oath, to steer the vessel of state." Assembly committees on education continued to be appointed. During this session of the Legislature, William Martin, of Pasquotank County, a member of the Senate Committee on Education, introduced a bill to establish and regulate schools in the several counties of the State. By the plan proposed schools were to be established in each military district. The county courts were to appoint "five persons of competent skill and ability" to have direction of school affairs in the various counties. Three local trustees, to be appointed by these county directors, were to employ the teacher and "designate such poor children in their neighborhood as they shall think ought to be taught free of any charge." These poor children were also to receive free books and stationery. The expenses of the schools were to be borne by a property tax of ten cents on the hundred dollars valuation and a capitation tax of fifty cents to be levied in each county. Each teacher was to be paid an annual salary of one hundred dollars from the county funds and also receive two thirds of the money collected from tuition. The bill passed its first reading in both houses, and passed its second reading in the Senate by a vote of 53 to 2, but on its second reading in the House it was postponed indefinitely.

Governor Branch in 1819 again called attention to the need for legislative action, declaring that the education of the youth of the State was a question which claimed attention above all others. In the same year an article in the *Blakely Gazette* pointed out that there was a prevailing sentiment in the State in favor of a general system of education, but that the sparse population rendered difficult the execution of any plan. Moreover, there was a diversity of opinion as to how schools should be supported. The Senate Committee on Education, to which had been referred that part of the Governor's message which concerned schools, made an interesting report at this time which suggested state aid for schools and the establishment of a school fund for educational purposes.

The question received no legislative consideration again until 1822, when Governor Gabriel Holmes addressed the Assembly somewhat at length on the subject. He urged obedience to the constitutional injunction to establish schools. "I fear, gentlemen, if those venerable fathers were to rise from their tombs, they would reproach us with supineness and neglect, and would not listen to our plea of want of power. We shall never know what power we have until we exert it." He also believed that agricultural education was seriously neglected, and urged attention to the demands of this form of training. His message had a slight effect: it was proposed that taxes on auctioneers be used to assist academies in the State, and a resolution was adopted which looked to securing educational aid from the national government. But both of the efforts failed.

In 1823 Governor Holmes again referred to the need for agricultural education and recommended the purchase of a small farm near the university to serve as a model for scientific and practical farming. At this session of the Assembly, J. A. Hill, of New Hanover County, introduced a resolution in the House to authorize the committee on education to inquire "into the expediency of establishing" a school system in accordance with the requirement of the constitution. In that same year the *Western Carolinian* editorially commented on the legislative neglect of education, pointed out that the great mass of the people of the State were deficient in the rudiments of education, and declared that "No appropriation which the Legislature could make would be so little objected to as one for the support of common schools. We do hope some member will make an experiment this session, and see what can be done in the Legislature on this subject." No legislative action was taken, however.

With the year 1824 there appeared an educational sentiment more vigorous and widespread than had before been seen, though the Legislature took no forward steps educationally. In his message to the Assembly Governor Holmes regretted that in spite of a treasury "abounding in gold and silver . . . collected from the people," no appropriation had been made for schools.

Surely, then, we cannot, consistent with good policy, hesitate to create a fund that will assist the parents of every denomination to initiate their offspring in elementary rudiments of learning. . . . The people are industrious and patriotic; they cheerfully subscribe to the necessary demands of the State upon their purse, without a murmur. They would gladly receive and greatly acknowledge your patronage for the improvement of their families. They have a right fully to anticipate your fostering care. . . .

Although he touched "the chord with almost hopeless expectations and frigid indifference," an unexpected response came in the form of an interesting report from the Senate Committee on Education. This report spoke eloquently of the evils of ignorance and of the advantages of "a general diffusion of useful knowledge" and concluded that the talents of the poor of the State should especially be provided for, since the wealthy already had the means of education. On this report was based a bill which proposed to create a fund for educational purposes. It was introduced by Charles A. Hill, of Franklin County, chairman of the Senate Committee, and bore the title, "A bill to create a fund for educating that part of the infant population of the State who shall from time to time be found destitute of the means of becoming otherwise properly taken care of in that particular." The sources of the fund were to be certain bank stock to be acquired by the State and certain license taxes. The management of the fund was also provided for in the bill. It passed the Senate on its third reading by a vote of 38 to 16, but was indefinitely postponed in the House without a division December 30.

Similar action was later taken in this body on a bill introduced by Samuel P. Ashe, of Cumberland County, which provided for a fund and a plan for the education of the poor children in the various counties of the State. By this bill schools were to be established in every county and were to be maintained by an annual appropriation from the state treasury which was to be apportioned by officials to be known as "County Commissioners for the Education of the Poor." These commissioners were to determine what children were entitled to share in this bounty and to make provision for them to be taught the rudiments of an English education. On its second reading the bill was amended and postponed indefinitely, January 3, 1825. On the same day a resolution was introduced in the House to appoint a committee to prepare a plan or system of public education for the instruction of children of "poor or indigent parentage" to be reported at the next session, and was passed as a joint resolution of the two houses. In his report to the same Assembly John Haywood, treasurer of the State, recommended the use of certain stock belonging to the State as the nucleus of a fund for education, "which might ultimately prove commensurate to the providing the means of education, throughout the State, for that portion of our citizens who may, from time to time, be found destitute of them." This would form at least a "hopeful beginning" and solve the problem of establishing schools without taxation.

Haywood's plan led to newspaper comments on the subject. The *Western Carolinian* editorially approved it and agitated legislative action, and articles in the same paper signed by "A. B." compared North Carolina's apparent indifference with the educational achievements of some of the Eastern States. The same articles recommended primary schools and the establishment of schools to train teachers. It was believed that the State was amply able to support an educational system. And at the same time an educational meeting was held in Edgecombe County and decision made to petition the Legislature in behalf of common schools; the appeal from the Edgecombe citizens was published in the *Raleigh Register*. Other newspaper articles appeared, and the public conscience showed signs of being awakened on the subject.

We have seen that the first signal victory for education in North Carolina came when the constitutional provision for schools was adopted in 1776. The second victory came in 1825 when the law creating a school fund was enacted. At the meeting of the Assembly that year, Governor Burton declared that education was more important than internal improvements, a subject which had been given legislative attention for eight years. Real freedom was impossible without education; education was necessary for the people to appreciate their political blessings. At this time a petition for free schools was presented from Beaufort County, and the Orange County Sunday-School Union asked legislative aid for its work. This petition, which was signed by forty citizens, recited that the society had under its care twenty-two Sunday schools with an enrollment of nearly one thousand "children, many of whom, — the children of the poor, — who would otherwise have been brought up in utter ignorance and vice, have been taught to read and trained to habits of moral reflection and conduct. The schools have been heretofore supplied with books for the most part by the charity of the public, and it is to furnish the necessary books, that your memorialists pray for such aid, as that the sum of twenty-five cents per annum may be paid for every Sunday-school learner under their care, out of the public taxes." The committee to whom the petition was referred considered it inexpedient to grant the request and the petition was rejected.

The committee appointed the previous year made its report on a plan for a general system of schools for the State. In most respects the plan proposed was similar to previous plans. Its most interesting feature was its provision for taxation for school support, and this provision meant immediate death to the plan. A few days later an attempt was made to create a school fund by lottery, but this likewise was defeated. But Charles A. Hill, of Franklin County, who had the previous year presented a bill to create a school fund, now reported to the Senate a bill to create a fund for the establishment of common schools in the State, which passed through the usual legislative channels without division in either house and regularly became law. The act was drawn by Bartlett Yancey, President of the Senate, and a former student of law under Judge Murphey. The provision of this act and the influence of the fund created by it will be treated in another chapter.

THE EARLY AGITATION 83

REFERENCES

Journals of the House and Senate; Public Laws of North Carolina; legislative documents; Coon, *Public Education in North Carolina, 1790–1840, A Documentary History;* Weeks, *Calvin Henderson Wiley and the Organization of the Common Schools of North Carolina;* Smith, *History of Education in North Carolina;* Report of the United States Commissioner of Education, 1895–96.

SUGGESTIONS FOR FURTHER STUDY

1. What was the final influence of the American Revolution on education in the United States?
2. How did the influence express itself in North Carolina?
3. What arguments are made in the messages of the governors during the early years of the national period for legislative establishment of schools?
4. Compare the constitutional provision for education in North Carolina with similar provisions in the constitutions of other States.
5. What States had made constitutional provision for schools before 1825? How many States had established school systems by that date?
6. What were the merits of the plan proposed by Murphey in 1817 for a school system in North Carolina? What were its weaknesses?
7. Compare that plan with the plan proposed for Virginia about the same time.
8. Compare Murphey's plan with the plan presented by Walker.
9. What was the Lancasterian system of education which Murphey recommended? What advantages were claimed for it? To what extent was the system adopted or used in North Carolina?
10. What is the historical relation between the Sunday-school movement and the public-school movement in the United States? Trace the historical development of the Sunday-school movement in North Carolina.

CHAPTER VI

THE LITERARY FUND

So universal is the acceptance of the free-school idea to-day that it is difficult to believe that it has developed through opposition and struggle or that any other educational theory ever found widespread support in democratic communities. But public sentiment in regard to public education, free and open alike to all, has undergone remarkable changes during the past century. Early in the nineteenth century, and even as late as the thirties, sentiment was more or less hostile to the principle of free schools, as that principle is now accepted. Not only were schools and the means of education at state expense rare, but taxation for educational purposes was everywhere difficult to levy. Efficient state supervision and control, now so rapidly developing, was practically unknown; laws which looked to encouraging free schools were permissive and hard to enforce; even the income from endowments created for free-school support was frequently used for other than educational purposes, and not infrequently the endowment itself was mismanaged and exploited for private ends. Indifference, contempt, and hostility confronted the early movements for establishing and maintaining systems of public free schools.

But the gradual growth of the free-school idea reveals the slow development of two important principles of education which to-day are present in every adequate and sound public-school system. The first of these is the democratic principle that education is the function of the State rather than a family function or a parental obligation, and that the responsibility of providing the means of education rests primarily with the State. The other principle is that the State has the power and the right to raise by taxation on the property of its members sufficient funds for adequate school support. Both of these principles are now generally accepted in North Carolina, though here as elsewhere they have won acceptance in the face of such bitter opposition and cold indifference that their period of intense struggle is now not only difficult to recount, but even more difficult, perhaps, to realize.

This remarkable change had its origin very largely in the establishment of permanent public endowments, popularly known as "literary" or "school" funds, the income from which was designed to apply to public-school support. Such funds have fostered and encouraged the growth of the present conception of education as a public duty. In almost every State in the United States the public-school system was begun and set in action through this popular method of support. Moreover, no feature of the public-school systems of the United States has rendered greater or more lasting service than public educational endowments, in destroying opposition to taxation for school purposes, in developing a wholesome educational sentiment, and finally, in stimulating local initiative and community enterprise. Historically, therefore, the origin, development, and influence of a public-school fund have an important place in a treatment such as this.

A variety of purposes or incentives for creating permanent public-school endowments appears, and a few of them may be noted here. Notwithstanding the conditions which at one time generally opposed free schools, public sentiment was never unanimous against them. There were a few public-spirited citizens in most communities who considered state education not only a necessary duty but a rare opportunity for promoting intelligent and efficient citizenship. The discharge of this duty called for funds, and there was almost everywhere a dominating sentiment against taxation for anything except the necessary expenses of government. Schools were not yet properly considered a state obligation. Therefore, the establishment of a permanent fund promised a means of escape from taxation for schools and relief to towns and communities from this burden. This seems to be the oldest aim or incentive for establishing a permanent public-school fund, and is illustrated by the act of 1795 which established such an endowment in Connecticut. The result was unexpected and unwholesome: the fund failed to make the schools free, the gradual increase in its income gradually decreased the tendency to raise local school taxes, and from 1821 to 1854 practically the only sources of school support in that State were the income from the school fund, gifts, and rate bills, which were not abolished until 1868.

Other States profited by the costly lesson Connecticut had learned. It was clearly demonstrated that an endowment should not entirely relieve a community from local burdens, but should stimulate and encourage local effort for school support. Any other principle is not only a moral injury to the community and to the cause for which the fund was provided, but means death to that cause if the people are relieved of all responsibility of assisting in its support. Therefore, another aim in establishing school funds was to encourage local taxation. The earliest example of this principle is found in the case of New York, where its founders never contemplated that the fund, established in 1805, should yield sufficient revenue entirely to support the schools. The principle here adopted was that of local taxation; before a community could participate in a distribution of the revenue of the fund an amount equal to its share had to be raised by local levy. This principle has been the one most generally accepted as the soundest and most stimulating to the cause of adequate school support, and is now, with some modifications, the one most extensively adopted in the various States. It was this principle which was adopted in North Carolina in 1839 when the fund was considered of sufficient accumulation to launch a school system; and on this principle the income of the fund was distributed throughout the *antebellum* period.

Other lawful objects to which the income of permanent school endowments may now be applied are numerous. In some cases it may be used for teachers' salaries, the expenses of summer normal schools, institutes, or other forms of teacher training; in others, for the construction and equipment of schoolhouses; in others for pupils' tuition, transportation, or textbooks, and in others still, for school supervision. The income from the present fund in North Carolina, by act of January, 1903, is applied exclusively to the purpose of building schoolhouses. Local communities may borrow from the fund one half the cost of the new building, repaying the amount in ten equal annual payments at four percent interest.

North Carolina's school fund, known as the "literary fund," was created in 1825. At that time eleven other States had created similar permanent endowments for public-school purposes: Connecticut in 1795, Delaware in 1796, New York in 1805, Tennessee in 1806, Virginia in 1810, Maryland in 1813, Georgia and New Jersey in 1817, and Illinois, Kentucky, and Mississippi between 1818 and 1821. New Hampshire created a fund in 1821, but it was not a permanent fund, and no permanent fund was established in that State until 1867. North Carolina was therefore the eighth of the original, and the sixth of the Southern, States to establish a permanent public endowment for educational purposes. The act creating the fund defined its sources as: —

> The dividends arising from the stock now held by the State in the banks of Newbern and Cape Fear and which have not heretofore been pledged and set apart for internal improvements; the dividends arising from stock which is owned by the State in the Cape Fear Navigation Company, the Roanoke Navigation Company, and the Clubfoot and Harlow Creek Canal Company; the tax imposed by law on licenses to the retailers of spirituous liquors and auctioneers; the unexpended balance of the Agricultural Fund, which by the act of the Legislature is directed to be paid into the public treasury; all moneys paid to the State for the entries of vacant lands (except the Cherokee lands); the sum of twenty-one thousand and ninety dollars, which was paid by this State to certain Cherokee Indians, for reservations to lands secured by them by treaty, when the said sums shall be received from the United States by this State; and of all the vacant and unappropriated swamp lands in this State, together with such sums of money as the Legislature may hereafter find it convenient to appropriate from time to time.

The same act vested the fund in the governor, the chief justice of the supreme court, the President of the

Senate, the Speaker of the House of Representatives, and the treasurer of the State, as directors of the endowment. This body was directed to invest the funds in the stock of any of the state banks or of the United States and to alter and change such investments in any way that would promote their value. The fund thus provided, when sufficiently accumulated, was to be applied to the instruction of the youth of the State in the principles of reading, writing, and arithmetic, to be divided among the counties in proportion to their free white population.

The growth of the fund was slow during its early period. When the first report of the literary board was made to the Legislature in February, 1827, the receipts of the fund previous to November 1, 1826, amounted to $12,304.95. At this time the State owned 2762 shares of stock in the Bank of the State, valued at $276,200, the dividends from which were then applied to the ordinary expenses of the government. It also held 1663 shares in the Bank of Newbern, valued at $166,300, and 2057 shares in the Bank of Cape Fear, valued at $205,700. The income from 1304 shares in the Bank of Newbern and 1358 shares in the Bank of Cape Fear, which the State held before 1821, was set apart and applied to internal improvements. The dividends arising from the remaining 359 shares in the Bank of Newbern, and 699 shares in the Bank of Cape Fear, were pledged to the literary fund. The board recommended "that the stock now owned by the State and purchased since 1821, and that which may be acquired in the Banks of Newbern and Cape Fear" be transferred to the literary board for educational purposes. If the fund were thus increased, the report stated, schools could soon be established.

The second report of the board showed that the receipts of the fund for the year ending November 1, 1827, amounted to $23,702.37, making an aggregate sum of more than $36,000 belonging to the fund at that time. The third report, dated December, 1828, placed the aggregate amount of the fund at $77,811.62. The board urged "a steady perseverance in the plan which is now in operation and which promises at no very distant period to realize the benevolent and patriotic expectations of those with whom it originated."

The income from the fund for 1829 was more than $16,000. In 1830 it was $30,152.88; the following year the fund amounted to $74,476.48, and on November 1, 1832, it amounted to $88,165.61. For the year ending November 1, 1833, the receipts of the fund were more than $28,000, making the total amount of the fund about $117,000. No expenditures had been made from the fund since 1828. The entire fund was therefore idle and unproductive during those years. The act creating the endowment gave the literary board authority to invest any part or the whole of the fund in the stock of any of the banks of the State, or in the stock of the Bank of the United States. The board was declining to exercise this authority largely because it was uncertain of the proper construction to be put on this part of the act. Problems of safe investments remained throughout the life of the fund one of its serious difficulties. Until 1838 they were in fact the chief problems confronting the board. Not until that date was the revenue of the fund appropriated for school support, and then the principle on which appropriations were made was simple. Each school district which raised by local taxation the sum of twenty dollars for school support was entitled to receive twice that amount from the income of the literary fund.

Criticism of the management of the fund was frequent and well founded. It was not unusual for drafts to be made on it for deficiencies in the public fund; and so common and continuous was this use of the educational fund that the state treasurer in 1832, himself a member of the literary board, urged some provision by which the fund could be preserved and improved. The following table shows the amounts due the literary fund from the public fund, at the end of certain months in 1832 and 1833: —

January	$2,937.20
February	51,271.68
March	52,913.25
April	52,766.05
May	58,380.11
June	60,823.92
July	60,455.30
August	64,339.88
September	56,762.66
October	5,198.42
December	14,125.05
January (1833)	24,547.69
February	66,016.75
March	12,982.49
April	12,742.73

When drafts were made on the school fund to supply deficiencies in the public fund, the amounts were replaced as soon as the taxes "afforded the means." But this use of the fund practically nullified the design of its founders; moreover, control of the fund was thus virtually taken out of the hands of the literary board. The treasurer said, commenting on the practice: —

To suffer thus to go to decay, and to be consumed, means liberally provided and set apart by previous Legislatures for the benefit of an after generation, resembles in some respects the conduct of an improvident heir, who wastes in mere indolence what has been saved, by the industry and economy of the ancestor, for the lasting improvement of the inheritance.

On November 1, 1834, the literary fund amounted to $139,403.99. With this amount 1200 shares of stock in the Bank of North Carolina were bought at a cost of $120,000, leaving an unexpended balance of $19,403.99 in the treasury to the credit of the fund. The receipts during the next year amounted to $29,670.72, which made a total of $49,074.71 in the treasury November 1, 1835. Out of this balance investments in more bank stock had been made to the amount of $46,600, and other disbursements during the year reduced the balance to $1167.08. The receipts during the year ending November 1, 1836, amounted to $32,642.71. Investments and other expenditures for the same period amounted to $29,964.70, leaving in the treasury the sum of $3845.09.

Nothing had yet been done toward the establishment of a system of schools. As has already been seen, there was a growing wholesome educational sentiment and a constant agitation for beginning some sort of educational plan; but the literary board seemed to regard its duties as being confined entirely to the management of the fund. The reports of the board were, therefore, financial rather than educational. Moreover, during this period the fund was considered by the State and private corporations and individuals as a convenient source for drawing or borrowing when in need. The literary fund was regarded as too small to support a school system, and the cause of education, having no powerful champions, suffered as a consequence.

But a decided change appeared after 1836, when the fund was greatly increased by the distribution of the surplus revenue in the federal treasury. Enormous revenues had accumulated as a result of unprecedented land sales and of the protective tariff; and under the leadership of Webster, who introduced the measure, an act was passed distributing the surplus on hand January 1, 1837, among the several States then in the Union, on the basis of their representation in Congress. The States were to agree to return the money when called on, provided not more than $10,000 should be demanded at any one time from any one State without sufficient notice, and all the States were to be called on for their respective parts at the same time. More than $28,000,000 was thus distributed.

North Carolina's share amounted to $1,433,757.40, and its disposition was determined by several important interests and conditions.[1] The first of these was financial and had to do with internal improvements. Previous state aid to this interest had not only proved unprofitable, but it had failed to decrease the need for better transportation facilities. Moreover, private companies and individual effort were ill-prepared to engage in such enterprises; and with the era of railroad construction at hand there was a growing demand for a combination of state and private capital. Such a policy had been recommended repeatedly. It had also been urged that the vast acreage of unavailable swamp lands belonging to the State be drained so as to be made pro-

[1] Boyd, "The Finances of the North Carolina Literary Fund," *South Atlantic Quarterly*, July and October, 1914.

ductive and profitable. But lack of funds prevented the State from inaugurating such a policy.

A decrease in the ancient and intense sectional rivalry between eastern and western interests also proved of influence in determining the disposition of North Carolina's share of the surplus revenue. This rivalry had for a generation existed as a result of an unequal distribution of representation in the Legislature, and demands for constitutional reform had as long been insistent. With the revision of the Constitution in 1835, this reform was secured and the conflict appeared less intense. Chance for united effort on public matters was now greatly enhanced. Moreover, the rise of the Whig Party revealed an important influence in North Carolina, where it adopted, and elected a governor in 1836 on, the progressive policy of increased state aid to internal improvements. These conditions and influences were purely political in character. Another equally important influence, perhaps, but of a different nature, was the depleted condition of the state treasury. In the year that the surplus revenue was distributed, North Carolina had a debt of about $400,000 and a record of expenses exceeding or equaling the revenues. And the literary fund was still insufficient for immediate educational service.

A joint legislative committee of twenty-six members, with William A. Graham, Whig, as chairman, was appointed to inquire into the best method of disposing of the share coming to North Carolina. The recommendation of the committee was that $900,000 be placed to the credit of the literary fund, and the remainder be applied to internal improvements. The opposition, representing the Democrats, proposed that the money be used to redeem the $400,000 debt of the State, to increase the literary fund and the fund for internal improvements, to drain and improve the swamp lands, and to assist in railroad construction. The plan finally adopted disposed of the amount allotted to North Carolina by appropriating $100,000 to the contingent expenses of the state government; the sum of $300,000 to redeem the public debt; the sum of $300,000 to the credit of the literary fund; the sum of $200,000 to drain the swamp lands; and the remaining $533,757.40 to the fund for internal improvements. The appropriation to the literary fund was to be invested in stock of the Bank of Cape Fear, and the $200,000 appropriated to drain the swamp lands was indirectly an appropriation to the same fund, since the income from these lands was to be applied to it when the entries were made. Eventually all of North Carolina's share became a part of the literary fund except the sum appropriated to the current expenses of the state government. But the $500,000 immediately placed to the credit of the fund was not the only increase of that endowment at this time. By further legislation, all the vacant swamp lands of the State were formally vested in the literary fund. Moreover, railroad stock owned by the State and amounting to $600,000, the revenue from certain loans made by the internal improvements board, and 4000 shares of stock in the Bank of the State of North Carolina, valued at $400,000, and 3000 shares in the Bank of Cape Fear, valued at $300,000, both the property of the State, were likewise vested in the literary board for educational purposes. The principal of the literary fund was thus increased about $1,800,000. In November, 1840, the total resources of the fund amounted to $2,241,480.05, and consisted of: —

Bank stock	$1,032,200.00
Railroad stock	600,000.00
Navigation stock	87,500.00
Railroad bonds	225,000.00
Notes of individuals and corporations	155,943.75
Swamp improvements	62,829.24
Cash on hand	78,007.06
Total	$2,241,480.05

The accompanying table on page 97 shows the amounts of the surplus revenue allotted to the other States and how the funds were used.[1]

With the distribution of the surplus revenue in 1837 the literary fund was considered sufficient to begin the support of or assistance to a system of common schools. By act of January 20, 1837, certain changes were made in the composition of the literary board so as to increase its responsibility. The governor, by virtue of his office, was to remain president with power to select with the advice of his council the other three members of the board. At the same time the House passed a resolution which instructed the Committee on Education "to inquire into the expediency of establishing a general system of free schools throughout the State," and the Senate likewise resolved that the literary board "be instructed to digest a plan for common schools, suited to the condition and resources" of the State, to be reported at the next session of the Legislature. The report was made December 4, 1838, and as a result the first public-school law of the State was passed January 7, 1839.[2] The principle of school support adopted by this

[1] Blackmar, *The History of Federal and State Aid to Higher Education*, Bureau of Education Circular of Information, no. 1, 1890, p. 46.

[2] This report of the literary board and the act of 1839 are treated fully in chapter VIII.

THE LITERARY FUND

State	Amount	How used
Alabama	$669,086.78	Education.
Arkansas	286,751.48	General purposes.
Connecticut	764,670.61	One half to education and one half to general purposes.
Delaware	286,751.48	Education.
Georgia	1,051,422.09	One third to education and two thirds to general purposes.
Illinois	477,919.13	Education and internal improvements.
Indiana	860,254.44	One half to education and one half to general purposes.
Kentucky	1,443,757.40	Education.
Louisiana	477,919.13	General purposes.
Maine	955,838.27	General purposes.
Maryland	955,838.27	Education and general purposes.
Massachusetts	1,338,173.57	General purposes.
Michigan	286,751.48	Internal improvements.
Mississippi	382,335.31	General purposes.
Missouri	382,335.31	Education.
New Hampshire	669,086.78	General purposes.
New Jersey	764,670.61	General purposes.
New York	4,014,520.71	Education.
North Carolina	1,433,757.40	Education and internal improvements.
Ohio	2,007,260.36	Education.
Pennsylvania	2,867,514.80	Partly for education.
Rhode Island	382,335.31	Education.
South Carolina	1,051,422.09	One third to education and two thirds to general purposes.
Tennessee	1,433,757.40	General purposes.
Vermont	669,086.78	Education.
Virginia	2,198,428.04	General purposes.

legislation was that of local taxation combined with appropriations from the literary fund; each school district which raised by local levy the sum of twenty dollars was to receive twice that amount from the income of the literary fund. Under this provision the endowment contributed during the first year of the law the sum of $2400: to Tyrrell County for thirteen districts,

98 THE PUBLIC SCHOOL IN NORTH CAROLINA

$520; to Cherokee County for sixteen districts, $640; to Richmond County for twenty-two districts, $880; and to Macon County for nine districts, the sum of $360. This means that the fund stimulated local taxation amounting to $1200 and that $3600 of public funds was expended for school support during the first year of the school system.

During the next twenty years the school system prospered and continued to increase in efficiency. The fund stimulated local educational effort throughout all parts of the State with the result that creditable expenditures were made for public schools. The table below exhibits the income and the disbursements from the literary fund, the amounts appropriated by it for schools, the amounts raised by local taxation, and the total amounts paid for public-school education between 1841 and 1861: —

Year	Income	Disbursements	For schools	Local taxes	Total paid for schools
1841	$121,613.02	$92,655.67	$32,836.12	$16,418.06	$49,254.18
1842	101,323.48	150,289.59	65,297.24	32,648.62	97,945.86
1843	135,453.45	130,407.76	46,424.92	23,212.46	69,637.38
1844	123,009.06	121,722.65	117,897.10	58,948.55	175,845.65
1845	112,246.24	64,362.51	61,566.01	30,783.00	92,349.01
1846	116,431.93	101,325.73	96,712.01	48,356.00	145,068.01
1847	122,556.47	106,830.81	96,511.31	48,255.65	144,766.96
1848	108,342.21	115,174.81	101,530.04	50,765.02	152,295.04
1849	105,388.29	116,893.42	99,499.38	49,724.69	149,174.07
1850	106,301.40	112,816.28	107,339.00	53,669.50	161,008.50
1851	129,255.24	94,596.41	81,329.61	40,664.80	121,994.41
1852	137,380.41	161,472.33	144,351.13	72,175.56	216,526.69
1853	192,250.75	139,865.16	120,545.63	60,272.81	180,818.44
1854	196,090.25	169,983.32	153,736.79	76,868.39	230,605.18
1855	146,753.35	202,689.50	82,688.88	41,344.44	124,033.32
1856	183,073.00	193,976.09	177,479.02	88,739.51	266,218.53
1857	278,767.87	300,528.53	180,751.38	90,375.69	271,127.07
1858	164,188.44	204,374.23	179,087.48	89,543.74	268,631.22
1859	158,442.04	209,156.68	172,051.69	86,025.84	258,077.53
1860	167,475.12	226,904.01	186,054.11	93,027.05	279,081.16
1861	154,839.37	150,749.68	131,886.75	65,943.38	197,830.13

There is perhaps no more lamentable and melancholy chapter in the history of American education than the record of the amazing carelessness and indifference with which public-school endowments have been managed. This record is practically universal of the pioneer days of public educational effort when education was not considered a proper public interest. Public educational funds were consequently not guarded with the jealous care which their importance and sanctity demanded. The manner in which such funds were managed is further convincing evidence of the harassing conditions and opposition which confronted the public-school movement in its early days.[1]

Few if any States entirely escaped from the evils of poor management and often exploitation of their school funds; even more rigid control proved to be no insurance of permanent endowments against loss, which was generally appearing. Almost every species of violation of public trust may be seen in the list of causes of loss to permanent public-school funds. In some cases the funds were grossly and shamefully diverted from the original designs of their founders. The history of the school fund of Missouri and of other States is a good illustration of this form of loss. In some cases the management of the funds was indifferently entrusted to incompetent officials and the result was unwise investments. This form of loss may be illustrated in almost every State. Another common cause of loss was insufficiently secured loans and defaulted interest. Fully $700,000 was lost to the school fund of Texas before 1900 through defaulted interest. Arkansas likewise suffered even a greater loss through practically worthless notes and bonds; and Alabama, Mississippi, and Missouri sustained losses

[1] See Swift, *Public Permanent School Funds in the United States*, chaps. v and vi.

in a similar manner. Notes given in Alabama between 1837 and 1874 for lands belonging to the school fund remained unpaid from thirty to seventy years, and many of them seem never to have been paid. The policies often employed in disposing of school-fund lands vary from inefficient and careless methods to those of questionable and clearly fraudulent character. Moreover, money derived from such sales not infrequently was unsafely invested.

Dishonest management and embezzlement by officers entrusted with the care of school funds represent other losses sustained by public education in the United States. Happily there are not many gross examples of this form of loss. Perhaps the most flagrant case is found in Tennessee where the state superintendent of schools between 1837 and 1840 used the fund for sinister private purposes. Through "wild-cat" bank schemes, loans to business associates, and through real estate operations, he succeeded in robbing the school fund of more than $120,000. Failures of banks in which school funds were invested, the use of school funds for paying the current expenses of the state government, and the repudiation by the State of debts due the school funds are still other forms of wrongs committed against education. In 1848 Vermont owed its school fund $224,000, which debt was repudiated; and Colorado twice repudiated an indebtedness to its school fund amounting to nearly a half-million dollars.

Before 1860 direct and permanent losses to the literary fund in North Carolina were not very considerable, but occasional carelessness in investing the funds in securities of declining value showed short-sighted management. Several misfortunes befell the endowment, however, during the *ante-bellum* period. The defalcation of the treasurer of the State in 1827 proved a temporary loss to the fund of about $28,000, though the Legislature later returned the amount with interest. A decline in dividends from the stock held by the fund in state banks somewhat retarded the growth of the fund before 1836 and proved of slight misfortune to the endowment. During the thirties and forties the fund was now and then used to meet deficits in the public fund,[1] and occasionally it was drawn on to meet interest charges on state bonds. By 1850 more than $122,000 had been drawn from the fund for deficits in the state treasury. In 1851 the sum of $81,000, in 1854 the sum of $152,000, and in 1855 the sum of $23,000, belonging to the literary fund, were used for expenses of the state government. These amounts were finally returned, but the frequent loss in interest charges, which were not always paid, and the manner of regarding the fund as a source of supply when emergency arose, are sufficient to condemn the practice as unwise and unjust.

With secession and the opening of the war in 1861 new perils threatened the fund which for many years had rendered such valuable educational service. From the outset it was apparent that vigorous efforts would be made to secure military revenues from as many sources as possible, and there was fear that the literary fund would be appropriated for war purposes. The fear was not ungrounded, for various attempts were made to obtain the fund to carry on the war. But through the efforts of Dr. Calvin H. Wiley, who had been state superintendent of public schools since January, 1853, the danger was averted and the fund remained untouched

[1] See p. 91.

for such uses. Dr. Wiley's anxiety for the schools led him in May, 1861, to address letters to the county superintendents in which he urged the use of their influence to help secure the endowment. Moreover, he obtained permission to meet with the governor's council just before the Legislature assembled, when the first executive recommendations for the emergency were matured. Dr. Wiley's description of the meeting is worth giving in full: —

The governor was in feeble health, wasting with consumption and the weight of public cares, and the meeting was at his residence. The superintendent was kindly received and patiently listened to on that memorable occasion, and then and there was fixed a policy which will ever be honorable to the State. It was suggested that the school fund of over $2,000,000 would seem large to some, and a ready means for the prosecution of the war and to save taxation, and that under these plausible pretexts the slumbering opposition to the schools would unite short-sighted friends, and by a temporary suspension aim to destroy them forever. And it was argued that though the fund was, indeed, a large one, in one sense, it was but an inconsiderable item in the expenses about to be incurred, and that if we were able to engage in hostilities at all we were able to do without it; that if it was desired to popularize the war it would be most injudicious to begin it by the suspension of a system which was the poor man's life, and which would be so essential to the orphans of the soldiers called to surrender their lives for the common good; and now, when it was aimed to vindicate Southern civilization before the world, it would surely be an unwise step to begin by the voluntary destruction of an efficient system of popular instruction; that no people could or would be free who were unable or unwilling to educate their children. True independence must be based on moral character and on popular intelligence and industrial development, and thus in the momentous struggle about to begin it would impart confidence to the public mind to see the State enter the contest with the apparent assurance

THE LITERARY FUND

that her interior interests were not endangered by her course; that war under any circumstances was destructive for the time, and that the pending contest might be long and exhausting; and that it was the part of wisdom and patriotism so to act that the end should find the fewest possible desolations to be repaired, and no permanent weakening of the elements of social elevation. These considerations prevailed, and the executive power of the State, represented by the governor and his council, entered into an informal but solemn agreement with the superintendent of common schools to oppose, with him, all attempts to seize the fund for war purposes, or to suspend the schools, and the compact was faithfully observed by Governor Ellis and his successors during the war and by their constitutional advisers.[1]

In November, 1861, the North Carolina Educational Association, which was organized several years before, memorialized the state convention, asking that by constitutional amendment the proceeds of the endowment "be sacredly and permanently secured to their original purposes." Meantime, the superintendent enlisted the influence of many of the county boards of education, and the attempt to appropriate the fund for military purposes was so bitterly fought that it was finally defeated. Thus the literary fund was saved to its original purposes. In September, 1861, however, an act was passed which repealed that section of the code which required the county courts to levy and collect school taxes. But the act was not to apply "to those counties where the justices, a majority being present, shall elect to lay such a tax." Thus released from the legal requirement to levy taxes for schools, some of the counties voted to use the money for military purposes, while others discontinued school support until the close of the

[1] Weeks, *Calvin Henderson Wiley and the Organization of the Common Schools of North Carolina.*

war. It seems that no distribution was made from the fund for school support after 1860 until 1862. In October of that year the sum of $100,000 was distributed; "and from evidence of a later date it seems that the income of the fund was temporarily used to meet the financial crisis brought about by the war." [1] But the schools did not entirely collapse until 1866.

Governor Vance appointed new trustees for the literary fund in 1862, but in a short time it seemed difficult to secure meetings of the board, and in 1863 the governor and one other member took entire charge of the management of the investments. Dr. Wiley had all along urged the trustees to make no change in the investments of the fund, and this policy was adopted and in the main followed throughout the war. The fund was, therefore, not heavily invested in Confederate securities; but it was invested very largely in stock in banks which had invested in such securities; and in the wreck which came to the banking system of the State in 1865, this part of the literary fund was largely lost. Moreover, it appears that about $650,000 was invested in state bonds, and the repudiation of the war debt by the state convention in 1865 destroyed this investment. The railroad stock and stock in the navigation companies were also practically without value. In 1866 the total income from the literary fund was only $776. Several plans were suggested by Dr. Wiley and other influential friends of education by which the fund could be reëstablished and the schools revived, but all appeals were without effect.

In 1869 all the railroad stock belonging to the fund and hitherto valued at $600,000 was sold for $148,000. The stock in the Cape Fear Navigation Company,

[1] See Boyd, *op. cit.*

THE LITERARY FUND

valued at $32,500, was sold for $3250, or for ten cents on the dollar. Bank stocks also belonging to the fund, and representing an investment of more than $1,000,000, was worthless. The money received from the sale of the railroad stock was invested in special tax bonds of the State and these were soon repudiated. The total loss of the fund, once so large and valuable, was nearly $2,500,-000. From this time forward any extensive public-school support by means of permanent endowments was largely a matter of history in North Carolina.

Although the legal existence of the fund created in 1825 practically ended with the adoption in 1868 of a new constitution, the fourth section of article nine of that constitution provided for an "irreducible" fund as follows: —

> The proceeds of all lands that have been, or hereafter may be, granted by the United States to this State, and not otherwise specially appropriated by the United States or heretofore by this State; also, all moneys, stocks, bonds, and other property now belonging to any fund for purposes of education; also, the net proceeds that may accrue to the State from sales of estrays, or from fines, penalties, and forfeitures; also, the proceeds of all sales of the swamp lands belonging to the State; also, all money that shall be paid as an equivalent for exemption from military duty; also, all grants, gifts, or devises that may hereafter be made to this State, and not otherwise appropriated by the grant, gift, or devise, shall be securely invested and sacredly preserved as an irreducible educational fund, the annual income of which, together with so much of the ordinary revenue of the State as may be necessary, shall be faithfully appropriated for establishing and perfecting in this State a system of free public schools, and for no other purposes or uses whatsoever.

With the return of home rule in 1876 a new constitution was framed which went into effect January 1, 1877. Section four of article nine provided: —

The proceeds of all lands that have been or hereafter may be granted by the United States to this State, or not otherwise appropriated by this State or the United States; also, all moneys, stocks, bonds, and other property, now belonging to any state fund for purposes of education; also, the net proceeds of all sales of the swamp lands belonging to the State, and all other grants, gifts, or devises, that have been or hereafter may be made to this State, and not otherwise appropriated by the State, or by the term of the grant, gift, or devise, shall be paid into the state treasury; and, together with so much of the ordinary revenue of the State as may be by law set apart for that purpose, shall be faithfully appropriated for establishing and maintaining in this State a system of free public schools, and for no other uses or purposes whatsoever.

Another section of the same article provided that the net proceeds from the sale of estrays; also, the clear proceeds of all penalties and forfeitures, and of all fines collected in the several counties for any breach of the penal or military laws of the State; and all moneys which shall be paid by persons as an equivalent for exemption from military duty, shall belong to and remain in the several counties, and shall be faithfully appropriated for establishing and maintaining free public schools in the several counties of this State: *Provided*, that the amount collected in each county shall be annually reported to the superintendent of public instruction.

By the constitution of 1868 and that of 1876 a new basis was made for the principal support of schools. State taxation, instead of the income from a permanent public endowment, was henceforth to be the chief means of supporting the public free schools of the State.

From 1870 to 1903 the principal sources of increase of the fund provided for in the constitution were proceeds of the sales of federal land grants not already appropriated by the United States or the States; the proceeds of the sales of swamp lands; and grants, gifts, and devises made to the State and not otherwise appropriated. As late as 1889 the entries from public lands averaged only about $5000 a year, and were gradually becoming less, and the income from the swamp lands was not considerable. Occasionally some of these lands were sold, but the prices received were small and the sums realized were of but little help in swelling the sources of school support. At the same time the fund owned North Carolina four per cent bonds, amounting to $99,250, from which there was an annual interest income of $3970. The total annual income from the holdings and sources of the fund was between $8000 and $10,000, but a distribution of it among the counties of the State was not made every year, as the school law provided. Whenever, in the judgment of the state authorities, there was a sufficient accumulation to justify a distribution, the fund was distributed for general school purposes on the basis of school population in the various counties. In 1889 the appropriation annually averaged about two cents per pupil of school age. Three years later the permanent fund amounted to $154,250. All of this yielded four per cent interest except $2000 which bore six per cent.

In 1903 there was in the hands of the state treasurer a fund of nearly $200,000 belonging to the state board of education, which had been accumulating for several years from the sale of swamp lands. About $150,000 of this was in state bonds which yielded an annual revenue of four per cent interest, but under the law only the interest on it could be used for educational purposes. From time to time this had been apportioned to the schools on the basis of school population, but the amounts were always so small that the distribution was scarcely felt. At its session in that year, Superintendent

J. Y. Joyner recommended to the Legislature that this fund be converted into a permanent loan fund as "a practical plan of securing in a reasonable time a comfortable and respectable schoolhouse in every rural district in the State. . . .

Addressing the Legislature, Dr. Joyner said: —

> The use of this sacred fund for any temporary purpose would, as I see it, be a crime against past, present, and future generations. . . . As long as it remains idle in the hands of the treasurer it will be a constant temptation to every General Assembly that happens to find a deficit that must be met. If used for any temporary purpose or to meet any temporary deficit, it will, in my opinion, be lost forever to the children of the State. Everybody knows the difficulty of getting the State to repay money that it borrows from itself.

The House and Senate Joint Committee on Education endorsed the recommendation of the State Superintendent, with the result that a special act was passed directing that all funds derived before that time from the sources enumerated in the constitution (section four of article nine), and all funds hereafter so derived, together with the interest on such funds, be set apart as a separate and distinct school fund to be known as the "State Literary Fund," to be used exclusively as a means of building and improving public schoolhouses, under rules and regulations to be adopted by the state board of education.

Under the rules adopted for regulating the loans for building schoolhouses, only half of the cost of a new house or of the improvement of an old one was to be lent to any one school district. Districts with a school population of less than sixty-five could not receive aid unless "sparsity of population" or "unsurmountable natural barriers" made such aid absolutely necessary. Preference was given first to needy rural communities and to towns of less than one thousand inhabitants; then to similar communities which were supporting their schools by local taxation; next to those communities which assisted themselves by private subscriptions; and the last class of districts to be aided by the fund were the large ones formed by the consolidation of smaller districts. The loans were to be made by the state board to the county board of education, payable in ten annual installments, at four per cent interest, and were to be secured by notes of the county board which were to be deposited with the state treasurer. Moreover, the loans became a lien upon the total school funds of the county, and the literary fund was further protected by regulations which authorized the state treasurer, whenever necessary, to deduct, from the funds due any county from special state appropriations for school purposes, an amount sufficient to pay any annual installment due the literary fund by any county. The county board was likewise similarly secured against default on the part of local districts. All houses built by aid from the fund were required to be constructed in strict accordance with plans approved by the state school authorities; and all counties and districts were required to observe strictly the rules and regulations governing the management of the loans.

The first loans from the fund were made in August, 1903. Up to December, 1904, loans amounting to $120,580 were made to assist 325 districts in 70 counties of the State. The new schoolhouses built during this time through assistance from the fund numbered 288. The majority of the districts aided were in distinctly rural communities or in village communities of less than 500 inhabitants. The benefits derived from the fund had already exceeded the expectations of its heartiest supporters. The value of the old buildings in the communities assisted was placed at $26,092, and of the new ones erected by aid of the fund at $297,540. It was early demonstrated that, under wise administration, it was possible "to secure during the present generation a respectable, comfortable, well-equipped public schoolhouse in every district of reasonable size in the State."

From August 10, 1903, to June 30, 1908, the sum of $390,985.50 was lent to 86 counties. The districts aided during this period numbered 871, and 787 new houses, valued at $975,293.30, were built. The old houses thus replaced were valued at only $144,564.50. For the biennial period ending June 30, 1910, the sum of $122,000 was lent to 65 counties for improving houses valued at $290,495. For the biennial period ending June 30, 1914, the total amount of loans made from the literary fund for purposes of building or improving schoolhouses was $207,447, which was an increase of more than $42,000 over the biennial period which ended June 30, 1912. Seventy-nine counties were aided by the fund between July 1, 1912, and June 30, 1914, and the total value of the houses built or improved was $674,842. The total amount of loans from the fund between 1903 and 1914 was $896,022.50. Ninety-eight counties had been assisted during this time in building or improving houses valued at $2,411,500. One fifth of all the schoolhouses in the State have been built or improved by the aid of the fund created by the act of 1903.

REFERENCES

Journals of the House and Senate; Public Laws of North Carolina; legislative documents; Coon, *Public Education in North Carolina, 1790–1840, a Documentary History;* Weeks, *Calvin Henderson Wiley and the Organization of the Common Schools of North Carolina;* Smith, *History of Education in North Carolina;* Swift, *Permanent Public School Funds in the United States; Report,* United States Commissioner of Education, 1892–93, vol. 2; Boyd, "The Finances of the North Carolina Literary Fund," in *South Atlantic Quarterly,* July and October, 1914; *Biennial Reports,* State Superintendent of Public Instruction, 1904–14; Bourne, *History of the Surplus Revenue of 1837;* Blackmar, *The History of Federal and State Aid to Higher Education in the United States.*

SUGGESTIONS FOR FURTHER STUDY

1. How did the creation of public-school funds aid the establishment of school systems?
2. What was the purpose of creating public-school funds?
3. What was the principle on which such funds were usually established?
4. How did permanent public-school funds aid local taxation?
5. What were the sources of the fund in North Carolina? How did they compare with the sources of similar funds in other States?
6. How did the principle of distributing the income of the fund compare with the principle of distribution used in other States?
7. How did the principle of distributing the income of the fund compare with the principle on which the present fund is used?
8. Why were the early public-school funds greatly mismanaged? How did careless management reflect the public attitude toward public education?
9. How was North Carolina's *ante-bellum* literary fund lost?

10. How did the distribution of the surplus revenue of the federal government in 1837 aid public education in North Carolina?
11. How has the state literary fund aided education in your county? How many schoolhouses have been built or improved in your county by aid from this fund?

CHAPTER VII
GROWTH OF EDUCATIONAL SENTIMENT (1825-1837)

WITH the creation of a school fund in 1825 the initial step was taken by the Legislature in obedience to the constitutional mandate to make provision for schools. Two reasons may be seen for this long delay. The belief was prevalent that current taxation for educational purposes would meet popular opposition, on the theory that education was not a proper function of government; and the element of charity read into state aid of schools was considered humiliating to those who accepted its benefits. These notions caused the State to hang back from any definite step by which common schools could be established by state taxation. Hostility to increased taxation was intense, and the passage of a measure calling for local or county taxation for school support would have been impossible. If schools were to be created provision for their maintenance had to be sought in other ways than by taxation, and the creation of a permanent public fund from the income of which schools were to receive aid seemed the only satisfactory plan. This method of school support had already been adopted in several other States.

The fund grew slowly at first and was naturally for several years inadequate to any considerable effectual relief of the need for increased educational facilities. At the next session of the Legislature several measures were introduced which looked to an increase in the fund, but all of them finally failed. At that time the State owned more than a half-million dollars in bank stock alone, only about one fifth of which was the property of the school fund. But all efforts to transfer the balance to the fund for school support failed. Moreover, other educational measures were defeated. A bill to establish a college, one department of which was to train teachers, and a bill to aid Sunday schools by appropriating a small amount to those which would teach indigent children to read, both met defeat at this session. The following year the first report of the literary board recommended the immediate establishment of schools and an increase of the fund, but no action was taken.

No legislation of especial educational importance was enacted during the next ten years, though the subject continued to be agitated and repeated efforts were made to secure educational improvement. As a rule the messages of the governors continued to recommend some legislative action in behalf of schools, and many plans were offered as a solution of the peculiar problem which the State was thought to be facing. But practically all efforts and plans failed. Failure marked the end of a movement in 1827 to promote the education of the deaf and dumb children of the State; no legislative attention was given to a plan proposed in 1828 to provide for the training of teachers at the state university; and the Senate at the same session defeated a bill providing for the education of the poor children of the State. Similar bills met the same fate in 1829 and again in 1830. And efforts to ascertain the number of children in the State without educational facilities and to increase the literary fund were also defeated in 1830.

In 1829 Governor Owen accompanied his message to

the Legislature with a plan for primary schools which had been submitted to him by Charles R. Kenney, who had observed the practical operation of schools in other sections of the country. In brief, the plan stated that North Carolina had as many college graduates as any other State in the Union except South Carolina, but was deficient in primary educational facilities, and proposed to divide the counties into districts and to give them power to raise by taxation money sufficient to build schoolhouses and maintain a school for four months each year. The plan also recommended an examination of teachers on the ground that their characters were "proverbially and justly bad" and usually consisted of men "unfit for anything else." A proper selection would remedy this evil. The custom used in New England of employing women teachers in the summer was also proposed. The excellencies of the plan were obvious. Five years later Hugh McQueen, a member of the Senate from Chatham County, introduced a bill which called for the collection of educational statistics and a transfer to school support of certain taxes levied for the support of the poor and also a tax on certain estates. Nothing came of either of the plans. McQueen's bill, however, attracted some legislative attention as well as newspaper comment. But its late introduction and the details of the bill meant its defeat.

The literary fund for many years after its creation was considered insufficient to render much aid in support of a general system of schools, and there appeared a willingness to allow it to accumulate as best it could without the addition of sources of income, which was constantly urged.

During these years of fruitless effort to promote education the population of the State was increasing, with the result that the children of the masses were growing up in ignorance. There seemed to be no voice to speak out of the wilderness and to point the way to correct educational action. Sentiment for and against schools and the means of education was also developing and expressing itself. Surprise was frequently expressed in the press of the State and elsewhere

> that a subject so interesting to every philanthropist, so superlatively important in a political point of view, and so loudly and imperiously demanded by existing circumstances in our State, should have continued so long without attracting the special attention and engaging the active exertions of our Legislature. . . . The dullness and incapacity which is permitted to enter our legislative hall, and disgraces us even in the national representation . . . evince most unequivocally the mental debasement of a large portion of our population.

The education of the masses was believed to be the only correct basis of agricultural and commercial prosperity and the surest guaranty of liberty. Another writer likewise censured the Legislature for spending its time "upon ephemeral objects" to the neglect of the "very salvation of the Republic." Still another declared that the Legislature was responsible for the

> chilling and sluggish apathy that penetrates into and pervades all our public measures for improvement. . . . Our physical, moral, and intellectual powers have never been unfolded, and never will be, until the people are redeemed by education from the state of ignorance to which they have been doomed by our penny-saving legislators. All the draw-backs of this State may be traced to this muddy source — want of general knowledge.

Dr. Joseph Caldwell, president of the state university, said, in an address before a convention in Raleigh in 1829, that the State was three centuries behind in education, the chief cause of which he declared to be the "fatal delusion" that "taxation is contrary to the genius of a republican government." The next year Governor Owen attacked the State's so-called policy of economy as fit only to keep "the poor in ignorance and the State in poverty." In 1833 Governor Swain in his message said: —

The apathy which has pervaded the legislation of half a century is most strikingly exhibited by the fact, that the mere expenses of the General Assembly have ordinarily exceeded the aggregate expenditures of all the other departments of the government, united to the appropriations which have been made for the purpose of internal improvements.

Two years later the Legislature was costing nearly half as much as the actual expenses of the state government. Governor Swain declared in his message in 1835: —

The history of our state legislation, during the first half-century of our political existence, will exhibit little more to posterity than the annual imposition of taxes amounting to less than a hundred thousand dollars, one half of which constituted the reward of the legislative bodies by which they were levied, while the remainder was applied to sustain the train of officers who superintend the machinery of government. The establishment of schools for the convenient instruction of youth, and the development and improvement of our internal resources by means beyond the reach of individual enterprise, will seem scarcely to have been regarded as proper objects of legislative concern.[1]

---

[1] The average annual expense of the Legislature during the early years of statehood was $15,000. In 1830 it was $40,000, and three years later it was $42,000. In this year the total expenses of the State were estimated at $160,000 with available resources amounting to only $140,000.

But sentiment was not altogether in favor of schools and internal improvements; occasionally a voice was raised against them. An open letter on the subject, addressed to the members of the Legislature just before the meeting of that body in 1829, and published in the *Raleigh Register* contained the arguments typical of the opposition: —

You will probably be asked, gentlemen, to render some little assistance to the university of our State. But I hope you will strenuously refuse to do this likewise. It is respectfully submitted to the wisdom above mentioned, whether our good old-field schools are not abundantly sufficient for all our necessities. Our fathers and mothers jogged along uncomplainingly without colleges; and long experience proves them to be very expensive things. The university has already cost the people not a little; and the good it has accomplished thus far is extremely doubtful; if I might not rather allege it to have been productive of mischief. College learned persons give themselves great airs, are proud, and the fewer of them we have amongst us the better. I have long been of the opinion, and trust you will join me in it, that establishments of this kind are aristocratical in their nature, and evidently opposed to the plain, simple, honest, matter-of-fact republicanism which ought to flourish among us. The branches of learning cultivated in them are, for the most part, of a lofty, arrogant, and useless sort. Who wants Latin and Greek and abstruse mathematics in these times and in a country like this? Might we not as well patronize alchemy, astrology, heraldry, and the black art? . . . In the third place, it is possible, but not very likely, I confess, that you may be solicited to take some steps with regard to the establishment among us of common schools. Should so ridiculous a measure be propounded to you, you will unquestionably, for your own interest, as well as that of your constitutents, treat it with the same contemptuous neglect which it has ever met with heretofore. Common schools indeed! Money is very scarce, and the times are unusually hard. Why was such a matter never broached in better and more prosperous days? Gentlemen, it appears to me that schools are sufficiently plenty, and that the people have no desire they should be increased. Those now in operation are not all filled, and it is very doubtful if they are productive of much real benefit. Would it not redound as much to the advantage of young persons, and to the honor of the State, if they should pass their days in the cotton patch, or at the plow, or in the cornfield, instead of being mewed up in a schoolhouse, where they are earning nothing? Such an ado as is made in these times about education, surely was never heard of before. Gentlemen, I hope you do not conceive it at all necessary, that *everybody* should be able to read, write, and cipher. If one is to keep a store or a school, or to be a lawyer or physician, such branches may, *perhaps*, be taught him; though I do not look upon them as by any means indispensable: but if he is to be a plain farmer, or a mechanic, they are of no manner of use, but rather a detriment. There need no arguments to make clear so self-evident a proposition. Should schools be established by law, in all parts of the State, as at the North, our taxes must be considerably increased, possibly to the amount of one per cent and sixpence on a poll; and I will ask any prudent, sane, saving man if he desires his taxes to be higher? . . .

You will doubtless be told that our State is far behind her sisters in things of this sort — and what does this prove? Merely, that other States are before us; which is their affair, and not ours. We are able to govern ourselves without reference to other members of the Confederation; and thus are we perfectly independent. We shall always have reason enough to crow over them, while we have power to say, as I hope we may ever have, that our taxes are lighter than theirs.

Evidence of growing sentiment in favor of improvement in educational conditions may be seen in the movement to organize a teachers' association in the State in 1830. A letter, signed by "Pædophilus" and addressed to "the friends of education and the cause of literature in North Carolina," was published in the *Raleigh Register* in July of that year. The letter pointed out the advantages offered by an organization of the teachers of the State, and suggested that a meeting be called in Raleigh the following December. No meeting was held, however, at that time. The following May the same paper referred to the preliminary call of the previous year and called attention to conventions for educational advancement which had been held in other States. It also stated that "a number of gentlemen desirous of promoting the general education of the people of this State, are solicitous of again calling the attention of the friends of education, and of teachers generally, to this subject, and for this purpose, propose to hold a convention at Chapel Hill, on the day before the ensuing commencement of our university." The meeting was held at that time and an organization formed, known as "The North Carolina Institute of Education." A meeting was held in 1832, but its proceedings are no longer extant and it is not known what work was undertaken at that time. The last meeting was held in 1833 when several subjects of importance were scheduled for consideration, among them being a system of elementary schools for the State. But no further meeting of the organization was held.

The year 1832 may be taken as another landmark in the educational history of the State. In that year appeared the well-known letters on popular education, addressed to the people of the State, by Dr. Joseph Caldwell, president of the state university. These letters, eleven in number, were the result of the work of a standing committee appointed by the Legislature several years before for the purpose of studying conditions in the State with a view to improvement. The committee never met; but the letters of Caldwell embodied his views on the subject of education. The substance of the letters appeared in the *Raleigh Register* in 1830, under the signature of "Cleveland."

Commenting on some of the difficulties in the way of educational advancement in North Carolina, Dr. Caldwell said: — [1]

When a people have continued long in one course of legislation, when they have frequently and habitually resisted essays made to diversify or enlarge it, any measure which looks beyond the limits of their ordinary action must conspicuously embody advantages great and numerous and unquestionable, if it would hope for complacent consideration, much more for final acceptance. Should an innovation in any instance gain their assent, and through malformation or mismanagement unhappily fail to secure its object, the event will be pregnant with disappointment to all future efforts at improvement. If, on the contrary, it should prove successful, even inveterate prejudice may be weakened and dissolved and many things become easy which before were impossible.

There is perhaps no art or science in which greater improvement has been made than in that of education in primary schools. It has assumed a character wholly different from that of former times, and from that in which it still appears among ourselves. The mode of communicating instruction, the variety of which it consists, the interest ever kept alive in the bosom of the pupil, the exclusion of corporal punishment with which it is most successfully conducted, the activity and versatility to which it trains the intellectual faculties, the life and force which it imparts to the human affections, and the wide range of thought and knowledge which it opens before the reason and curiosity of the pupil, transcend the anticipated pictures even of an indulged imagination. Could we witness it in its processes and effects, its superior excellence would assuredly occur to us with a conviction as complete, as every one now feels in favor of the gin in preference to the fingers in the process of cleaning cotton, of the steamboat compared with sails or oars, or of a locomotive engine carrying its numerous

[1] These letters are published in Coon, *Public Education in North Carolina, 1790–1840, A Documentary History*, vol. II.

tons at twelve miles an hour, contrasted with the labor and plodding movement of wagons and horses, of which unhappily to our incalculable loss we are still fain to avail ourselves, over the sharp pinches, the floundering water pits and jolting obstacles of highways on which the hand of improvement has never operated. Nothing certainly is wanted but this ocular demonstration, to the resolute and instant adoption of all these astonishing and inestimable improvements which distinguish the generation of men and the age to which we belong, above the bygone ages and generations of the world. But to witness the present perfection of the schoolmaster's art is not our privilege, for its examples are too remote. And this presents an obstacle to any system of elementary schools we can recommend for the children of our State.

Another obstruction meets us in our aversion to taxation beyond the bare necessities of government and the public tranquillity. Any scheme of popular education must be capable of deriving existence originally, and of maintaining it perpetually, without taxing us for the purpose, or we are well aware that we shall not as a people consent to its establishment.

A still further difficulty is felt in the indifference unhappily prevalent in many of our people on the subject of education. Vast numbers have grown up into life, have passed into its later years and raised families without it: and probably there are multitudes of whose forefathers this is no less to be said. Human nature is ever apt to contract prejudices against that which has never entered into its customs. Especially is this likely to be the case if there have been large numbers who were subject in common to our same defects and privations. They sustain themselves by joint interest and feelings against the disparagements and disadvantages of their condition. It becomes even an object to believe that the want of education is of little consequence; and as they have made their way through the world without it, better than some who have enjoyed its privileges, they learn to regard it with slight if not with opposition, especially when called to any effort or contribution of funds for securing its advantages to the children. Such are the woeful consequences to any people who, in the formation of new settlements, have not carried along with them the establishment of schools for the education of their families. So strangely may the truth be inverted in the minds of men in such circumstances, that they become avowed partisans of mental darkness against light, and are sometimes seen glorying in ignorance as their privilege and boast. When a people lapse into this state, and there is reason to fear that multitudes are to be found among us of this description, it must be no small difficulty to neutralize their antipathy against education, and enlist them in support of any system for extending it to every family in the State.

I might mention further, as one of the greatest obstructions, the scattered condition of our population, over a vast extent of territory, making it difficult to embody numbers within such a compass as will make it convenient or practicable for children to attend upon instruction.

A most serious impediment is felt in our want of commercial opportunities, by which, though we may possess ample means of subsistence to our families, money is difficult of attainment to build schoolhouses and support teachers. Could the avenues of trade be opened to this agricultural people, funds would flow in from abroad, and resources would be created at home, which would make the support of schools and many other expenses to be felt as of no consequence. Excluded as we now are from the market of the world, the necessity of rigid economy is urged against every expenditure however small, and the first plea which meets us, when the education of children is impressed upon parents, is their inability to bear the expense. This is one principal reason why it has been thought that among all the improvements upon which we are called to engage for the benefit of the State, commercial opportunity shall be first. With the enlargement of funds, every difficulty would vanish in the way to such improvements as are rapidly elevating other States to distinction and opulence. . . .

I have already mentioned seven distinct causes of embarrassment in the organization of any plan for popular education. It were easy to extend the enumeration, but these will suffice to show the serious obstacles that meet us in the formation of a system of primary schools, to stagger our hopes of its acceptance with the people. An eighth, however, I must not omit, on account of its very great influence. It is seen in the aversion with which we recoil from laws that exercise constraint upon our actions. We are a people whose habits and wishes revolt at everything that infringes upon an entire freedom of choice upon almost every subject. It would be easy to elucidate how this has come to be a trait so deeply marked in our character, but its reality is unquestionable. Provision for general instruction can scarcely be effected, without some compulsory measures regulating the actions of individuals into particular channels directed upon the object. Every such measure is felt to be an entrenchment upon the indefinite discretion to which we tenaciously adhere, when a relinquishment of it is not absolutely indispensable.

In considering plans for overcoming the educational backwardness of the State, the letters declared: —

It will be forever vain to meditate plans of legislative action, if we persist in looking to means, which the people have given prescriptive evidence that they will never adopt. Why continue to press schemes from year to year, involving the necessity of taxation? Such projects may serve to amuse, to distract, to weaken. Party spirit, which is the bane of all wise and sound policy, is perpetuated from year to year, assumes a standing character, and is propagated among the people, poisoning the fountains of legislation. The halls of the Assembly become an arena to fight over again the same battles, in which it often happens that the best interests of the country are connected with the degradation of defeat. Success is made the test of merit. The strength of a cause is estimated, not from the benefits with which it is pregnant to the State, but by the comparative numbers enlisted in its support or subversion, by adherence to a party, the agitations of hope and fear, and the delusions of artificial excitement. The triumphs of victorious opposition, even to an object so sacred and all important as the education of the people, are capable of covering the object itself with ignominy, through an indiscreet and persevering connection of it with loans and taxes to which our established feelings are in revolting and irreconcilable aversion.

The laws and measures which have been urged upon us by the most unquestionable patriotism, and by minds of every rank in ability, and which have owed their prostration to the taxes proposed for their execution, who could attempt to enumerate? They lie entombed in the mouldering records of our legislative assemblies. Were each to occupy the space of earth usually allotted to a fellow mortal, no repository of the dead in the wide range of our State would be ample enough for their receptions. Let us take warning from their fate, and look to other means.

Thousands of parents are ready to second any practicable system by which education may be accessible to their children. Let it be offered to their voluntary acceptance by the best methods of instruction, and at the least expense, and they will grasp with eagerness the proffered privilege. How can we imagine that a people like ourselves, living in an age of knowledge everywhere distributed through a thousand channels, can continue indifferent to its opportunities. There is not a wind of heaven, come from what quarter it may, which wafts not to our ears improvements and discoveries that fill the world with activity and interest.

A discussion of the three usual methods of education — the voluntary plan, legislative aid by means of taxation, and a combination of voluntary and state aid — followed in the third letter. It is in this letter that educational practices in the State at that time were freely remarked upon and strictures made on the teaching profession: —

The first method is the one which we now practice. It consists in the origination and maintenance of a school in any neighborhood, by a voluntary combination among as many of the inhabitants as will agree. Its insufficiency is proved by all our past and present experience. A school house is to be erected at the common expense; a site for it is to be chosen with the consent of all; a master is to be found; a selection and approbation if there be more than one, is to be discussed and settled; his compensation and support must be fixed to the general satisfaction, and the time of continuance must be stipulated.

Here are six principal points on every one of which dissension of opinions, feelings, and interests may spring up, to produce weakness or defeat. It is unnecessary to enlarge upon the perplexities that meet us at every step, and the discouragement of failures and disappointments, until at last in a vast number of instances, the object is relinquished in despair.

The evil which is the greatest of all, is the want of qualified masters. It may be difficult to obtain a teacher at all, but it is pretty certain in the present state of the country, not one is perfectly fitted for the occupation. Do we think that of all the professions in the world, that of a schoolmaster requires the least preparatory formation? If we do, there cannot be a more egregious mistake. For if any man arrived at years of maturity, who can read, write and cipher, were taken up to be trained to the true methods of instructing and managing an elementary school, by a master teacher who understands them well, he could scarcely comprehend them and establish them in his habits in less than two years. This is not to speak with looseness and extravagance on the subject; and we need only to examine with opportunity of information, to be convinced of it as a practical truth. Yet in our present mode of popular education, we act upon the principle that school-keeping is a business to which scarcely any one but an idiot is incompetent, if he only knows reading, writing, and arithmetic. If in almost every vicinage there happens to be one or a few who have more correct opinions, the numbers who think otherwise carry it over their heads, and our primary schools are kept sunk down to the lowest point of degradation, and education is disgraced by our own misconceptions and mismanagements.

In the present condition of society and of public opinion, the occupation of a schoolmaster, in comparison with others, is regarded with contempt. It would be wonderful were it otherwise, when we look at the manner in which it is very often, if not most usually, filled. Is a man constitutionally and habitually indolent, a burden upon all from whom he can extract a support? Then there is one way of shaking him off; let us make him a schoolmaster. To teach a school is, in the opinion of many, little else than sitting still and doing nothing. Has any man wasted all his property, or ended in debt by indiscretion and misconduct? The business of school-keeping stands wide open for his reception, and here he sinks to the bottom, for want of capacity to support himself. Has any one ruined him-

GROWTH OF EDUCATIONAL SENTIMENT

self, and done all he could to corrupt others, by dissipation, drinking, seduction, and a course of irregularities? Nay, has he returned from a prison after an ignominious atonement for some violation of the laws? He is destitute of character and cannot be trusted, but presently he opens a school and the children are seen flocking into it, for if he is willing to act in that capacity, we shall all admit that as he can read and write, and cipher to the square root, he will make an excellent schoolmaster. In short, it is no matter what the man is, or what his manners or principles, if he has escaped with life from the penal code, we have the satisfaction to think that he can still have credit as a schoolmaster.

Is it possible, fellow citizens, that in such a state of things as this, education can be in high estimation among us? Is it strange that in the eye of thousands, when education is spoken of, you can read a most distinct expression that it is a poor and valueless thing? Can we rationally hope that so long as a method of popular education as this shall be all to which we look, the great body of the people will become enlightened and intelligent? Will they be qualified to act in all the various relations of parents and children, brothers and sisters, masters and servants, neighbors, members of the community, citizens of the State, subjects of Providence, and heirs of immortality? In all these capacities every child that grows up into life must necessarily act, and the teacher whose habits, views, and dispositions do not qualify, and whose conscience does not urge him to instill into his pupils the principles, excite the emotions, and select the books best fitted to them all, is totally defective in the business of a schoolmaster, and has need to learn the first elements of his art. If any difficulty occurs as to the largeness of the qualifications of a common teacher, which seem here to be required in excess, it is a subject on which I propose to explain more fully afterwards, and will hope for a reference at present to the further remarks to be made upon it.

Every species of business may be executed with various degrees of ability, and men may differ in their opinions of such as possess skill of a higher order in their professions. But respecting such as possess no talent, no qualification, none can mistake. All must feel one common overpowering conviction that their pretensions are despicable. Let any profession be wholly consigned to occupants so wretchedly destitute of every qualification in skill or principle, let it be known to the people only in such defective and degrading forms, and how can it be otherwise than contemptible, and all that is connected with it of little or no worth? . . .

That education in our primary schools should be held in low estimation, is but a natural consequence of the circumstances in which it is acquired. It never can be valued so long as they continue. The resources to which we have been left through our whole progress as a people, being of this character, the consequence is well known that thousands, and perhaps tens of thousands, are left to grow up unable to read at all. Experience has made it undisputable that the plan which we have practiced, if plan it can be called, is a total failure so far as North Carolina is concerned. Can evidence be wanting of its deplorable consequences, when it is by no means rare to hear men directing upon education a derision which would imply that they can deem it a glory and a privilege to be without it? I have been placed in circumstances, and there are few I fear who have not been similarly situated, where it would be dangerous to the election of a candidate to have it thought that he had any pretensions to information or culture, at least beyond a bare capacity to read. And some miserable being, to secure the great object of his ambition, has frontlessly presented it as a sure and glorious passport to success over the head of a rival, who was so unfortunate as to have had some education, that he belonged to the class of the ignorant, with whom the greater part considered it their glory to be ranked.

We see, then, the consequences of educating children by such wretched methods as we commonly practice. Thus it will always continue to be, so long as these methods are retained. We dress up the occupation of a schoolmaster in rags. It appears in hideous deformity by our own arrangement. It is no wonder if that which we intended for the figure of a man cannot be thought of otherwise than as a laughing-stock, a byword, or a scarecrow, and then education is put down as a questionable subject. Nay, it becomes a thing of scorn and reproach. The repulsive and disgraceful forms in which it appears have been given to it by ourselves, in the crudity of our own misconceptions. Where is the subject or the personage that may not be exposed to derision and rejection by a similar process?

And how shall the confidence and the affections of the people be regained? It is by stripping off the offensive and contemptible disguise, and presenting Education in all the beauty and excellence of her proper character. No sooner shall this be done than all will fall in love with her. Her presence will be courted as the privilege and ornament of every vicinage, and under her patronage the clouds and mists that lower upon us will be dissipated.

Other letters discussed the public-school system of other States and pointed out those features which would be practicable for conditions in North Carolina. Provision for training teachers was regarded as a necessary feature of any system which the State should adopt, and a thorough plan for a school in which such provision could be made was considered in detail. The demand for trained teachers would then increase and "the walls that shut in our people from the light of day" would be broken down.

Certain social and economic conditions during these years had produced a general feeling of uncertainty and depression, with the result that progressive policies of internal improvements and education were difficult to formulate and execute. These conditions had variously revealed themselves. In 1790 the State ranked third in population; ten years later it had declined to fourth, and by 1830 to fifth, place among the other States of the Union. Moreover, the value of lands was also on the decrease: in 1815 it was more than in 1833, although a million acres had been entered by the latter date. Slaves were increasing faster than the white population; emigration continued a persistent and alarming problem, thousands of people leaving the State every year in search of better opportunities; and the want of better commercial opportunities closed the avenues of trade to a people almost entirely agricultural, proving a most serious impediment to social progress.[1] The report of the committee on internal improvements in 1833 recited many of these conditions and discussed the inauguration of a state policy by which the evils which resulted from the previous policy of the State could be cured. Among other things the report said: —

Upon comparing the present languishing condition of the agricultural resources of North Carolina with the improved and prosperous condition of even the most inconsiderable members of the Union, the picture portrays the contrast, characteristic of a community worn down by the hand of adversity, in colors too strong to be concealed. That in North Carolina, it is apparent the reward of labor has ceased to be a stimulus to industry and enterprise; that agriculture has ceased to yield to the landowner a compensation equivalent to the expense attending the transportation of his surplus produce to market. The consequent result of this state of things is, that real estate throughout the country has so depreciated in the hands of farmers as to be considered not to possess a fixed value estimated upon its products. Hence our citizens are daily abandoning the places of their birth for situations in other States less healthy, and often not superior in fertility of soil; but which, by the improvement of those States, rendered so by the fostering aid of legislative patronage, the facilities to wealth and the means of acquiring the necessaries of life, the profits of labor hold out stronger inducements to agricultural pursuits than is to be found in North Carolina. Nor does the evil stop here. The tide of emigration, which never ebbs, not only carries with it a great portion of the enterprise and prime of our youth, but much of the productive and most valuable description of the State's wealth. These are facts of "ominous import," which should admonish us to guard against the fatal issue with which

---

[1] Boyd, "The Finances of the North Carolina Literary Fund," in *South Atlantic Quarterly*, July and October, 1914.

they are pregnant. Can it be our interest so to shape our policy as to render our State the mere nursery for the Western and Southwestern States? Surely not. We do not thereby lessen the political influence of the State in the councils of the general government, but we evidently weaken the ties of patriotism of our citizens to the land of their nativity.

The social relations of family connections evidently constitute the most lasting cement of the political permanency of any country. Indeed, what else is it but the social ties of family connections, when rendered happy and prosperous by their own industry, that stamps a value upon society? Or will it be contended that the present scattered condition of the family connections of North Carolina has a tendency to increase either the happiness or the devotion of its inhabitants to the interest of the State? Go into any neighborhood, and inquire of the seniors or heads of families, how many children they have raised, and in what State do they reside, and in nine cases out of ten, the answer will be, "I have raised some six or eight children; but the major portion of them have migrated to some other State"; and adds the parent, "I am anxious to sell my lands, to enable me to follow them." Thus, it will appear that the lands of nine tenths of the farmers of the State are actually in market; and what does it arise from? Evidently from the fact that the distance to and expense of sending the staple products of the soil to market, so far lessen the profits upon agricultural labor that the farmer has no inducements to effort. Therefore, it is that all our farmers are land-sellers, and not land-buyers.

The cause of these evils is apparent; but no less so than is the remedy. Throw open the agricultural interest of our State to the action of trade or commerce; open its widespread avenues, by constructing railroads from the interior of our fertile back country to markets within the State, at least, so far as nature in the distribution of her favors has rendered them feasible; connect by railroads the rivers of the State at given points, whereby the produce of their fruitful valleys may be sent to an export market. This done, and it will reflect to the State all the substantial benefits to be derived from an export dépôt — such at least as will locate a capital within its influence, equal to the amount of exports.

By concentrating the commerce of the State to one point, it will remove an evil which but few are apprised of. The produce should be received at the export dépôt in sufficient quantities so as to furnish a cargo, without subjecting the shipper to the increased expense arising from delay, a privation in the outset which often renders the voyage unsuccessful. Hence the necessity of adding to the aggregate quantity of export articles at the shipping port.

The laggard progress of internal improvements the report charged to the Legislature: —

But your committee hath the gratification to perceive that this important subject has in a great degree undergone the inquisitorial examination of the people, whose decision in all matters of public interest has ever been found in unison with the general welfare.

The people now perceive that they have endured a state of privation, which sad experience shows to be a downward course, and when longer forbearance would be but an aggravation of the evil. But the people, knowing their interest, with a voice not to be resisted hath proclaimed aloud that the period has arrived when *something ought, something can,* and *when something must be done* to arrest the progress of our down hill march.

Public expectations have become awakened, all eyes have been turned upon the present session of the General Assembly, and now look with patriotic solicitude for the anticipated favorable result of its deliberations. With regard to the ability of individual efforts to accomplish the desired results of public improvements, there can be no difficulty in perceiving that they cannot raise the required funds. Our citizens, subjected as they evidently are, and have ever been, to an expense almost equal to the market value of a great portion of their surplus produce in getting it to market, must be ill-prepared to engage in enterprises, which from their importance should be justly considered undertakings of state magnitude. It is, therefore, apparent, that if the improvements of the State are to be effected at all, they must be by the aid of the State, and not by private companies. The expression of public opinion by the people, in their recent numerous primary meetings, has given ample testimony of what the public expectations are with regard to the two-fifths principle. The unanimity of the internal improvement convention, held in November last in Raleigh, in which forty-four counties were represented, and of which [there] were but five dissenting votes to the magnificent scheme recommended by that body to the consideration of the General Assembly, should be viewed as conclusive as to the sentiments of the people upon the subject.

In criticism of the continued policy of the Legislature the following newspaper article, signed "Old Field," which appeared about this time, is significant: —

Mr. Editor: In your last paper I observed a piece taken from the *Family Lyceum*, which contains a great deal of matter upon the subject of the school funds in the different States. What a mirror is it to the eyes of a North Carolinian! We see from that, that she, upon this, as upon all other subjects of importance to her citizens, is almost a century behind her sister States. True, she has a small school fund, but how is it applied? Do we use it for the purpose of bringing within the reach of the children of the poor the means of education? No, but we borrow from it, from year to year, to pay our members of Assembly! How humiliating this must be to the pride of every public-spirited citizen. The State of North Carolina borrowing money to pay her members of Assembly, from a fund set apart for the education of the poor! Shame upon our law-givers. Can we expect to compete with our sister States, in the march of improvement now going on, while many of our citizens remain ignorant even of the alphabet? Can we expect to arouse them to the importance of internal communication, by means of canals, or railroads, while they remain ignorant even of the names of these mediums of conveyance? Surely not. A child must crawl before it can walk. . . . Our citizens must learn how to spell internal improvements before they can comprehend the meaning of the term.

I have thrown out these desultory remarks, in the hope, Mr. Editor, that some person more able than I am, would urge the importance of some system of common schools, to the citizens of our State. It is high time we were thinking upon the subject. . . . It is one of vital importance to our welfare.

In the same year, 1833, the Committee on Education and the Literary Fund reported to the Senate that no system of schools could be established with the funds then on hand, and recommended an increase in them. To do this a resolution was offered to appropriate thirty thousand dollars to drain certain vacant and unappropriated swamp lands belonging to the literary fund. This would bring into market a large quantity of valuable property which would otherwise remain unavailable and worthless and would enormously increase the resources of the fund. By such action the benefits of education could be furnished to "every cottage throughout the country" from the fund the aggregate amount of which was then considered too small to launch a system of schools. But in spite of the recommendation and the popular belief that something could be done to improve conditions, no legislative action was taken at this session. The next year a bill was introduced to make surveys and to sell certain portions of the lands belonging to the literary fund, but nothing came of the recommendation. At the same session a creditable scheme for schools was introduced in the Senate, and although this bill likewise met defeat it made sufficient impression on the Legislature to be printed in the laws of that year.[1] The press had praise for the proposed legislation and called it one of the most important measures ever presented to the Assembly. The *Raleigh Star*, after discussing the important features of the bill, said:—

The late session was not very propitious to the fate of a measure so novel in its character, and so important in its principles. It came in after the political resolutions and the convention bill, and of course had necessarily to give place to them. But it was only lost in the Senate by a majority of six

---

[1] McQueen's Bill.

votes, after an explanation of its principles by Mr. McQueen, in a speech of about an hour's length; and immediately after the bill had been disposed of, the senator from Burke, Mr. Carson, rose in his place, and moved that the bill be printed and appended to the laws of the State, and that the remarks of the introducer of the bill be published along with it. The first part of the motion prevailed unanimously; but Mr. McQueen would not consent to the last. We hope, however, that he may yet be prevailed upon, by the importance of the subject, to write out his remarks for the press, that the people may have the benefit of the useful information and cogent arguments which they contained. A stronger recommendation than the order taken upon the bill and remarks by the body to whom they were submitted, could not be given; for we believe it is the first time that either a *bill* or a *speech* received such a distinguished mark of approbation by our Legislature.

No educational legislation was passed in 1835, the Assembly committees not even making a report on the subject. Governor Swain discussed the matter in his message, however, referring to the small provision which the State had made for education and internal improvements. At the session of 1836–37 a memorial was presented from some citizens of Fayetteville who "witnessed with pain and mortification the depressed condition which each section of our State presents, when compared with that of her sisters of our happy Union"; and Governor Dudley, in his inaugural address to the Assembly, said: —

As a State, we stand fifth in population, first in climate, equal in soil, minerals, and ores, with superior advantages for manufacturing and with a hardy, industrious, and economical people. Yet with such unequaled natural facilities, we are actually least in the scale of relative wealth and enterprise, and our condition daily becoming worse — lands depressed in price, fallow and deserted — manufacturing advantages unimproved — our stores of mineral wealth undisturbed, and our colleges and schools languishing from neglect. . . .

It was said that there were then in the State fully 120,000 children between the ages of five and fifteen who were "destitute of a common-school education. In some parts of the State, many large families are found, not one of whom, parents or children, can read their alphabet; and in others, whole neighborhoods of forty or fifty families exist, among whom but few individuals can read their Bible." From press and pulpit the need for schools and increased facilities for education was being discussed, and the whole subject was becoming more and more absorbing in its interest.

Several important educational steps were taken at the session of the Legislature of 1836-37. One of these was the plan adopted for disposing of the surplus revenue distributed by act of Congress in 1836; another was the passage of a law which vested certain swamp lands in the literary board and appropriated the sum of $200,000 for their drainage and improvement; and still another, equal in importance to these, was the direction given to the literary board to digest a plan for a state school system and to report to the next session of the Assembly. These steps, all of an educational significance, marked the dawn of a new era in education and social progress in the State. The principal of the literary fund was now greatly increased with a resulting expansion of its revenues. The share of North Carolina in the surplus revenue from the federal government amounted to $1,433,757.40, all of which was eventually applied directly or indirectly to the cause of education. The literary fund was thus increased to nearly two million dollars, and steps were at once begun for launching a creditable system of common schools.

REFERENCES

Journals of the House and Senate; Laws of North Carolina; legislative documents; Coon, *Public Education in North Carolina, 1790-1840, a Documentary History;* Smith, *History of Education in North Carolina;* Weeks, *Calvin Henderson Wiley and the Organization of the Common Schools of North Carolina.*

SUGGESTIONS FOR FURTHER STUDY

1. Account for the fruitless effort to establish schools between 1825 and 1837.
2. What were some of the conditions of this period that retarded educational progress?
3. In what way were the educational conditions of the time the product of social, economic, and political conditions?
4. How do the arguments in favor of education during these years compare with those advanced in its favor between 1800 and 1825?
5. What were the merits of the plan offered by Charles R. Kenny in 1829? Compare that plan with the plan offered by Hugh McQueen in 1834.
6. What were the defects of most of the plans offered during these years for establishing a system of education?
7. How do the Caldwell letters reflect the educational sentiment of the leaders of the time?
8. In what respect is the letter opposing legislative aid to education (see p. 118) representative of the sentiment hostile to educational advancement?
9. What evidence do you find that the popular attitude toward schools, teachers and teaching during the period discussed in this chapter was changing?

CHAPTER VIII

THE BEGINNINGS OF PUBLIC EDUCATION (1838–1852)

THREE distinct periods, corresponding to as many different periods in our social and economic development, characterize educational development in the United States. The first is that of the transplanting of European institutions, traditions, and customs to American soil, from the first settlement to the middle of the eighteenth century or a little later, when political, social, and economic conditions in the mother country affected the colonies. The second period is one of attempted modification or adoption in an effort to meet the demands of a new and radically different environment, and extends from about the middle of the eighteenth century to about the fourth decade of the nineteenth century. The third is the period of the building up here of a system of education, distinctively American, to meet the new conditions into which the nation had come, and extends from the thirties to near the close of the nineteenth century. We have already traced the educational history of North Carolina through the first and second of these periods.

The third period shows a gradually developing faith in the power of the people; Jeffersonian democracy was now rapidly culminating. The period is characterized by the gradual separation of public education from ecclesiastical control; by the gradual development of the ideal of local control; and by what is probably even more noticeable, a gradual but sure growth toward the

THE BEGINNINGS OF PUBLIC EDUCATION

ideal of democracy. During this time public schools passed over to the State; the old academies rapidly changed into public high schools, colleges became largely non-sectarian, and state universities were organized and developed. It is during this period, also, that we find a more general expansion of state constitutional provisions for education than previously existed, which was one result of the development of the democratic theory of government. Specific and definite language was substituted for general educational terms in the constitutions. There was also an extension of the franchise and an increase in the number of elective officers. It was during this period that we find the establishment of the first normal school, the creation of the first state board of education, the office of the first superintendent of public instruction, the maintenance of the first teachers' institutes, and the establishment of the first school libraries. Everywhere there was a new impetus to educational thought and practice.

Conditions in North Carolina were showing the same marked change as appeared in other sections of the country during the early years of this period. Important political and social changes had produced a new educational ideal. The friends of education were numerous and gradually increasing and for several years had agitated a movement for public schools. Conditions were now more favorable than ever for undertaking such an enterprise; resources were at hand, and there was no lack of will and intelligence to apply them with liberality and discretion.

We saw that the Legislature of 1836–37, however, was not quite ready to enact a law establishing schools.[1]

[1] See p. 136.

But certain important educational measures were passed at that session: a part of the surplus revenue was applied to educational purposes; an appropriation of $200,000 was made to drain and improve certain swamp lands belonging to the literary fund; and the literary board was directed to digest a plan for a system of schools to be reported to the next meeting of the Legislature.

In his message to the Legislature at the beginning of the session, 1838–39, Governor Dudley urged the establishment of schools and the employment of a state superintendent. Early in the session several resolutions were passed relative to the subject, and the report of the literary board was also early received in both houses. This report was extensive, thorough-going, and detailed, and suggested a plan for common schools "suited to the conditions and resources of the State"; and on this report was based the first public-school law of North Carolina. On this law, ratified January 8, 1839, and its revisions, was developed the creditable *ante-bellum* system of schools which was attracting wide attention at the outbreak of the Civil War. The importance of this law justifies a full reproduction of it at this point: —

Be it enacted by the General Assembly of the State of North Carolina, and it is hereby enacted by the authority of the same, that it shall be the duty of the sheriffs of the several counties of this State, when they advertise the next election for members of Congress, to give notice, at the same time, by public advertisement in every election precinct that an election will be held to ascertain the voice of the people upon the subject of common schools; and all who are in favor of raising by taxation, one dollar for every two dollars proposed to be furnished out of the literary fund, for the establishment of common

THE BEGINNINGS OF PUBLIC EDUCATION 141

schools in each school district, will deposit their vote with the word "school" written on it; those opposed to it will vote "no school" upon their ticket; and all who vote for members of the house of commons, shall be entitled to vote; and it shall be the duty of the poll keepers to count the votes given at each precinct for school or no school, and to return the same to the sheriff who shall count together all the votes; and if a majority shall be found in favor of schools, it shall be the duty of the sheriff to furnish a certificate of the same to the next county court of his county; and any sheriff failing to comply with the requisitions of this act, shall suffer all the penalties imposed by law for failing to discharge his duty in any election for members of Assembly.

II. Be it further enacted, that the several courts of pleas and quarter sessions in each county of the State of North Carolina, shall, in such county as shall determine to accept these terms, at the first court that may happen after such election, a majority of the justices of such county being present, proceed to elect not less than five nor more than ten persons, as superintendents of common schools, for such county; and in such election, it shall be necessary for a choice that each of the persons elected shall receive a majority of the votes of all the justices present.

III. Be it further enacted, that said superintendents or a majority of them, shall meet within a reasonable time thereafter, and shall have power to choose one of their number as chairman, and shall proceed to divide their respective counties into school districts, for the purpose of establishing common schools, containing not more than six miles square, but having regard to the number of the white children in each, so far as they can ascertain the same: *Provided, nevertheless*, that no greater number of school districts shall be laid off in any county than shall be equal to one for every six miles square of inhabited territory in said county.

IV. Be it further enacted, that said superintendents shall number the districts, and make return thereof to the first county court in their several counties, which shall be held after the first day of January, one thousand eight hundred and forty; and it shall be the duty of said superintendents in making their return, to designate, as well as they may, their natural boundaries and prominent objects of the boundary of each said districts; and it shall be the duty of said court to cause such return to be recorded in the registrar's office of said county.

V. Be it further enacted, that the aforesaid boards of superintendents, in each county, after completing the divisions as aforesaid, shall appoint not less than three, nor more than six school committeemen, in each district, whose duty it shall be to assist said superintendents in all matters pertaining to the establishment of schools for their respective districts.

VI. Be it further enacted, that if any person who shall be thus appointed to serve as superintendent, shall refuse or neglect to do so after having accepted this appointment, he shall forfeit and pay the sum of fifty dollars, to be recovered by action of debt, in any court of record in this State; and such penalty, when recovered, to be paid over to the president and directors of the literary fund, and to be appropriated to the literary fund; and it shall be the duty of the county attorney for the State, to prosecute suit in all such cases, for and on behalf of the president and directors of the literary fund.

VII. Be it further enacted, that in any county where a majority of the votes have been for common schools, and a certificate of the same has been furnished by the sheriff to said superintendents of common schools, it shall be the duty of the superintendents to transmit the same, with a certificate of the number of school districts in their respective counties, to the president of the literary fund.

VIII. Be it further enacted, that in every county in the State, where the vote shall be in favor of common schools, it shall be the duty of the said county courts, after the first terms that shall happen after the first Monday in January, one thousand eight hundred and forty, a majority of the justices being present, to levy a tax to the amount of twenty dollars for each district in said county, in the same manner that other county taxes are now levied for other county purposes, to be paid over to the school committee of the respective districts, upon the certificate of the chairman of the board of superintendents.

IX. Be it further enacted, that forty dollars out of the net income of the literary fund, for the year one thousand eight hundred and thirty-nine, is hereby appropriated to each dis-

THE BEGINNINGS OF PUBLIC EDUCATION 143

trict in said counties where the vote shall be in favor of the establishment of common schools, which shall be paid by the public treasurer, upon the warrant of the governor, upon the certificate of the chairman of the board of superintendents of said counties, that taxes have been levied to the amount of twenty dollars for each school district in their respective counties and that schoolhouses have been erected in each district sufficient to accommodate at least fifty scholars.

X. Be it further enacted, that every county which shall refuse or neglect to levy a tax, and build the schoolhouses herein specified, shall at any time hereafter be entitled to receive the forty dollars hereby appropriated to each district, upon complying with the terms hereinbefore specified.

XI. Be it further enacted, that if in taking the next census of the United States, Congress shall fail to provide for ascertaining the number of inhabitants, and especially of white children, in the several school districts of North Carolina, it shall be the duty of the governor, as president of the board of common schools, to make such arrangement with the marshal of the United States for the district of North Carolina, or with his deputies in the several counties or with such other person or persons as he may deem proper, to cause such census to be ascertained, together with any other information which he may deem important to the establishment of a just and equal system of common schools throughout the State: and to communicate the same together with a full report of the returns of the superintendents in the several counties and the proceedings of the board of common schools under this act.

XII. And be it further enacted, that it shall be the duty of the county trustee, or the agent of public accounts in each county, to transmit to the governor as president of the board of common schools, a full and accurate statement of the whole amount of taxes levied and collected in his county for the years one thousand eight hundred and thirty-nine and one thousand eight hundred and forty (excepting the public revenues paid into the public treasury by the sheriffs), specifying in such statement what were the subjects from which taxes were levied and how much from each source of taxation; also a full and true account of the disbursements of the moneys so collected, showing specially what amounts have been paid for the prosecution of insolvent criminals, and their maintenance in jail; and that such statements shall be returned to the governor on or before the first day of December, one thousand eight hundred and forty; and if any county, trustee, or other agent of public accounts shall fail to make return as aforesaid, he shall forfeit and pay the sum of two hundred dollars, to be added to the fund for common schools; and it shall be the especial duty of the solicitor of each county to sue for the same if any failure shall occur in his county.

The educational campaign waged in the spring and summer of 1839, previous to the elections in August, showed a healthy and widespread sentiment in favor of schools. Among the discussions the newspaper comments are of considerable interest.[1] The *Raleigh Star* pointed out the educational backwardness of the State and urged the people to spread the sentiment for schools. It made a peculiarly strong appeal to parents: —

They have here, no matter what may be their poverty, a system which offers to them, in addition to the free education of their offspring, the highest gratification which a patriotic feeling parent can desire — *that of seeing their children endowed with sound learning, established in good morals, and qualified for the responsible duties of popular government.* To those poor youth of our State who are aiming at honor and eminence, the appeal to embrace the advantages of this system comes with twofold power. Their ignorance is not to them a reproach — nor will they acquire learning under this system as pensioners upon the public bounty. [The system recommended itself as worthy of confidence, continued the editorial.] "Support it, if you would strengthen the pillars of representative government: Abandon it, if you would quench that Promethean fire which returned the light of freedom in the western world!"

The *Carolina Watchman* called attention to the fact that "seven eighths of the money paid as county taxes

[1] See Coon, *Public Education in North Carolina, 1790–1840, a Documentary History*, vol. II, pp. 893 *ff*.

by the people of North Carolina is laid out in payment for court-houses, jails, whipping-posts: in the maintenance of insolvent persons, and for bringing offenders to justice"; and argued that the school tax would not be a burden. The *Raleigh Register* also argued in favor of adopting schools, declaring that education would found "on a secure and permanent basis the welfare and honor of the State," decrease the number of dangerous demagogues, and advance the prosperity of the State. The *Rutherfordton Gazette* and the *Newbern Spectator* likewise lent their influence in favor of the plan for schools and answered some of the arguments of the opponents. Moreover, individual citizens and county officers were energetic in the campaign to secure a favorable vote on the subject throughout the State.

Elections to ascertain the voice of the people on the subject of schools were held in August, 1839. The majority of the counties adopted the scheme outlined by the school law, approving the principle of supporting schools by a combination of local taxation and the income from the literary fund. The plan failed to be adopted in seven counties: in Rowan, Lincoln, Yancey, and Davidson in the west, and in Edgecombe, Wayne, and Columbus in the east. Those counties which voted for schools were to levy a tax amounting to $20 for each school district which was to be supplemented by twice that amount from the proceeds of the literary fund.

The sum of $1200 was immediately raised by local taxation for school support which was supplemented by the sum of $2400 from the literary fund, making a total of $3600 of public funds which went at once to support the schools.[1] The long agitation for schools had now

[1] See p. 97.

146 THE PUBLIC SCHOOL IN NORTH CAROLINA

passed, and the State was beginning her noteworthy *ante-bellum* educational career.

The actual condition of affairs in the State when the first school law went into effect is vividly given by Dr. Calvin H. Wiley who became the first superintendent of schools in North Carolina. Writing in 1881 he said: [1]

According to the census of 1840, one third of our adult whites, by their own statements to the enumerators, were unable to read and write. This is one fact. By the side of this was the fact that our sisters had nearly outgrown us in population and improvements, and yet it was well known to some, and is now a matter of common information, that no part of the world enjoyed greater natural advantages. Our resources from soil and climate, from minerals and timber, fisheries and water power were varied and immense; our colonial and revolutionary history and traditions were honorable; from the establishment of American independence there was no purer government on earth than that of our own State and municipal system, and society was moral, peaceful, and secure. . . .

But development everywhere around us was more rapid than here, and thus, comparatively, our course was downward. We labored under one disadvantage, and that was the want of streams navigable into the interior; but in other places railroads were superseding rivers as commercial highways. The exuberant soil and cheap lands of the West allured immigrants, and rapidly covered that vast region with industrious people; but there was no such exodus from other states as from ours, and some of our Northern sisters, with sterile lands and harsh climate, were in the van of improvement, while States south of us, under scorching suns and enveloped in a malarial atmosphere, were not only outstripping us, but constantly draining us of our capital and enterprise. . . .

Concerning the introduction of the school system Dr. Wiley said: —

[1] "History of the Common Schools of North Carolina," in the *North Carolina Educational Journal*.

THE BEGINNINGS OF PUBLIC EDUCATION 147

This population was tenacious of old habits, conservative to the point of stubbornness, with no neighboring precedents or examples, and no persons trained under such systems. The experiment was an absolute novelty in this region, the cause occupied little of the thoughts of Southern statesmen, and it began among people inured to light taxes and the less inclined to be taxed for education from the fact that there was a large school fund. The accumulation of the fund was a practical and strong teaching against current taxation, and since its inception the principle of distribution was changed from the basis of white to that of federal population, and thus an element of sectional jealousy and strife was added to other inherent trials. The idea of a charity system was connected with it, rendering it obnoxious to many interested in it, and there were no appliances for the instruction and training of the vast number of managers and teachers immediately needed, while many of the "old field" instructors, as the teachers of primary subscription schools were called, received it with jealousy, prepared to make war upon it.

From time to time the school law was revised or supplemented with a view to improvement, the first act of this kind being passed in January, 1841, for the "better regulation of the common schools." By this law the net annual income from the literary fund was to be distributed to the various counties on the basis of their federal population, and the county court was authorized to levy a school tax not to exceed one half of the estimated amount which the county was entitled to receive from this source. Three district trustees were to be elected by popular vote for every district in the county and these officers were to have general charge of the local schools — to provide the houses, take the school census, employ teachers, and visit the schools. The curriculum included "any branch of English education," and the schools were open to all white children between five and twenty-one years of age. Counties which rejected the schools in

1839 were by this act given opportunity to vote on the matter again with the same privileges and rights allowed under the original act. Counties voting against schools were to have invested for them by the literary board whatever sums they would have received under the ratio of federal population. Teachers were exempted from road, military, and jury duty while teaching. A penalty of $50 was prescribed for neglect of any duty on the part of county officers.

The chief of the many obvious defects of the system during its early years was the lack of any efficient central supervision. Until 1853, when Dr. Calvin H. Wiley became superintendent, the literary board was the chief executive head of the schools; during this time the champions of education labored blindly, the system being left very largely to the direction of local officials, who, though interested, were not fitted by training or experience to guide the work wisely. Many other evils grew out of this fundamental defect. Returns of school statistics from the counties were irregular and incomplete and published reports of educational progress were rare as a result. There was no provision for special reports from the literary board, and information on the subject of schools was lacking. Different counties developed different habits in the control of their schools with the result that there was little tendency to encourage a general state system. Moreover, the permissive character of the legislation was a serious evil. The law left it to the counties to say whether or not schools would be adopted, and since the plan was a novelty, many of the counties took their time in disposing of the matter. It took six years after the first schools were established for all the counties to adopt the system. And as late as 1844 the justices

THE BEGINNINGS OF PUBLIC EDUCATION 149

in some of the counties which had adopted schools failed to levy a school tax on the ground that the law made it a discretionary rather than an imperative duty to do so. The idea of charity which attached to the common schools also hindered their progress, helping "to raise a barrier between the upper and lower classes of society. It seemed as if these schools were to erect a fence between the two. It prevented many from sending their children to these schools," and, declared Dr. Wiley, kept many intelligent people from taking any active part in their management.

The friends of the schools soon saw the defects of the system and repeatedly urged legislative correction. Until 1853 there was no way to ascertain the number of schools in operation or any other facts concerning them; "for there were no means by which the system could observe its own deficiencies, ascertain its own progress, and record its own experience." To remedy the permissive provision for local taxation, Governor Graham in 1848 suggested that the counties be required to raise one half of the amount to be received from the literary fund before being entitled to the appropriation from that source. The literary board also believed such a requirement essential to the success of the schools, saying: —

It seems, however, to be expedient to require of each county imperatively to raise by local taxation, annually, a sum equal to at least one half of that received from the State, to the end that schools may be maintained a sufficient portion of each year in the several districts, and to withhold from any county her share in the State's distribution until her chairman shall make the report now required of him by law.

The requirement was not made, however, and this

defect persisted throughout the *ante-bellum* period and for many years longer.

The change in the principle of distribution of the income from the literary fund was also unfortunate. By the act which created this endowment in 1825 the basis of distribution of the income was that of the free white population. By act of January, 1841, this basis was changed to that of federal population. Not only did this change add an element of sectional jealousy, but, as Governor Manly suggested in his message to the Legislature in 1860, the change carried

on its face a violation of the spirit and object of the injunction of the constitution; is a breach of the public faith given by the Legislature of 1825; is at variance with the rule in other Southern States; divides the fund not according to public necessity, but the wealth of the people, and is in itself unequal and unjust.

Another difficult problem confronting the school system was that created by the jealousy of the academies and "old field" schools which were numerous in the State in 1850. The important place occupied by these schools may be seen from a description of them made by Dr. Wiley during his superintendency. They were

taught by persons widely variant in character and qualifications. Some of these were seminaries of learning of a high order, conducted by men of mark in their day, and whose labors have exerted a wide and lasting influence for good, not only in this but in many other States; but the large majority of teachers instructed only in the elementary branches of spelling, reading, writing, and arithmetic. English grammar was not taught, perhaps, in a majority of the schools, and geography as a general thing was an unknown science. The textbooks in every branch were few, unattractive, and often very defective; but one good result of the want of readers was the general use of the holy scriptures, and especially of the New Testament. The teacher, in most cases a law to himself and a neighborhood oracle, knew little of the methods of his brethren in other places, and never regarded himself as an element of a general system; and his progress was only in the mechanical art of writing, and from years of practice many became masters in penmanship and naturally looked with contempt on their brethren of a new generation whose qualifications were mental and who had not spent a lifetime in learning to make graceful curvatures and flourishes with the quill.

A further description made in 1855 [1] furnishes other interesting facts concerning this type of school: —

The schoolhouses were few and far between, located in the more thickly settled neighborhoods, and bad as our common schoolhouses, not at all equal to them as a general thing in comfort and convenience of arrangement, while there was not a house of any kind expressly dedicated to the purposes of teaching for every ten miles square of territory in the State.

The teachers as a class were indifferent scholars; and I say this with high respect for a race among whom there were some useful and devoted public servants and benefactors. But much as we complain now, salaries then were a good deal lower than what they now are; and even had they been equal or larger, the advantage in this respect would still belong to the modern cash incomes, promptly paid, over the uncertain earnings, which were often long delayed and part of which was very frequently paid in barter. There were a great multitude of little collections to make, and men of active business habits were not eager to engage in a calling whose small profits were as hard to collect as they were to make. The lazy, the lame, the eccentric, the crippled, were but too often the "old field teachers"; and while many of them could not write their own "articles" (as agreements between teachers and parents were called), a collection of those written by the masters would form a literary curiosity as unique in style, spelling, and chirography as any contribution of the kind that could now be made by any class of teachers.

The studies pursued were spelling, reading, writing, and arithmetic; and if those who applied themselves to them in the

---

[1] Leg. Doc., Session 1854–55.

152 THE PUBLIC SCHOOL IN NORTH CAROLINA

old school succeeded better as men and women than those who now study in our common schools, it is another illustration of the advantages of early hardships, while the praise is due mainly to the energy, industry, and perseverance of the pupils and not to the schools.

Grammar and geography were almost wholly unknown in the best of these schools, and many of our middle-aged people who now read the newspapers teeming with news, from the four corners of the earth, all knit together with railroads and telegraphs, feel and complain of their ignorance of the latter study, and would give much to be able to trace upon the map the connections and bearings of countries formerly seldom heard of and now mixed up with their nearest political and religious interests and affecting the prices even of their produce and labor.

The method of teaching was extremely primitive; to look on the book and make a decent droning noise of any kind, not out of the common key, would insure immunity from the all-potent rod, while this habit of noise, pleasant as it is as a reminiscence, because it was the music of our early years, was anything else than an advantage to those who really wished to bend their minds to study. Hence all these, and all who claimed to be such, were allowed to pursue their studies out of doors; and among the white heads with which the sunny landscape would blossom, perhaps one in every ten would be following out some useful train of thought or diving into the mysteries of Dilworth and Pike. He would "work out the sums" for all the others, and, as blackboards were unknown, the scholar had but to run in, hold up his slate to the teacher, get an approving nod, and return to his amusements. There were no lectures, few explanations, no oral instruction; to get through the book was the great end, and to whip well the paramount means. Few and indifferent as these schools were, they were not generally kept for a longer term than the great majority of common schools now are, and the attendance was equally uncertain and irregular. The schools were generally limited to a quarter of three months during the coldest part of the winter, and as families with two to six children would subscribe half a scholar, the house would often be jammed with sixty students and as often hold fifteen or twenty.

THE BEGINNINGS OF PUBLIC EDUCATION 153

Half a scholar! Why, can't we remember when five children would biennially get the benefit of the teaching due half a scholar for three months; that is, when one and a half months' schooling every year, or every two years, would be divided among three to five children making six to ten days or more apiece! *The good old times!* which, divested of all romance, of all the tender fancies which naturally cluster around the recollections of all childhood, were times which tried the soul of those who wished to gain a good education and which throw their still lingering shadows upon the present age.

Progress toward reform began to be made in 1850 by Governor Manly and other friends of the schools. In his message to the Legislature that year,[1] the governor criticized the school system for deficiencies in organization, accountability, and general management. He said: —

For a period of ten years about $90,000 have been placed annually in the hands of the various school committees of the State, a sum larger than the whole amount of the State's revenue paid into the public treasury during that period. This large sum, forming an aggregate of nearly a million of dollars, has within this brief period been spent, and yet no adequate provision has been made, much less enforced, for even informing the people or their representatives of what has become of it or how it has been spent.

Other charges were made against the inefficiency of the system. In 1849 the governor had published all the laws relating to education and distributed them throughout the State, together with an appendix of precedents and forms for the convenience of the school officials. Under the law the chairman of each board of county superintendents was required to furnish to the literary board, within the first two weeks of November, an annual written report of his school accounts and of other school

[1] Leg. Doc., 1850-51.

154   THE PUBLIC SCHOOL IN NORTH CAROLINA

statistics, such as the population, enrollment, and length of school term. Only seven officials complied with the law within the time allowed; and at the time the governor reported to the Legislature in 1850 only about half of the counties had performed the duty. For the incomplete returns fully $90,000 was left unemployed in the hands of the county officials; and probably twice that amount for school purposes lay idle in the entire State, to say nothing of additional amounts in the hands of former officials. The discovery of this condition led the governor to say, continuing his message: [1]

> It may be safely stated that thousands of dollars remain from year to year in the hands of superintendents, and if a rigid settlement were enforced the public would be astounded at the aggregate sum thus withheld from its legitimate destination.

The governor attributed the "general listlessness" in the State to the absence of close supervision, and urged the immediate appointment of a central officer to superintend the entire system.

The condition which was found in North Carolina in 1850 is strikingly similar to the condition which Governor Wise called attention to in Virginia in 1857. It was found that the amounts of school money continuously in the hands of the superintendents of schools in that State were more than one third of the total amount paid out by them for school purposes. Moreover, on the county quotas drawn at the beginning of the year, the county superintendents received a commission of five per cent and also had continuous use of at least one third of the entire quota without any interest charge.

[1] Page 20.

At the current rate of interest this was not an inconsiderable sum. From 1852 to 1856 the average annual sum expended by the superintendents was about $159,000, and the average annual balance left in their hands was $52,678, amounting for the five years to more than $211,000 on which they received a commission of five per cent. The superintendents also had the use, without interest charge, of more than $52,000, which annually lay unemployed for school purposes. Governor Wise's criticism drew attention to the evil and caused immediate reform to appear urgent.

Lack of central supervision accounted for the chief weaknesses of the *ante-bellum* school system in North Carolina. Measures for the appointment of an executive head had been introduced in the General Assembly of 1848–49, but they were rejected. By acts of January 29, 1849, the courts of pleas and quarter sessions were "authorized and empowered, in their discretion," on recommendation of the county boards of superintendents, to levy annually, when the school tax was levied, an additional tax not to exceed $250 for the purpose of "employing a suitable and competent person" to visit the schools of the county, under rules and regulations to be prescribed by the county board. Provision for licensing teachers by a county examining board, appointed by the county board, had also been made two years before. There was still urgent need, however, for more central supervision of the school work of the State. At the General Assembly of 1850–51, Calvin H. Wiley, who was a member of the Legislature from Guilford County, introduced a bill which provided for a state superintendent, but the measure failed. Two years later he was again a member of that body and through his influence an act was passed creating the office of superintendent and defining his duties.[1]

This new officer was to be appointed by the Legislature for a term of two years at a salary of $1500 to be paid out of the literary fund. He was to collect accurate and full information concerning the conditions and operation of the schools in each county in the State; to inquire into the causes which promoted as well as those conditions which retarded the schools; to consult and advise with teachers; to enforce the school laws; to see that the school funds were properly applied; to report to the governor annually of the educational progress of the State; to instruct the state examining committee concerning the proper qualifications of teachers; to see that returns were properly made from the various counties; to attend meetings of the state board; to deliver educational addresses, and in other ways promote the cause of schools. He was also required to codify the educational laws of the State. In seeking a man for the position the Legislature naturally turned to Wiley who had been so influential in securing the legislation which created the office, and who was qualified, by training and experience, as well as by his interest in education, for educational leadership. The reorganization of the schools under his direction and their rapid growth during the next decade will be treated in the following chapter.

[1] Act of December 4, 1852.

THE BEGINNINGS OF PUBLIC EDUCATION

REFERENCES

Journals of the House and Senate; Public Laws of North Carolina; legislative documents; Coon, *Public Education in North Carolina, 1790–1840, a Documentary History;* Weeks, *Calvin Henderson Wiley and the Organization of the Common Schools in North Carolina;* Smith, *History of Education in North Carolina.*

SUGGESTIONS FOR FURTHER STUDY

1. What were some of the difficulties in the way of establishing a school system in North Carolina before 1840?
2. Why is the period from 1840 to 1852 called the "experimental period"?
3. Compare the school laws of this period with the present law of the State.
4. Criticize the principle of school support in North Carolina during this early period.
5. Note Wiley's comment on the introduction of the school system in 1840. (Page 147.)
6. When did your county adopt the plan provided for in the first school law?
7. What were the actual educational conditions in the State in 1840?
8. What was the attitude of the academies toward the new system?
9. What was the chief weakness of the school system established by the law of 1839?

CHAPTER IX

THE EDUCATIONAL REVIVAL UNDER WILEY (1853-1865)

IN the preceding chapter it was noted that the second quarter of the nineteenth century was the beginning in the United States of a period of educational development which is marked by a growing tendency to democratization. The close of the first half of that century is distinguished for an educational awakening which is unique in the history of this country. But this revival, so frequently and conspicuously located in New England, where it was most noticeable, was not confined exclusively to any one section of the country. Attempted reforms in educational theory and practice were but a part of the general reform program in the development of democratic ideals. Educationally the storm center of this reform was perhaps in Massachusetts and Connecticut, where Horace Mann and Henry Barnard were conspicuous leaders and where educational progress was rather spectacular. But a gradual change from English ideals, transplanted here in colonial days, was taking place in other sections of the country as well as in New England during this period. Awakened sentiment for popular education appeared in New York, Pennsylvania, New Jersey, Delaware, Ohio, Indiana, Illinois, and Michigan, and in some of the Southern States. But slavery and its natural hindrances to a rapid development in public education, and the absence of a strong middle class in the South, somewhat delayed the revival of education in that region. And yet there the ground for a reorganization of educational effort was being rapidly and properly prepared, public opinion was being educated, statesmen of vision and broad educational traditions appeared who were eager to enlarge and extend educational facilities, and a general movement for free-school systems was rapidly gaining on the eve of the war. But for that strife and its disastrous results the educational historian would have a different story to tell of the South and her *ante-bellum* educational efforts.

The educational revival in North Carolina was in large measure promoted and strengthened by the leadership of Calvin H. Wiley; and the history of public education in the State from 1853 to the war is in the main his biography and the history of his noteworthy educational achievements. Wiley was already widely known and popular in the State when he became superintendent of the schools, having already had an extensive and varied experience. He was born in Guilford County, February 3, 1819, of Scotch-Irish descent. As a boy he showed an extraordinary intellectual ambition for the time and was given whatever educational opportunity conditions afforded. He was sent to Caldwell Institute near his home, where he was prepared for the state university, from which he graduated with the class of 1840. Later he studied law, was admitted to the bar, and located in Oxford, Granville County, for the practice of his profession. In addition to his legal duties he became interested in journalism and edited the *Oxford Mercury* from 1841 to 1843. A few years later he was offered the editorship of a Whig newspaper in Charlotte, but this position he declined. In 1851 he became assosociate editor of the *Southern Weekly Post*, a newspaper published in Raleigh and devoted to civic, educational, and industrial improvement. In 1850 he entered politics as a Whig member of the Legislature, and it was in this capacity that he began certain educational reforms which finally won for him an enviable reputation as an educational statesman of rare vision and qualities of leadership. A brilliant career doubtless awaited him as a politician and statesman, but he retired from that field of service at the age of thirty-three to become the first superintendent of the schools of the State. Though a Whig, he was elected to his position by a large majority of a Democratic Legislature, in December, 1852, and assumed the duties of his office, January 1, 1853.

The absence of any effective supervision between 1840 and 1852 made his task peculiarly difficult. From fragmentary reports found here and there before 1853, it is clear that county officials were notoriously negligent of their duties, a defect which continued for several years after Wiley became superintendent, in spite of his efforts at improvement. Moreover, teachers were scarce, poorly equipped, and migratory, and the great diversity of habits among the people of the State made reasonable uniformity in school affairs well-nigh impossible. But from the day Wiley entered the office until 1866, when it was abolished, conditions so improved that at the outbreak of the war in 1861 the State laid just claim to educational leadership in the entire Southern States. This was accomplished largely through the resourcefulness, versatility, and indefatigable toil of the superintendent.

During the thirteen years of Wiley's incumbency he labored consistently for a complete reorganization and improvement of the educational forces of the State; and, considering the obstacles against which he worked, his achievements challenge favorable comparison with those of Mann and Barnard. His first great care was to arouse interest in the cause of popular education, and this he did by means of his annual tours through the State. These educational campaigns extended through all the counties from Murphy in the extreme western, to Currituck Court-House in the eastern, part of North Carolina, the trips usually being made by private conveyance and at Wiley's personal expense. During his first year in office such campaigns called for fully half of his salary. Later, however, facilities for travel improved and less time and money were required for this part of his duties. While on these lecture tours he did not always receive the encouragement which his sacrifices and the cause for which he labored deserved. But his courageous heart was never daunted. Before the outbreak of the war his leadership was so greatly appreciated that his services were in demand not only in the State, but calls frequently came to him from other States for lectures, addresses, and educational advice.[1] Virginia, South Carolina, and Georgia sought to copy the educational example of North Carolina, and Wiley was invited to appear before the Legislature of Georgia for the purpose of aiding that State in improving its school system.

Wiley's task was not easy, however: there was much misinformation concerning public education, many misconceptions of the work which the superintendent was trying to promote, and too often a healthy educational spirit was lacking. The system was not without

[1] See p. 63.

its enemies who made attacks both on the schools and on Wiley; sectional, partisan, and sectarian prejudices also increased the difficulty of management. There were fears, which even the superintendent seems to have entertained, that the law of 1852 would be repealed. Rumors to this effect were especially current in December, 1854. But the fears were without substantial foundation and Wiley was reëlected without any opposition. Through all these troubles, however, the energetic and faithful educator so directed the educational system as to discover its friends and strengthen the feeble-hearted. He had also to "purge" the idea of public education "of the fatal taint of charity once adhering to it," and to lift it "from the position of a beneficence to a class to that of a fundamental interest of all the State." These efforts met with encouraging success from the start. He was soon able to decrease the danger threatened by politics and denominationalism, to enlist the interest of academies, high schools, and colleges, and to retain the admiration and friendship of his influential political opponents.

Much of the superintendent's time was taken up with mere routine. His correspondence with school officers alone was enormous, and at a time when typewriters and fountain pens were not in use. Moreover, he was not allowed a clerk to aid him in a position heavily burdened with the routine of exacting clerical details, but was forced to draw liberally on his own meager salary to make provision for this part of his duties. But he made use of the public press as freely as possible and through articles in the various state papers was able to give suggestions to teachers and to instruct the school officers in the local communities.

Many of the conditions which faced the superintendent when he began his work in January, 1853, are described in his first report which appeared in January of the following year: —

The first officer of the kind in the State — expected by some partial friends to do more than it was possible for mortal to do, while other honest men thought it was impossible to do anything — seeing in the light of the past but a dim and uncertain light, and in the condition of the present a widespread field of apparent chaos, brooded over by doubts and despondency, it was impossible for me not to err.

But he begged the public to be charitable and to consider the difficulties of the work, urging immediate legislative remedy of the defects which he discovered. He visited about half of the counties in 1853. He said in his report for that year: —

I determined to go to every county seat in the State, and during much of the past year I have been traveling, giving notice some days before of my intended visit.... My inquiries from various parts of the State, from Currituck to Cherokee, — and the letters and returns made to me from officers and friends of the system, — all corroborate this statement. The most universal information given is, that in the past year a new start has been taken, and new life has been felt: hope and animation have revived, new friends have been made, and old friends have resolved to work with redoubled efforts.

Certain interesting facts concerning the progress of schools and education in the State also appear in this report. In 1840 there were in North Carolina 2 colleges and universities, about 140 academies and grammar schools, and 632 so-called primary or common (subscription) schools. The enrollment in these institutions was 158 in the higher institutions, about 4398 in the academies, and 14,937 in the other schools, making a total of 19,483. At that time there were fully 57,000 illiterate white adults in the State. In 1850 there were 13 institutions for higher training, and perhaps 300 academies. The number of primary or common schools was not definitely known. The enrollment in the colleges and universities and in the academies had greatly increased by 1850 as had also attendance at the common schools. In that year 100,591 white children were attending some educational institution in the State. During the decade from 1840 to 1850 the white population increased only 12 per cent, but the increase in the number of children attending schools was nearly 500 per cent. In 1853, when the first official returns of the work of the common schools were made, there were fully 2500 common schools in North Carolina with an enrollment of about 95,000. "I am fully warranted," declared the superintendent, "in asserting that the average ignorance among the generation now coming on, will be at least *fifty per cent* less, or only one half as great as among those now on the stage of active life in North Carolina." The school population of the State at that time, however, numbered nearly 195,000.

In 1853 there were 82 counties in the State and 2828 school districts. All the counties made more or less complete reports except Chowan, Currituck, Jackson, McDowell, Madison, and Tyrrell. From two of these, Jackson and Madison, which were new counties, reports were not expected, as they were still under partial control of the parent counties, Haywood and Buncombe, and had not assumed independent educational organizations. Schools were taught in 2169 districts in 1853. The reports showed that the great majority of the teachers were men and that the average monthly salary was about eighteen dollars. The average term was about four months. The sum of $180,000 in public funds was expended in that year for school support, of which amount $120,000 came from the literary fund and $60,000 from local taxation.[1]

The scarcity of teachers in the State when Wiley became superintendent was another difficulty which hindered rapid progress of education. But from his instructions to the county examining committees it was evident that the superintendent meant every year to elevate the standard of teaching qualifications. Examining committees had been provided for since 1847; and by the act creating the office of superintendent the principal features of the previous act were retained and improved. These examining boards were required to hold three meetings every year to examine applicants to teach. Certificates were valid for only one year at the time and in the counties where issued, and only those teachers who were properly certificated could participate in the benefits of the public school funds. The superintendent constantly urged strict conformity to the law so that the teachers would gradually improve. He also sought to encourage women to become teachers. He believed, for certain classes, women would "make the best teachers. They are more patient, more easily win the affections of the young, and are more likely to mold to virtuous and refined sentiments, the plastic nature of childhood."

As a further means of improving the professional qualifications of the teachers he urged the formation of library associations. "How many teachers in North Carolina have read one single book giving an account of the ex-

[1] See p. 98.

perience and improvements in their profession in other places?" he asked, in calling attention to the need of legislative assistance in this important work. "If only one third of the common-school teachers of North Carolina could be induced to read the most indifferent work on teaching, what a vast change would be perceptible! Opposition to new-fangled innovations, is well to a certain extent, but . . . the experience of all the world does us no good, as we know nothing of any experience but our own. Scatter judiciously over the State good copies of any good work on teaching and it will create a revolution." Wiley's continued effort to encourage improvement among the teachers finally led to the formation of the state teachers' association.[1]

Three things necessary to the success of the school system were discussed at length in Wiley's second report made in December, 1854.[2] First of all, there was needed "a stricter and more uniform and patient attention to the execution of the law." In the second place, the improvement of teachers by "some systematic means," called for "careful attention, wise oversight, and constant exertion." "There has been great complaint in regard to them; and I know it to be a fact, that this incompetency and their want of fidelity in many, many cases, have given just cause of complaint. This is a real sore, and one of the severest which now afflicts our system; and the character of these teachers has done much to disgust a large class of citizens with our system, and to cause intelligent people to refuse to send to the schools, or to interest themselves in their success."

The third thing which called for attention was what Wiley called "discipline," a term which he used not in a

[1] See p. 176.   [2] Leg. Doc., Session 1854–55.

narrow sense, however. By it he meant general school organization, and in his discussion of this "vital point" he urged improvement in the program of studies, in the classification of the pupils, in equipment and apparatus, in textbooks, in methods of teaching, and in other features of the system.

How often do I hear the complaint that teachers consider that they have to *fill out merely* a certain number of days, and make it their greatest object to *kill* time instead of *improving* it! How often is it charged that our old routine is observed, and no bad habit forgotten and no good one acquired! How often is it said that parents are put to expense and children put back by a constant change of books, while there is no effort made to classify the children, and a school of fifty scholars will have forty classes, each class thus having but a very few minutes to recite in, and the teachers no time for lectures, explanations or oral instructions. Seven hours are enough for school hours in the twenty-four — and ten recitations, fifteen at the farthest, is [sic] as many as can be well made and heard in seven hours, except recitations by those learning their letters.

Here he advocated that the teachers

adapt themselves in manner, tone, ideas, and illustrations to every age and every grade; and from the child learning its letters to the most advanced youth, all are pleased, all are at home, and all are interested, all learn as children learn in the family circle, study and innocent pleasure being so blended that it is hard to say whether they are making pleasure a study or study a pleasure.

Of course we will not reach this point for a long, long time; but we can have blackboards for mathematical recitations, we can have public examinations to interest students and parents, and try the capacity of teachers; we can have the state looking in at each school house, and its voice heard daily; we can discard antiquated books, books with new-fangled isms. . . .

There is evidence that the schools were gradually

gaining the sympathy and respect of the educational and political forces of the State: —

Professors in colleges, male and female, reposing a confidence for which I am grateful, have tried to strengthen my hands, and I have felt proud of the fact that since my term of office began common schools have enlisted interest and received respect in every male college and nearly every female one in the State, and from the conventions of both political parties. Such influences are lasting and pervading; they must in time give a new tone to every society, and it is not one of our least misfortunes, that heretofore college professors and college students, as well as a large class of [other] intelligent people, were either indifferent to common schools, or treated them with actual contempt.

A decided improvement was noticed in the general operation of the school system in 1854. Most of the counties made returns to the superintendent showing that salaries were gradually increasing, that women were slowly entering the teaching ranks, and that there were in the State about three thousand school districts and nearly as many houses in most of which schools had been maintained during the year. The school population and enrollment were somewhat larger than the year before. "The information generally received . . . is that the schools are improving, that hopes are reviving, interest in them deepening and spreading, and the grade of teachers being elevated."

Many other signs of improvement were evident in the superintendent's third annual report which covered the year 1855.[1] The official returns from the various counties had been received earlier than usual and were fuller and more satisfactory. There was a gratifying contrast between the reports for that year and the previous years,

[1] Leg. Doc. 9, Session 1856–57.

and a noticeable tendency on the part of school officers to a more faithful performance of their duties. The superintendent had examined the school systems of other States and had also collected the opinions of officers and teachers at home, and he felt encouraged at the comparisons. But much work remained to be done, and the task was delicate and difficult.

Tender nursing, good food, and regular habits in the system were all-important: every change was to be closely observed, every irregularity touched with a most cautious hand, every effort used to make the schools grow in efficiency and usefulness as well as in public affection. . . . It was easy to give opiates and tonics: but how was the glow of permanent health to be infused into a system, not mortally sick, but wasted and emaciated with obstinate, complicated chronic disorders?

In spite of the imperfections of the system, however, "there has been a real revolution, an entire and radical change of things for the better in the last three years." The standard of the teachers had "unquestionably greatly advanced," and fully "nine tenths of the children of the State, it is hoped and believed, attend the common schools at some time or another — and certainly fifteen sixteenths of our youth are getting an education of some sort."

Seventy-five counties reported their school statistics on time and sixty of these in conformity to the law. Fifteen counties were deficient in certain minor details of information, and ten lacked the certificates of the finance committees and of the clerk of the county court to the financial statement. Fully 130,000 children were enrolled in 2800 schools, and about 2000 teachers had been regularly licensed during the year. This was a noteworthy evidence of progress. Four years before there were probably not more than two hundred teachers in the State who had been once examined and certificated. It was estimated, however, that in spite of this improvement there were approximately five hundred who were teaching without legal certificates in 1855. The average school term was four months and "the average salary, everything considered, is nearly as high as it is anywhere in the United States." Besides being "certain cash," the salaries of teachers were much "higher than the wages of teachers in the old-fashioned country schools were — the school houses are better, and the average scholarship higher," and the teachers were annually improving. The superintendent declared that female teachers in the common schools of North Carolina "received higher salaries than in any other State in the Union."[1]

There is everywhere, more confidence, more hope, more life, more public spirit, a greater sense of responsibility — and the tendency this way is increasing. Inveterate difficulties in a number of counties have been healed, it is hoped and believed permanently cured. With the improvement of teachers, wages have advanced, the number of school districts not taught has decreased, and the average time of keeping schools open has been lengthened, and the number of children taught greatly increased — while colleges, academies and high schools have been induced to lend their influence in *favor* of instead of *against* this great system, and politicians and parties have come to recognize in it the great hope of the country.

---

[1] The statistics which he gave in this connection showed the average monthly salaries of men and of women teachers in the public schools of several States to be as follows: Connecticut, men, $18.50, women, $8.50, including board; Illinois, men, $25, women, $12; Indiana, men, $23.01, women, $15.62; Iowa, men, $19.61, women, $9.39; Massachusetts, men, $37.76, women, $15.88; New Hampshire, men, $17.38, women, $7.83; Pennsylvania, men, $19.25, women, $12.03; Wisconsin, men, $21.10, women, $10.87; North Carolina, men, $21, women, $18.

Certain means of general and permanent improvement in the school system were suggested. The school law needed to be made more generally known and its objects more widely understood. A more rigid enforcement of the laws was also advocated. There was need of pervading "the public mind, especially the young mind of the State, with more accurate and interesting information concerning its history, its resources, and its institutions." The professional qualifications of the teachers also needed to be gradually elevated. But there appeared no specific remedy by which this could be immediately accomplished; curative means necessarily had to be slow. Normal schools could not immediately solve the problem — the schools themselves, the superintendent believed, were the agency through which an adequate supply of comparatively competent teachers could be furnished. Finally, there was need for an interchange of ideas and needs of the teachers and the various school officers, and some organ or channel of communication was recommended. To supply this the superintendent urged the formation of a state teachers' association and the establishment of an educational journal.

The most important means of training teachers for the public schools of the State during this period was furnished by Braxton Craven at Normal College, in Randolph County. He became principal of Union Institute in 1842 and immediately his interest in all phases of public education, especially that of training teachers for the public schools, began to grow. At that time there was no executive head of the school system in the State and teachers were without the means of preparation and training for the important work which they were called upon to do. Of his fitness for training teachers, Professor E. C. Brooks says: —

It is quite probable that no man of his generation was a more thorough student of educational problems and had a keener insight into the needs of the common schools than had Braxton Craven. The greatest essential need in America in the forties was for teachers who knew how to organize a school, classify pupils, and instruct them in the elementary branches. Craven was a tireless worker, omnivorous reader, and a careful student. He collected all the information on those subjects to be found in Europe and the United States, and in 1848 he was ready to begin a plan of teaching training at Union Institute that, within a few years, attracted the attention of the entire State. In introducing the normal feature into his institution he was following the practices in New York and other States, where teacher-training classes were organized in connection with academies and supported in part by state appropriations. That feature was popular in Union Institute, for in 1850 he wrote that the normal class that had been in training the previous year was very large.[1]

In 1850 Craven published in pamphlet form a very comprehensive plan for teacher training. Discussing needed reforms in education in the State, he said: "We must have normal schools. We can never reach any eminence without them. All endowments and enactments will be in vain without skillful workmen to put them into operation." The treatise was widely distributed in the State and created a strong opinion in favor of legislative aid to the training of teachers. When the General Assembly met in 1850 Union Institute was changed to Normal College and authority was given the institution to issue certificates to its graduates, as "sufficient evidence of ability to teach in any of the common schools in this State, without reëxamination of the

[1] "Braxton Craven and the First State Normal School," in *Trinity Alumni Register*, vol. I.

county committees." Two years later a new charter was granted Normal College, with the governor and the state superintendent *ex officio* president and secretary, respectively, of the trustees, and a loan of $10,000 was made to the institution from the literary fund. The following year the college opened with 195 students, and the teacher-training courses, now the most important work of the institution, required three years for completion. From this time until 1859, when the name was changed to Trinity College and all state relations severed, Normal College continued its work of preparing teachers for the public schools of North Carolina.[1]

In this great work Braxton Craven, who was instinctively a teacher, was the moving spirit. Teaching was almost a passion with him; he regarded it as an art great and difficult to master. Much of his educational philosophy is sound to-day:

> He is the best teacher in any given case who arouses the student to energetic action, directs his efforts in the right way to consistent, worthy, and noble ends; causes him to form manly, tasteful, and proper habits, and creates within him a thirst for knowledge and personal excellence that will bear him firmly through all the allurements of dissipation, the dazzling splendor of prosperity, or the deep, dark gloom of poverty.

And again he says: —

> If a teacher cannot clothe with fascination the symbolic columns of the spelling book, the maxims and stories of the reader, the principles and problems of arithmetic, the definitions and exercises of grammar, and all other subjects he proposes to teach, he has embarked in the wrong profession, and should at once and forever abandon that for which he is not qualified.

---

[1] Craven's efforts to promote public education led him into educational journalism, and in 1850 he began publishing the *Southern Index,*

174 THE PUBLIC SCHOOL IN NORTH CAROLINA

In 1855 the school law was revised and somewhat improved though its principal provisions remained practically the same as before.[1] The revision was intended largely to simplify the law, to provide for improving the quality of the teachers, and to secure more faithful service from other school officers. This action of the Legislature showed a healthy public sentiment and a ready and sympathetic response to the appeals and exertions of the superintendent. Everywhere his influence was seen in the supplementary school legislation. In most cases he was the author of the school laws enacted after his election to the superintendency.

The fifth report on the work of the schools appeared in January, 1858, and covered the year 1857.[2] There was much evidence that the schools were gradually improving. "The change in public sentiment among all classes of the people is marked and cheering," said Wiley, who felt greatly encouraged. Eighty of the eighty-five counties made fuller and more satisfactory reports than had been made in any previous years, and the returns showed marked advancement. The school population numbered 220,000 and the enrollment in the common schools was 150,000. Several thousand more were taught in academies, select and private schools, at home, and in Sunday schools. There was a school in every district and a schoolhouse for nearly every school.

a bi-monthly sixteen-page magazine for teachers. It had a short life, however, and in December of that year was changed to the *Evergreen*, a purely literary magazine, which was likewise short-lived.

[1] Act of February 10, 1855.
[2] Wiley's fourth report was made in November, 1856, soon after his third report appeared. It was more of a special than a general report and dealt largely with the need for teachers' library associations and with the importance of the educational journal, which first appeared the previous September. Few new or important statistics were given.

These houses are in reach of twenty-nine thirtieths of all the children of the State. It is now a fixed habit to have a school every year or once in every two years at these houses; and these schools are taught by persons of whom at least nineteen twentieths are annually examined as to moral and mental qualifications by respectable and intelligent committees in the counties where they teach. There are in the State not less than three thousand five hundred schools — and twenty-four out of every twenty-five of all the white children of the State are obtaining an education.

The common school property of the State was valued at $350,000. The schools were operating at an annual cost of $250,000, ninety-five per cent of which went to pay teachers' salaries.[1] The number of teachers examined and certificated in 1857 was 2500.[2] The superintendent believed that not more than fifty teachers were employed in the public schools who did not have the proper licenses. Three fourths of those legally certificated taught grammar and geography. The average school term was four months, the average monthly salary paid teachers was $24, and the average attendance was about forty pupils to the school.

There appeared about this time two other noteworthy signs of general improvement in educational conditions in North Carolina. One of these was the establishment of an educational magazine as the official state teachers' organ, and the other was the formation of a teachers' association. For several years Wiley had advocated the creation of these auxiliary agencies and finally his efforts were crowned with success; and as head of the

[1] Corrected returns show that about $271,000 was expended on the common schools in 1857.

[2] The difference between the number of teachers and the number of schools is accounted for by the fact that many teachers frequently conducted as many as two or more schools in a year.

176 THE PUBLIC SCHOOL IN NORTH CAROLINA

school system, president of the teachers' association, and editor of the teachers' journal, he served the State in a threefold educational capacity.

The organization of the teachers, officially known as the "Educational Association of North Carolina," sprang from preliminary teachers' meetings held in Goldsboro in May, 1856, and in Salisbury the following October. Both of these assemblies were large and harmonious and were attended by the leading teachers and friends of education in the State. At the meeting in Salisbury a permanent association was formed, and the first annual session was held in Warrenton in July, 1857. At this time the constitution was formally adopted and plans perfected for a career of great usefulness. Several county affiliated teachers' societies immediately applied for constitutions. Other annual meetings of the association before the collapse of the Confederacy were held in Statesville, in 1858; in Newbern, in 1859; in Wilmington, in 1860; in Greensboro, in 1861; and in Lincolnton, in 1862. Wiley was the chief spirit in the formation and direction of the organization and through his leadership the coöperation and support of public men, lawyers, ministers, and teachers were secured for public education. The annual meetings were filled with discussions of normal schools, textbooks, school equipment, methods of teaching, the course of study, grading the schools, and other important subjects. The association was incorporated by the Legislature at its session in 1860–61,[1] and was assisted by the state treasury to the amount of $600 a year. At the outbreak of the war it was rapidly extending itself through the organization of local county associations. Through this agency,

[1] Act of February 23, 1861.

EDUCATIONAL REVIVAL UNDER WILEY

as through educational journalism, the superintendent was developing and strengthening the common school cause, which was constantly growing in popularity and usefulness.

Wiley also worked to secure further educational advancement for the state through the *North Carolina Journal of Education* which he likewise fathered and fostered with marked devotion. In this auxiliary agency, which during its early career fluctuated in success, Wiley not only put much time and energy but several hundred dollars, which he finally lost. The plan of the magazine was outlined in the superintendent's report for 1855. In the summer of 1856 he succeeded in selling the advertising space to reputable publishers (G. and C. Merriam and A. S. Barnes and Company) for a sum sufficient to defray the entire cost of thirty-five hundred copies of a quarterly magazine of thirty-two octavo pages. The superintendent was highly gratified at its promise of success, and the *Journal* appeared in September, 1856, but failure to retain the advertisers caused it to suspend after the first year. Meanwhile, however, the educational association was formed and steps were taken to promote the magazine through this body. Under its auspices the *Journal* began to appear again in January, 1858, with Wiley as editor-in-chief, assisted by J. D. Campbell and a board of editors representing all the educational interests of the State, both public and private. The magazine proved unexpectedly popular and was supported alike by public-school officials, college professors, and others whose contributions on educational matters helped to fill its pages. Through it Wiley made every effort to advance the cause which was nearest his heart. Legal provision was made in 1860 by which copies of the magazine were sent to all school officers and paid for by the public-school funds, and its influence was thus widely extended throughout the State. The *Journal* continued until near the close of the war when difficulty of securing paper, and the destruction of the plant in which the magazine was printed, forced it to suspend. Considering that one half of its exchanges were compelled to suspend two years before, it is indeed remarkable that the publication was able to continue so long and in the face of such discouraging difficulties.

In his report for 1858, the superintendent said of these agencies: —

The State Educational Association, embracing all the educational interests of the State, is now on a firm foundation; and one of its chief objects is to stimulate the cause of common schools. Its organ, the *North Carolina Journal of Education*, has been pronounced by competent authority, one of the best periodicals of the kind on the American continent; and while its circulation is increasing among the officers and teachers of common schools, energetic efforts have been adopted to push it, if possible, into nearly all the districts of the State.

Of the progress of the schools in 1858 the superintendent said in his sixth report: —

Some of the hopeful manifestations which are not only felt by one in my position, but can also be made appreciable to the common apprehension are: *First*, an evidently increasing sense of responsibility on the part of the subordinate officers. *Secondly*, more energetic and enlightened action on the part of boards of county superintendents. *Thirdly*, the general, gradual, but certain elevation of the standard of teachers' qualifications. *Fourthly*, obvious influences for good among all classes, and in various places, caused by increasing efforts to disseminate useful information and statistics. *Fifthly*, the successful formation of associations intended to combine the exertions of the friends, of all classes, of general education. *Sixthly*, the general disappearance of all prejudices, and in-

EDUCATIONAL REVIVAL UNDER WILEY

veterate difficulties arising from honest prejudice, and from ignorance. *Seventhly,* an increased and increasing animation and hopefulness on the part of friends of the cause among all ranks of society, and in every part of the State.

Most of the counties in 1858 made official returns sufficiently complete and early enough to enable a reliable estimate of school conditions to be made. The school population now numbered approximately 225,000 and 155,000 were enrolled in 3700 common schools. This estimate was "based on certain data and cannot be an exaggeration," the superintendent declared. The average school term and the average salary paid teachers were practically the same as reported the previous year. The average expenditure for each county was $3114, and the total for the State about $265,000. A continued improvement was evident in the qualifications for teachers and in the enforcement of the law on certification. Concerning the success of the system reference was made to the schools of Madison County, "a rugged mountain country, as broken, perhaps, as any part of the peopled area of the United States. It has no navigable streams, not much arable soil, or mineral wealth, or rich pasture land — and for much of the year, the climate is cold and bleak." The school population of this county was, males, 1226, females, 1068; and 1131 boys and 884 girls were attending the common schools. "What a light is here beaming among those barren and craggy heights!" exclaimed the superintendent.

Wiley's seventh report, covering 1859,[1] showed returns from eighty-one counties. The five delinquent counties were Alleghany, Anson, Haywood, Johnston, and Lenoir, in all of which certain incidental causes

[1] Leg. Doc. 9, Session 1860–61.

explained the failure to make returns on time. In spite of the delayed reports from these counties there was a manifest improvement in the character and efficiency of the local school officers of the State. The school population in seventy-four counties was 186,000, and for the entire State it was estimated at 230,000. The school attendance in seventy-seven counties was 108,000 with an estimated enrollment for the entire State of 155,000. Seventy-nine counties reported 2758 schools in operation; seventy-one counties showed that 2066 teachers had been licensed; the average school term was four months, and the average monthly salary paid teachers was $28.[1] The receipts for school purposes in seventy counties were $279,000 and the expenditures in the same counties were $235,000. Local school taxes collected averaged about $1238 to the county, making a total for the State of more than $100,000; and expenditures for school purposes averaged about $3300 to the county, making a total for the State of about $285,000. There was a growing tendency to build new and better schoolhouses, and improvement in the qualifications of teachers was likewise growing. Among the recommendations made to the Legislature, the superintendent urged the State to furnish means of placing the *Educational Journal* and the State Teachers' Association on a firmer foundation, and to elevate the standard of teachers by enlarging the course of study, by requiring more thoroughness in the subjects taught, and by requiring teachers to avail themselves of the opportunities offered for improvement

[1] A comparison of the average monthly salaries paid in other States at this time is suggestive: Massachusetts, $34.75; Connecticut, $23.75; New Hampshire, $19.72; Ohio, $20.42; Wisconsin, $20.97; Illinois, $24.57.

through the *Journal* and the state and county educational associations.

The eighth annual report of the work of the schools, for 1860, appeared a little more than two months before the State seceded.[1] The close similarity in statistics in this and in the reports for the three previous years was evidence of the gratifying regularity of the operation of the school system. Eighty-one counties reported statistics for the year. It was estimated that the school population numbered 221,000, that 150,000 children were enrolled in more than 3000 schools, and that more than 2700 teachers had been licensed during the year. It was also estimated that more than $100,000 had been collected in local school taxes. The school term was practically the same as in 1859, but the average monthly salary paid teachers was somewhat less than in the previous year.[2]

The ninth annual report, for the school year 1861-62,[3] was made December, 1862,[4] and showed that sixty-five counties made more or less complete official returns of school statistics. A school population of 118,802 was reported in forty-six counties, and fifty-nine counties reported a school attendance of 52,018. The superintendent believed that 65,000 children were actually enrolled in the common schools of the State. More than 1200 teachers had been licensed, and more than 1500 schools were reported in operation, with an average term of nearly three months. The actual disbursements for common schools in sixty counties amounted to

[1] Leg. Doc. 10, Session 1860-61.
[2] In 1860 the average monthly salary was $26.
[3] The Legislature of 1860-61, for the sake of convenience and uniformity, changed the school year.
[4] Leg. Doc. 9, Session 1862-63.

$117,924. By this time counties had been released from the obligation of laying taxes for schools, and the small amounts received from the distribution of the literary fund income were insufficient to maintain schools as long as usual. The superintendent urged on the local authorities the following course of action: to keep in perfect order the framework and machinery of the system; to supply the places of male teachers called to the war with qualified female teachers,[1] and to continue schools wherever competent female teachers could be secured; to license only the competent and loyal ones; and to maintain as high a standard of qualifications as the conditions would allow.

In spite of the difficulties caused by the excitement of the times and the absorbing interest in the war, which naturally decreased the attention given to school affairs, the educational machinery continued to operate with surprising consistency. The schools still lived, but official returns gradually decreased in completeness. In his report for 1863 [2] the superintendent gave statistics for that year as follows: thirty-six counties reported a school population of 95,259, and fifty counties reported 35,495 children in regular attendance in 1076 schools; forty-four counties reported 872 teachers who had that year been properly certificated; the average school term was three months; teachers' salaries averaged $25 per month; female teachers were on the increase; depreciation of the currency caused financial embarrassment for the schools; and on account of the more reliable class of citizens being at war, active district committees were difficult to secure. With all these obstacles, however,

---

[1] Teachers were subject to conscription in North Carolina.
[2] Leg. Doc. 9, Session 1863.

in the darkest hour of the Confederacy, with every nerve and muscle wrought to the highest tension in a disastrous and unexampled struggle for life, the State still maintained a school system surprisingly vigorous and useful. The superintendent believed that fully 50,000 children were that year enrolled in the common schools of the State.

Faith in the schools and in the outcome of the struggle led Wiley to continue his annual recommendations to the Legislature and his suggestions to local officers for school improvement. The great defect of the schools, according to the superintendent, was their horizontal character, "furnishing one kind of education for children of all ages, and of every degree of advancement." But the schools had elevated the standard of popular intelligence, and had increased the demand for higher schools. At the meeting of the teachers' association in Newbern, in 1859, graded schools and teacher training were among the principal subjects discussed. A committee was appointed to investigate the matter of graded schools and to make a report at the next meeting. A plan was accordingly formulated and approved by that body the following year, and a bill based on it was before the Legislature when the war began. Wiley labored for the passage of the measure, but its permissive character, as well as many other defects, finally brought the plan to naught. A similar bill was introduced in the Assembly in 1863, passed the House, and was reported favorably by the Committee on Education in the Senate. But lack of time forced it to be tabled, and there the measure rested until the following year, when an act to grade the schools was passed.[1] In this connection it should be noted

[1] Act of December 23, 1864.

that just before the outbreak of the war a movement was begun to establish a graded school at Wilmington, and an enthusiastic public meeting was held for the purpose in April, 1860. The tendency to train teachers through institutes was also rapidly gaining at the same time.[1]

A wholesome educational sentiment continued during the war and every possible effort was made to foster and preserve the schools. In the summer of 1861, soon after hostilities began, the press of the State urged renewed efforts to prevent a suspension of the schools. "In the name of the good people, and especially the children of the State, let none of the schools be abandoned, if possible," advised the *Raleigh Standard*. And the *Charlotte Democrat* declared that "the children of the State must be taught to read and write, war or no war." In November, 1864, in his message to the Legislature, Governor Vance said: —

> The subject of our common schools is one which I beg you will not forget amid the great concerns of war.... I earnestly recommend to your consideration the whole subject, and especially the system of graded schools advocated by the superintendent, for which memorials will be presented by the literary board and the Educational Association of North Carolina. I also suggest that regular teachers be exempted from state military duty whilst employed in teaching. Though fully aware of the importance of their vocation, I have not felt

---

[1] The first institute held in the State was conducted at Graham, in Alamance County, in May, 1860. The work was in charge of W. H. Doherty, who conducted a private school at Graham, and continued for one week. Doherty came from Antioch College, Ohio, where he had been associated with Horace Mann, and opened a school in Graham about 1855. In 1861 he went to Newbern where he had charge of an academy which also had a normal feature. In 1859 the Wilson Female Seminary had normal classes and the Goldsboro Female College had similar work in 1860.

EDUCATIONAL REVIVAL UNDER WILEY

at liberty to excuse them under existing laws.[1] The common schools should surely be kept going at any cost; and if sufficient inducements can be offered to disabled soldiers and educated women to take hold of them, the necessary males should be exempted. ... It is with pride that I observe the publication in our State of various new schoolbooks, creditable alike to the authors and to the public which has demanded them. Our great system of common schools is, after all, our only true and solid foundation for public education and demands your constant and fostering care.

Throughout the dark days the schools continued to operate with unexpected regularity and consistency, and as late as April, 1865, when Johnston surrendered, the superintendent was receiving official returns from the various counties. But the gradual depreciation of Confederate currency and the loss of the school funds finally brought disaster to the schools. The literary fund had remained untouched for military purposes, but Confederate securities had been encouraged throughout the war, and it was difficult to change the form of investments. The principal of the school fund was invested in bank and railroad stock [2] and there it seemed reasonably safe. But the banks had themselves invested heavily in Confederate securities, and in the wreck which came to the banking system of the State at the close of the war, the literary fund was lost. With it went the principal means of school support and the basis of the State's creditable school system.

Wiley's eleventh and last report was made in January,

[1] By act of 1863 college professors "and teachers in academies were exempted from service in the home guards." Persons "engaged in editing or publishing classical or common-school books and all persons actually engaged in printing or binding such books" were also exempted from military service.

[2] See chap. VI.

1866,[1] but little information concerning the operation of the schools during the last year of the war is given. The old régime was rapidly passing, and the system of schools into which Wiley had put so much earnest labor soon collapsed with the fall of the Confederacy. During the dark days which followed, while efforts were being made to reëstablish the relations of the State with those of the national government, other matters absorbed public interest and schools and the means of education received little attention. With the constitutional convention of 1868 and the process of congressional reconstruction, attention turned again to education. The story of its fortunes and the operation of the schools during that period will be told in another chapter.

From the foregoing treatment of public-school education in North Carolina it can be seen that the law of 1839 and its revisions, in spite of the weaknesses of the system thus provided for, made creditable provisions for educational enterprise. State, county, and local district organizations were formed and the plan of school support, by a combination of local taxation and the income from the literary fund, proved well suited to the conditions of the time, and proved popular and efficient. The literary fund, as was seen in Chapter VI, stimulated a healthy sentiment in favor of local taxation, which was rapidly increasing at the outbreak of the war. It was estimated that more than $100,000 was collected in local school taxes in 1860. In that year about $280,000 of public funds was expended on public-school education. In 1859 the estimated school population was 230,000 and 155,000 children were enrolled in school. The aver-

[1] Leg. Doc. 47, Session 1865–66.

age monthly salary paid teachers was $28, and the average school term was four months. These facts appear especially striking when it is considered that the average term in the State as late as 1900 was less than in 1860, and that the average salary paid teachers in 1900 was only about $22.50.

The educational achievements of these years were due in large measure to the untiring labors of the superintendent, and to his genius for leadership and organization. We have already noted his threefold educational services as superintendent, editor of the educational journal, and director of the state teachers' organization. But his activities were not confined to these enterprises, however extensive in reforms they may have been. Another effective means of disseminating reform and improvement was through his annual reports which began in 1854 and continued until 1866. These reports were intended to give information concerning the condition of the schools and the progress they were making; to discuss the weaknesses of the system and to make suggestions for improvement; and finally they were used as a means of creating and directing public opinion on the great subject of universal and free public education. In these reports and in Wiley's prolific writings in the *North Carolina Journal of Education* are found his practical educational doctrines. His philosophy of education was not complicated. Throughout one very definite point of view is held: that public education is the only sure and safe foundation in a democratic society, and that a "system of common schools for a great and growing state is a vast and sublime moral organization." While these doctrines may now appear commonplace and trite, it must be remembered that when Wiley urged them they were not familiar, and that their gradual acceptance in North Carolina is in no mean measure due to the work of her pioneer educational statesman and leader.

Through his textbooks Wiley rendered still another important service to the cause of education in North Carolina. Before his election as superintendent of the schools he had published at his own expense *The North Carolina Reader*, which went through several editions and became a standard in the schools until after the war. When it first appeared the book was received with enthusiasm and was adopted by all classes of teachers. One of the noteworthy services rendered by the book was the wholesome spirit which it created and fostered among the masses of the people of the State. When Wiley became superintendent he disposed of his interest in the work, but other volumes were later produced under his direction, and these became, along with the first book, very extensively used as readers in the schools during the *ante-bellum* period.

Wiley's educational ideals were lofty. He believed that education should be universal, free, and open alike to all, both rich and poor. So devoted was he to this principle that at the close of the war he was very decided in his advocacy of the education of the freedmen.[1] He also believed that public education could easily be so well developed that aristocratic ideas, as they were reflected in the patronage of private schools, would die away and the superiority of the public school be universally recognized. In this respect he shows a striking similarity to Horace Mann. Finally, Wiley was deeply religious, and he sought to apply to education everywhere the ideals of the Christian faith.

[1] See the *Greensboro Patriot*, March 26, 1879.

Religion and education must go together; and while contemplating the possibility of a future generation of North Carolinians wholly enlightened and universally able to take care of themselves, in a worldly point of view, I cannot but feel a deep solicitude that it should not be an infidel generation, devoted to Mammon, and ready to abase itself to all the strange gods which the wicked inventions of men may create. . . . It is my desire that all children shall be taught to read, and taught by those whose lives illustrate the beauties of a heart disciplined to good; and that when enabled to read they be allowed to read for themselves the revelations of Heaven's will to man.

While Wiley achieved much in the stimulation of interest in education and in making friends for the cause, his work did not stop there. He was a practical reformer and was concerned with the material as well as with the spiritual side of education. His reports were full of recommendations and suggestions for improvement in the school machinery and the material equipment. Nothing rejoiced him quite so much as to be able to report the improvement of an old or the building of a new schoolhouse. He was likewise eager to improve the textbooks in use and to develop, by scientific training and the application of sound methods of teaching, a body of intelligent and active teachers. In most of these respects he was able during his thirteen years of distinguished service to effect noteworthy reforms and to place the schools in the sympathies of all classes. He showed familiarity with the systems of public schools in this country and in Europe, and saw much merit in the Prussian system to which he frequently referred.

He remained in office after the war until the ordinance of October 19, 1865, of the constitutional convention, declared vacant all state offices which were in existence April 26 of that year. His final report was made in January of the following year, and two months later the office of superintendent of schools was abolished by the Legislature.[1] He soon retired to private life. In 1869 he was appointed general agent of the American Bible Society for a part of Tennessee, and later for the Carolinas, in which work he continued until his death. In 1872 and again four years later he was proposed as the Conservative candidate for the superintendency of schools. In the former year he was kept out by political disability, and in the latter he refused to be a candidate because the public schools had been brought into politics. During his remaining years he was active in local educational matters. He was largely instrumental in establishing the graded school in Winston and served as chairman of the school board of that city until his death, January 11, 1887.

REFERENCES

House and Senate Journals; Public Laws of North Carolina; *Annual Reports* of the Superintendent of Public Instruction, 1853–66; *North Carolina Journal of Education*, 1856–63; Brooks, "Braxton Craven and the First State Normal School," in *Trinity Alumni Register*, vol. i; Weeks, *Calvin Henderson Wiley and the Organization of the Common Schools of North Carolina;* Smith, *History of Education in North Carolina;* Knight, *The Influence of Reconstruction on Education in the South.*

[1] Act of March 10, 1866.

SUGGESTIONS FOR FURTHER STUDY

1. In what respects were the educational problems which faced Horace Mann similar to those which confronted Calvin H. Wiley?
2. In what respects were their educational achievements similar?
3. Compare Wiley's philosophy of education with Mann's educational philosophy.
4. Compare Wiley's theory of education with the theory of education held by Braxton Craven.
5. What contribution did Braxton Craven make to public education in North Carolina?
6. What were Wiley's most permanent contributions to public education in North Carolina?
7. What influence did his work in North Carolina have on public education in other Southern States?
8. Why were so few women engaged in teaching in North Carolina before the war?
9. What were the defects of the school system between 1853 and 1860?
10. What percentage of the school population was enrolled in the public schools just before the war? What percentage of the school population is in school to-day?
11. What progress was made in educational journalism in North Carolina before the war?
12. What other auxiliary educational agencies were at work in the State during the *ante-bellum* period?
13. What attempts were made to establish public high schools in North Carolina before 1860?
14. What were the facilities for training teachers in the State before the war?

CHAPTER X

ANTE-BELLUM EDUCATIONAL PRACTICE

THE actual practice of any educational system is always more difficult to describe than the theory and laws on which the system is built, and the more remote the period the more difficult is an adequate description of its practice. Scarcity of concrete illustrative materials of no more remote a time than the *ante-bellum* period makes a description of actual educational practice of the system discussed in the preceding chapter more of a task than would at first appear. The poor system of bookkeeping of the time, for example, renders an intelligible treatment of the fiscal features of the school system no easy matter. Moreover, officials, either ignorantly or through negligence, often failed to record in permanent form minor but historically important details of the operation of the system. However, by a study of the few illustrative materials accessible, a fairly adequate conception may be formed of educational practice in North Carolina before the war. In the practical operation of the school system at that time, the curriculum, schoolbooks, material equipment, and methods of teaching are among the more interesting features. The principle of school support, by local taxation and the income from the literary fund, has already been pointed out.

The curriculum of the *ante-bellum* system was very narrow, generally including little more than reading, writing, arithmetic, and spelling, with now and then a little geography, grammar, and history. The subjects on which teachers were usually examined were reading, writing, arithmetic, and spelling. Wiley urged that the female teachers be examined on these and that the male teachers be required in addition to show ability to teach the subjects of grammar and geography. But this requirement was not generally made, though these "advanced" subjects were sometimes taught in some of the schools, as was also the subject of history. Texts in this subject served rather as reading-books, however, than as guides for historical study.

Uniformity of textbooks during the *ante-bellum* period was unknown in North Carolina. One of the evils of the system was the "multiplicity and frequent change of textbooks, by which expenses were accumulated on parents and guardians, the progress of the school retarded, and teachers greatly embarrassed by having large schools with nearly every child in a class by itself." Wiley urged improvement of this condition and worked to drive out poor books, to prevent frequent and unwise changes, and to secure the use of a uniform series. Uniformity, the superintendent believed, would decrease expense and enable a form of student classification which would not otherwise be possible, especially when a great variety of books were in use. To secure this improvement he early recommended uniform books. He was unable to secure the adoption of uniform books, however, and a great variety of texts in the subjects taught continued to be used throughout the period. This great variety of texts and of authors reflects something of the actual educational conditions of the time.

Wiley urged uniformity of books as a means of improving school conditions in the State, and recommended those which in his opinion were suited to the schools. The list consisted of: Webster's *Speller;* Wiley's *North Carolina Reader;* Parker's *First and Second Readers;* Davies's *Arithmetics;* Emerson's *Arithmetic;* Mitchell's *Intermediate Geography* (North Carolina Edition); Bullion's *Grammar;* Worcester's *Comprehensive Dictionary;* and Wiley's *Common School Catechism.*[1] In spite of their official recommendation these books were by no means all of those actually used in the public schools of the State before the war. In addition to Webster's famous book, which occupied first place in North Carolina as in other States, the following were among other spellers extensively used in the State during the period: — Barry's *Speller*, Burton's *Speller*, Cobb's *Speller*, Comly's *Speller*, Dilworth's *Speller*, Emerson's *Speller*, *The Eclectic Speller*, Ely's *Speller*, Fenning's *Speller*, Hazen's *Speller and Definer*, Kirby's *Speller*, Marshall's *Speller*, Mayo's *Speller*, Murray's *Speller*, *The National Spelling Book*, *The United States Speller*, *The Universal Speller*, *The Union Spelling Book*, Town's *Spelling Book*, *The Western Speller*, and Wood's *Speller*.

Spelling-books during the *ante-bellum* period were not intended primarily for the purpose of teaching spelling, but served the threefold purpose of spellers, readers, and moral instructors. The most famous of all the texts on the subject was Webster's, popularly known as the "Old Blue Back," which was universally used in the schools

---

[1] It is interesting to note that in the same year that Wiley recommended these books for use in North Carolina (1853), the following books were recommended, by a convention of school officials and teachers in Augusta County, Virginia, for use in the schools of that State: Webster's *Speller;* McGuffy's or Mandeville's *Readers;* Brown's or Bailey's *English Grammar;* Mitchell's or Smith's *Geography;* Colburn's or Davies's *Arithmetics.*

of this country until comparatively recent years. Even young people of to-day are familiar with or have heard of this celebrated book. It had a wide circulation from the first, and at the time of Webster's death in 1842 a million copies were being distributed annually. The influence of the book can hardly be estimated. Spelling became a fad almost simultaneously with its appearance in 1783, and "spelling-bees" soon came to be a popular school exercise. In North Carolina, as in other sections of the South where schoolbooks were scarce, it was often one of the first books put into the hands of the child when he entered school, and served as a good combination of primer, speller, reader, and moral guide.

Among the primers in use in the State during the *ante-bellum* period were *The American Primer*, *The Baltimore Primer*, Cobb's *Primer*, Hanson's *Symbolical Primer*, *The Juvenile Primer*, *The New York Primer*, *The New England Primer*, *The Philadelphia Primer*, *The Union Primer*, *The United States Primer*, *The Washington Primer*, Webster's *Primer*, and Worcester's *Primer*. Of these *The New England Primer* was for a long time one of the most popular and was in use in North Carolina and other Southern States for a long time after it had fallen into neglect in other sections. Scarcity of textbooks here probably helped to maintain a place for it. The book was "almost entirely a religious and moral miscellany of verse and prose gathered from all sorts of sources. Prominent in the miscellany is a picture alphabet — a series of twenty-four tiny pictures, each accompanied by a two or three line jingle," which was a very old method of teaching the alphabet. The jingles were doubtless thought to lend themselves to teaching certain religious beliefs.

The list of reading-books was even larger than the number of primers in use in North Carolina before the war. Reading, together with ciphering and writing, occupied the major portion of the curriculum, and during the *ante-bellum* period almost any printed matter which could be furnished the children served as a textbook in the subject. The following are some of the material reported as "readers": Bingham's *American Preceptor*, Blair's *Reading Exercises*, Baxter's *Call*, *Bible and Sabbath School Books*, *Class Readers*, *Child's Library*, *Child's Book*, Cobb's *Reading Books*, *Columbian Orator*, *Come and Welcome to Christ*, *Eclectic Reader*, Emerson's *Readers*, *Evening Entertainment*, *Fascinating Companion*, *Family Story Book*, Hall's *Western Reader*, Hervey's *Meditations*, *Juvenile Readers*, Kay's *Reader*, Murray's *Introduction*, *Reader and Sequel*, *Moral Instructor*, *National Reader*, *New England Reader*, *The New York Readers*, Nos. 1, 2, and 3, *New York Expositor*, *New Testament*, *Orator's Assistant*, *Panorama of Arts*, *Panorama of Trades*, *Parley's Tales*, Parley's *Reader*, *Popular Lessons*, *Pleasing Companion*, *Pilgrim's Progress*, Scott's *Lessons*, *Southern Reader*, *The Spectator*, Town's *Little Thinker*, *United States Readers*, *United States Constitution*, *The Virginian Orator*, Miss Edgeworth's *Early Lessons*, *Mother at Home*, *Child at Home*, *Parents' Cabinet*, *Cabinet Library*, *Robinson Crusoe*, and others. Of these Murray's *Reader*, published in Haverhill, Massachusetts, in 1825, and *The New York Reader*, No. 3, published in New York in 1828, were the most extensively used. All readers of the period were intended to assist young people to read "with propriety and effect, to improve their language and sentiments, and to inculcate some of the most important principles of piety and virtue."

Because of the high esteem in which mathematics was held as a practical science, arithmetic held perhaps the most important place in the curriculum, and, as in other subjects, a great variety of texts were in use. Among those most frequently reported in use, texts by the following authors may be mentioned: Adams, Beattie, Colburn, Daboll, Dilworth, Emerson, Fenn, Fenning, Fisher, Fowler, Gough, Jess, Jones, Niles, Park, Pike, Ray, Root, Slocomb, Smiley, Smith, Stockton, Walkingham, Walsh, Webster, Willard. Of these Colburn's *First Lessons in Intellectual Arithmetic,* which appeared in 1821, Thomas Dilworth's *The School-Master's Assistant,* which appeared earlier, and the works of Jess and of Pike, earlier still, were among those most extensively used in North Carolina during the *ante-bellum* régime.

On account of the monopoly of the curriculum by the minimum essentials of an English education — reading, writing, and arithmetic — geography found rather tardily the position which it now occupies in the curriculum of the elementary school. Even the higher schools neglected it as a separate study until far into the nineteenth century. When it first appeared in the lower schools it was not treated as a subject distinct in itself; neither was it intended, as it is to-day, to impart a knowledge of world movements, of current events, or of the economic and commercial relations of man. Like the earlier histories, books on geography served as readers rather than as texts on the subject of the earth as the home of man. Frequently, however, geographies must have been used in the capacities of readers and histories also. Not a few of the texts in use in the early nineteenth century could have served one purpose quite as well as another.

In these capacities, as readers and as histories, a great variety of texts were in use. Among them books by the following authors seem to have been most widely known and used: Adams, Carey, Cummings, Frazer, Guthrie, Huntingdon, Moss, Morse, Olney, "Peter Parley," Smiley, Willett, Willard, and Woodbridge. Of these the work of Morse, the pioneer American geographer, and the work of Olney were apparently the most popular. Morse's book, *The American Universal Geography*, was a sketchy, fragmentary combination history-geography of the whole world, treated historically, geographically, economically, educationally, religiously, politically, morally, and socially. Olney's *Geography and Atlas* was accepted as a standard text on the subject immediately after its appearance in 1828, and for forty years or longer it found a place in North Carolina. Moreover, the book almost immediately had the effect of changing the current method of teaching the subject. Olney, who was a practical teacher, emphasized the tendency toward "home geography."

Textbooks on grammar did not, as geographies and histories, serve well as readers, and that subject, as we know it to-day, also came slowly into the schools. The early texts were unduly intricate and difficult to explain or to understand, and the subject was regarded as more or less meaningless as well as dreary. Children were therefore little interested in it. The prefaces of many of the earlier works were often apologetic, deploring the lack of interest in such an important subject. The primary purpose of grammar was to teach the correct use of spoken and written language, but, like geography, it was also meant to serve a moral and religious purpose. Grammar was not a required subject in the public schools in North Carolina during the *ante-bellum* period, teachers were not examined on it, and the subject was therefore not widely taught. Occasionally, however, county officials reported a few "grammar and geography" pupils.[1] in some of their schools. With the few who were studying the subject a great variety of texts were used. Among them the following authors may be mentioned: Ash, Bingham, Boardman, Brown, Bullion, Comly, Greenleaf, Harrison, Ingersol, Jandon, Johnston, Kirkman, Lowth, Murray, Merton, Olney, Sanford, Scott, Smith, and Webster. The work of Murray and that of Kirkman were the most generally used.

History likewise found a place tardily in the curriculum of the public schools of the State, and when it first appeared as a school subject it was largely used as material for teaching reading. The value of the subject as a means of furnishing a broad interpretation of the world was not recognized, neither was it believed that the subject was capable of making direct appeals to human interests, to curiosity, to the imagination, or of developing enlightened patriotism or strengthening intellectual habits. Many of the early texts contained neither maps nor illustrations. The function of early history teaching was often believed to be ethical and religious, though the methods used were often unsafe even for these purposes.

Few books on historical subjects appeared in the schools of North Carolina until the late thirties, and then they were used largely as readers. Among those most generally in use were works of Adams, Frost, Goldsmith, Goodrich, Grimshaw, Hale, Jesse, Millot, "Peter Parley," Pitkin, Pinnock, Webster and Worcester. Ancient,

[1] See pp. 200-203.

mediæval, European, universal, general, and ecclesiastical, were words which often described the texts in use. Most of these works were often the merest outlines, a characteristic often observable in histories until near the close of the nineteenth century. Moreover, teachers were poorly prepared to teach history, and there was but little to recommend a place for the subject in the schools. Poor books, poorly prepared teachers, and classrooms so inadequately equipped that they never suggested the subject, were not conducive to lead pupils to study history or to acquire the wholesome habit of reading historical material.

Of the material equipment of the schools, qualifications of the teachers, and interest in public education in the State before the war, the following pages contain fairly representative descriptions which are taken from the reports of the chairmen of the school officials of Burke, Alamance, Union, and Wilkes Counties to the state superintendent for the year 1857. These reports are representative of educational conditions in the State during the closing years of the *ante-bellum* period. The last selection is from one of Wiley's early reports and contains his own criticism of schoolroom practices of the time.

(Burke County, 1857)

I visited the following schools, and have the honor to report as follows, to wit:

No. 1. There is no district schoolhouse in this district, and no school going on, but they have used the money heretofore by teaching in a rented house.

No. 2. Has a good house, rock chimney and glass windows. Taught by Mr. ———, an excellent teacher of the lower branches of English education. He knows nothing of grammar and geography.

No. 3. An excellent house with rock chimney and glass windows. Taught by Miss ———, five grammar and geography scholars. She governs well, because she governs by affection.

No. 4. Has a neat schoolhouse (new). Taught by Miss ———; governs well; a good rock chimney, and well lighted; all right.

No. 5. Is a pretty good house, wants some repairs. Taught by Mr. ———, and does very well.

No. 6. A very good house, rock chimney; six grammar and geography scholars. Mr. ———, a pretty good teacher, has the school.

No. 7. Has no district schoolhouse, having recently lost a very good house by fire, accidentally. A school has been lately taught in a storehouse, which is on the school lot. It was well taught. Seven grammar and geography scholars.

No. 8. An excellent house, with two rock chimneys. The school is well taught by Miss ———, daughter of our sheriff. Eight grammar and geography scholars.

No. 9. Taught by Mr. ———, an excellent young man. Good house, rock chimney. Has six grammar and geography scholars. All is right here, and school well governed.

No. 10. Is a pretty good house, but wants some repairs, taught by Mrs. ———. This lady is an excellent tutoress, and lives near the schoolhouse — devotes great attention to her school, and governs well. I think her No. 1 as a teacher. She has eight grammar and geography scholars.

No. 11. Is a small district, without a teacher or house.

No. 12. Taught by Mr. ———, an excellent teacher; good house, with rock chimney and glass windows. Nine grammar and geography scholars.

No. 13. A good house, rock chimney and glass windows. School to commence soon under the tuition of Mr. ———, who is now teaching in No. 12.

No. 14. An excellent house, rock chimney, well lighted with glass windows, taught by the Rev. Mr. ———, one of our best teachers. Thirty grammar and geography scholars.

No. 15. A new, good schoolhouse. An excellent teacher has been teaching; not now teaching, but will soon re-commence his school. All right here.

No. 16. A good house; teacher absent a while; rock chimney, well lighted. No difficulties here.

No. 17. An excellent house, good rock chimney and glass windows. School well taught. Ten grammar and geography scholars.

No. 18. The district had a house nine years after the school law went into operation, near the center. It was conducted in peace and harmony until the house was burnt down; since then there has been a school taught in a house given for the purpose. Some dissatisfaction still exists about the location of a house by the committee, but I think these differences can be settled and the school will go on.

No. 19. A good teacher and good house. Things all right.

No. 20. Good house, an excellent rock chimney, well lighted, good teacher, school well taught.

No. 21. Good house and pretty good teacher. All right.

No. 22. Rich Mountain district. Tolerable good house. All right. Teacher has been teaching, but stopped his school for a while.

No. 23. Stacey district has a very good house, with rock chimney, good glass windows, and taught by a Mr. ———; all in good order.

No. 24. A very good house with rock chimney and glass windows, taught by Mr. ———, a good teacher.

No. 25. Taught by Mr. ———; a neat good house, with rock chimney and glass windows. Six grammar and geography scholars. School well conducted.

No. 26. Mr. ———, teacher; an excellent new house with rock chimney and glass windows; school well conducted. Four grammar and geography scholars.

No. 27. An excellent house, rock chimney and windows of glass. Five grammar and geography scholars. All right.

No. 28. No district school at present, but expect one will be erected soon. A lot of land is given, and will be conveyed to the committee soon. Mr. ——— is now teaching in a house which has been procured for the purpose. Five grammar and geography scholars. No difficulties.

No. 29. Brindleton is an excellent house, with rock chimney and glass windows. Taught by Mr. ———, an ordinary teacher.

ANTE-BELLUM EDUCATIONAL PRACTICE 203

No. 30. Rain Hill is an excellent house, taught by Mr. ———, a very good teacher, and all right.

No. 31. Is an excellent house, well lighted and school now being taught. No troubles or difficulties.

No. 32. Is a pretty good house, school being now taught by an excellent teacher.

No. 33. School taught by Mr. ———, an able man; pretty well taught. An excellent house, with rock chimney and good light. All right.

No. 34. In this district they have had a school every year, except the present year, in a house procured for the purpose, but not a good one. The committee will probably cause a good house to be built pretty soon.

No. 35. This is a very good house, and has a school now taught by Mr. ———. Nothing wrong in this district.

No. 36. School taught by Mrs. ———, a most excellent tutoress. A very good house, everything neat about it; rock chimney, etc. Nine grammar and geography scholars.

No. 37. School taught by a young man, Mr. ———. An excellent house, new, and good rock chimney and glass windows. Seven grammar and geography scholars.

No. 38. This is the district in which the difficulty arose and in which I recommend a division, as stated in No. 22. A school has been taught by Mr. ———.

No. 39. School taught by Mr. ———; a very good teacher; a good house. All right.

In submitting this report to the board of superintendents and to the state superintendent, it gives me great pleasure to state that I found the houses much better than I expected, and the manner in which the schools are conducted far better than I ever expected to find them in my lifetime. There appeared everywhere throughout the county a good spirit among all classes. Every assistance was rendered to get me on from one district to another, and not one dime was charged by any person for expenses, and every necessary comfort rendered me; which was extremely grateful to the feelings of an aged man.

In conclusion, I will respectfully remark that I had but one thing to regret in this visit, to wit: that so few of the districts taught a *silent school*. I told the teachers that I had no power to reform; this belonged to the district committees. But I used every effort which reason and fair argument suggested, to remove the prejudice which exists on that subject. Some two thirds of the districts teach a *noisy* school.

(*Alamance County, 1857*)

I came home last night from a tour visiting our school districts and houses, and am glad to find your favor of the 24th inst. at the post-office. We had a very cold, windy day yesterday, and this morning is quite cold, the thermometer standing at 20 degrees, and so I concluded I would give you some account of my progress in visiting, and ask your counsel on several matters relative thereto. I have visited about one half the schoolhouses, and find them in better condition than I expected, and have been treated with courteous attention by all. I purchased a set of the schoolbooks and paid for them, one set for each district, and left them with each committee, with a catalogue, in order that the parents of the children might know the prices, and where they might be had.

I have taken much care to select one of the most public-spirited of each committee to act as foreman; those having the largest family of children to attend the schools, and enjoin it on them each to see that the schoolhouses are kept in good comfortable repair, and also to keep the sample books and catalogues. I have found, where all three of the committee have to attend to the requirements, they will all neglect to do their duty; and hence the necessity of giving it to one, under the instruction of the joint committee. They all appear to be well pleased with the plan of procuring books and the mode proposed to procure them.

I have measured the dimensions of the houses and the land attached and taken deeds, and classed the houses in five grades, Nos. 1, 2, 3, 4, 5; as yet I have had but one of No. 1, worth $175; No. 2, from $100 to $140; No. 3, from $75 to $100; No. 4, from $50 to $75; and one No. 5, worth only $25. So far the school houses and land average about $100 each; the number in the county 48. The houses are generally sufficiently large in extent or size. I have a small book in which I record the quality of each, with a view to bring about some district pride.

I am requiring of the teachers to furnish, in addition to the printed forms, the number and names of the scholars taught and the length of time each was taught, and to designate the five most attentive and obedient and apt to learn, by attaching Nos. 1, 2, and so on to their respective names.

I have been trying to take the number of black and white polls, and the quantity of land in acres embraced in each district, and also the value of it, so as to ascertain the amount of tax collected from each for school purposes.

(*Union County, 1857*)

Your circular for the present year came to hand a few days ago. With its contents I am much pleased, and hasten to comply with your request; and I herewith send you a rough and hastily made map of our County of Union, and its common-school districts. I do not wish to consume time making apologies because my map is such a commonplace excuse, but I must make some explanation.

Our county was formed in 1842, but continued with the counties of Anson and Mecklenburg as to common-school matters until 1850; we then set up for ourselves. In 1851 we laid off the county into school districts, four miles by four miles square (by survey); your humble servant was made chairman, and has so continued. We now consider our school districts as being too large and inconvenient as well as too populous (many of the districts numbering from 100 to 140 children); and we have it in contemplation to re-district our county in the course of this summer and fall, and we are intending to bring the matter to the notice of our county court for their approval — not that we, the county superintendents, doubt of having a right to do so, but for courtesy only. For when the county was first districted the court generously made an order to pay the expenses of the laying off, amounting to something over $200; and at that time there was no school tax laid in this county, but as there is now, we do not expect the county to pay, and shall take the expenses from the school funds raised in the county. (Will this be right?) As to the form and size of the districts — on this subject I would be very glad of the opportunity to consult with you; but I will try to give you my views and plan as well as I can, which are to lay off the districts in regular hexagon form, or six equal angles containing twelve square miles, so that the center of each district will only be two miles from each corner. Our present number of districts is forty-one; by this plan, it would be fifty-six. Our county contains six hundred and sixty-seven square miles, and has within its limits a number of large creeks, which will necessarily cause derangement of the regular plan, and also add to the number of districts. This, sir, is the outline of the plan I had expected to district by; and if you can help me to an idea, I will be thankful to you for it.

You make some allusion to chairmen visiting schools, etc. I will take the liberty here to give you some account of the way and manner that I have proceeded. In the fall of 1854 I visited seventeen of the districts, when the schools were going on, gave such advice as I thought necessary, and settled a number of difficulties that had arisen in the schools; took account of the number of children in attendance, scolded about the bad seats, open houses, smoky chimneys, etc., called on committeemen and extorted promises to have repairs attended to, most of which I believe was done. The summer and fall of 1855, from family affliction, I attended only two or three — nothing worth naming; in 1856 I visited twenty-two schools, and I should have been glad, had it been called for, to have made a report to you of the improvement which appears to be going forward in our schools. When you make the allowance that our county is a good way behind in education it is gratifying to know that in every district I was at, where the teacher was competent to teach grammar and geography, there were students pursuing them, and I do not now recollect that a solitary complaint was made in the county the past year. I know I have run on with a great deal of egotism, but I am writing for the eye of none but my much respected superintendent, and that is my apology. One who I know takes so deep an interest in education generally is entitled to the highest commendation.

Should we succeed and our county be re-districted by a competent surveyor (my age forbids me), I will endeavor, as soon as possible, to comply with your request more fully.

(*Wilkes County, 1857*)

Your esteemed favor of the —— was duly received, and, according to your request, I should have written you long before this; but my professional engagements have been so pressing that I have found it impossible to write sooner, and now write away from my office . . . while waiting upon the sick.

According to appointment, our "Educational Meeting" came off and, as the first effort of the kind in this county, may well be called a great "success." I had visited as many as ten of our voting precincts, involving a ride of over two hundred miles — had extended a very earnest and special invitation to our magistrates, ministers of the gospel, school teachers, committeemen, and all friends of education in our county, to come out and let us form a society of such numerical strength, character, and influence, as would at the very outset place us on a firm and successful career. I am proud to say that I realized a more hearty response than I at first anticipated — a large and imposing delegation of the magistracy of our county, and a representative from almost every district either of the committeemen or some friend of common-schools being present.

Although it was court day, and there was political speaking, yet we so arranged it that our meeting was organized immediately at the close of the discussion. I had made an effort to have a *speaker* provided, but did not succeed — had therefore to officiate myself; and after calling a temporary president, I proceeded to explain more fully the object of our meeting, to point out some of the advantages likely to result from this movement, and then I read your letter, as you requested. I then called over the names of all our committeemen, invited the ministers of the Gospel and the teachers and magistrates to come forward and take seats (as by an article of our constitution they were already members by virtue of their office).

After consulting with some of the friends of our cause, we concluded to draw up and adopt a constitution for the present, according to my promise, and hereafter alter or substitute, as occasion may require. I accordingly drew up the accompanying preamble and constitution, copying the state form as far as I could. This I submitted, article after article, accompanied with suitable explanations, and it was adopted. I then proceeded to nominate and elect individually our board of officers.

After the president took the chair, and our association was fully organized, I submitted a few suggestions concerning the introduction of the *Bible* in our schools — having ascertained that this matter had been so neglected that it amounted almost to a prohibition — premising that I had obtained, partly by *donation* and partly by purchase, a sufficiency of books to give *one* copy of the Bible and ten copies of the Testament to *every school district in the county*. I urged with earnestness and zeal the great importance of this movement — enjoined it upon the teachers to attend to this matter — and called upon the committees to help us carry forward the plan. My remarks were listened to with profound attention on this point; and I have reason to believe will not only command the approbation of our school officers, but will contribute something toward the accomplishment of this much needed measure.

I then detailed a plan we were trying to introduce to prepare and encourage our teachers, i.e., of raising a "Public Circulating Library," a scheme the teachers were gladly availing themselves of, but which was much desired and much needed by many others — as placing the means of information and preparation in the hands of the teachers, introducing standard books, etc., into our community. I was anxious to obtain subscribers, as many as possible, outside the corps of teachers. As this was the last business we did, and as the county candidates were urging us through, I did not get as many subscribers as I think, under other circumstances, might have been obtained. I have, however, from all sources, about $70 subscribed. I hope to be able to raise $100 — if so, it is the intention of the board to subscribe another $100 — this will give us a pretty fair start. If I succeed in this matter, I will trouble you again in making out a catalogue of books, etc.

Previous to adjournment it was agreed to set apart the 4th of July in every year to hold our annual meetings, and that called meetings will be held as often as required by the president. This, with a few other desultory proceedings, closed our meeting.

I have thus, my dear sir, in my intervals while in attendance upon the sick, endeavored to give you a sketch of our "First Educational Meeting" in Wilkes County — a sketch imperfect in all its details, and in which I regret that my own name and efforts should occupy so conspicuous a place; but am assured that you will not refer it to any egotism on my part, but to the deep and abiding interest that I hope I, in common with yourself, feel in this matter.

I think I may safely assert that our corps of teachers, though not prepared as well as even the law requires, and not making the advancement it is desirable they should do, go out to their fields of labor *impressed* more deeply and thoroughly than perhaps ever heretofore, with the importance and immense responsibility of their calling.

The imperfect manner in which our school districts were originally run off, their irregularity both in numbering and size, renders it necessary to re-arrange and re-district our county; and we expect to have this done the present fall — having the districts made uniform in size, the number in regular order, and the lines and corners marked. When this work is done, I shall be glad to supply you with a map of our county, and I have no doubt but what it will greatly facilitate our school operations.

The following, taken from one of Wiley's earlier reports, will throw a little light on his own idea of defects in the schoolroom: —

I have met with persons who thought my course of instruction — that is, the series of books recommended — too simple; and I found that these persons could not answer one fourth of the important questions which could be asked and answered out of Webster's *Spelling Book*. All pupils, when reading, ought to have by them, for constant reference, a dictionary; and when teachers exercise the students in spelling, from memory (and they ought to do it often), they should give out the words from a work of this sort, and give also the definition. Arithmetical recitations on the slate should be universally abolished; and there is no one thing so important in a schoolroom, and few things cheaper than a blackboard. In the hands of a good teacher it is absolutely indispensable: it serves for arithmetical recitations, for practice in shaping figures and letters to those beginning to write, and is useful in lectures, as affording a place to make illustrations in the view of the whole school.

Blackboards were doubtless very scarce in the public schools of the State before the war and they continued scarce until many years afterwards. Throughout the period Wiley urged improvement in material equipment and in methods of teaching, and in these things he brought about considerable progress. In the late fifties there was a rapidly growing tendency to improve schoolhouses, and throughout the period there was a noticeable improvement in the teachers.

REFERENCES

Legislative Documents of North Carolina; Legislative Documents of Virginia; *Annual Reports* of the Superintendent of Public Instruction, 1853–66; the *North Carolina Journal of Education;* Johnston, *Old-Time Schools and School-books;* Coon, *North Carolina Schools and Academies, 1790–1840, a Documentary History;* numerous old textbooks. Most of the books referred to in this chapter are in the Library of Congress, and many of them have been examined by the author.

SUGGESTIONS FOR FURTHER STUDY

1. How much more extensive is the public school curriculum to-day than it was before the war? How has it expanded during the past twenty years? How have school books improved during that time?
2. What is the advantage of uniform school books? Compare the books recommended by Wiley in 1853 with those in use in the public schools of the State to-day.
3. What are the characteristics of a good spelling-book? What was the method of teaching spelling before the war? What is the weakness of the methods in use to-day? What was the value of the old-time "spelling-bees" or "spelling-matches"?

ANTE-BELLUM EDUCATIONAL PRACTICE

4. Compare the early readers with those in use in the State to-day.
5. Why did arithmetic occupy such an important place in the *ante-bellum* curriculum? What was the purpose of teaching the subject? How did the early method of teaching the subject differ from the present method or methods? What are the characteristics of a good textbook on arithmetic?
6. Why did geography come slowly into the public schools? How did the purpose and use of early geography teaching differ from the purpose and use of the subject to-day? How has the method of teaching geography changed in recent years? Account for this change. In what respect is geography a "practical" subject? A "moral" subject? A "cultural" subject?
7. How have textbooks on grammar changed in recent years? How have the methods of teaching the subject changed? What is your criticism of so-called "formal grammar"?
8. Why was the value of history as a distinct school subject not early recognized? What was the purpose of the subject when it first appeared? What is the purpose of the subject to-day? In what way does history serve as a subject for moral training? What are the characteristics of a good textbook on history? What are the qualifications of a good teacher of the subject?
9. Why were all textbooks of the early period arranged so as to furnish moral and religious training?
10. How has the material equipment of the schools in your county increased in the past ten years? How have the qualifications of the teachers in your county improved in that time?
11. What agencies are at work to improve the public school-houses and grounds of your county? Why should local school-houses be built in accordance with plans approved by the state department of education?
12. How has county supervision improved in your county during the past ten years?
13. How does local educational interest express itself in your county?

CHAPTER XI

THE BEGINNINGS OF RECONSTRUCTION

ONE criticism which the student of American educational history is forced to make of the average treatment of the origin and development of our public-school system is in the great variety of loose and inaccurate statements concerning *ante-bellum* educational effort in the Southern States. Another is in the more or less arbitrary geographic and chronologic divisions made in the story of public educational development in the United States at large. There may be a certain convenience in such divisions, but they are often made at the expense of justice and fairness to the principle on which educational interest expressed itself prior to 1860. For example, Massachusetts is often considered the prototype of scholastic endeavor in all New England in colonial days and during the early years of the nineteenth century; the educational customs of Virginia are frequently considered representative of the educational theory and practice which prevailed in the entire Southern States before the war; schools and education in Pennsylvania are usually taken as a type for the middle eastern section of the country; and New York is ordinarily given an educational classification to itself.

In such historical treatments, which are more or less arbitrary and often contrary to facts, numerous loose and general statements concerning education in the United States before 1860 have appeared. One of these statements has concerned educational sentiment and educational effort and practice in the southern part of the country prior to the Civil War. It has become popular to assert that there was no system of public education in these States prior to the congressional plan of Reconstruction; that little effort for education had been made in the South before that time; and that this lack of educational tradition for all the people was largely responsible for the war and its deplorable aftermath. Such education as was given in the South during *antebellum* days was believed by some to have been based on wrong principles which finally produced the secessionist and rebellious spirit. It was also believed that the poor whites of the South were in dense ignorance and that this ignorance had been exploited by unprincipled leaders and made the foundation for the Confederacy. It was further believed in some quarters that the white leaders in the South frequently opposed public education for the masses of the people, and that all classes opposed the education of the negroes after their emancipation.[1]

The evidence on this matter is abundant. The war had scarcely closed before this belief was finding expression throughout the country. The speeches in the annual meeting of the National Teachers' Association, which was held in Harrisburg, Pennsylvania, in August, 1865, were burdened with the idea that the lately closed rebellion had been a "war of education and patriotism against ignorance and barbarism." In his opening speech, "The Educational Duties of the Hour," the president of that organization said: —

All through the loyal States our principal institutions have prospered to a most wonderful degree. How has it been with

---

[1] Fleming, *Documentary History of Reconstruction*, vol. II, chap. IX.

the States in rebellion? Scarcely an institution of learning survived.... In all the free States the public-school system prevailed, and in most was administered with great efficiency, giving a good education alike to the poor and the rich.... How was it in the States where the institution of slavery prevailed? There was no common-school system. Exceptions there were in some of the cities — but as a general fact, the statement is correct. The children of a large portion of the population were, by law, prohibited the advantages of an education, and a large portion of the free population were virtually shut out from the means of early culture.... Thus has our land been deluged in blood. Sagacious politicians of the South saw the tendencies, and attributed the evil to the quality of Northern education. Without stopping to defend the character of our educational processes at the North, let it be observed that the root of the difficulty lay not in this direction, but in the fact of a diffused and universal education at the North and a very limited education at the South. No two sections of country, though under the same government, can dwell together in peace and harmony, where the advantages of education are widely dissimilar....

There is but one alternative — education must be diffused throughout the masses of the South. Black and white — "poor white" and rich white — all must be educated. Not to educate them is to prepare for another Civil War....

Before the war no Southern teacher dared to discuss the whole truth at the South.... Can we not as educators go boldly into the Southern States and teach the truth and the whole truth? If not, I pray God that martial law may prevail in every Southern State, till Northern men, or any other men, may discuss educational, social, political, and moral and religious topics in any part of the South as freely as in Faneuil Hall. This right we must have....

The result of the war was also regarded by many as affording rare opportunities for extending "universal education" in the States lately in rebellion. The entire South was now viewed as a vast missionary field, and this view was one of the defenses of the policy adopted

THE BEGINNINGS OF RECONSTRUCTION 215

for "reconstructing" that region. In spite of the genuineness of much of this sentiment, the decade following the close of the war shows much misdirected missionary zeal and visionary effort. With the exception of the Peabody Board Trustees, whose work has had a lasting beneficial influence on education in the South, the most of these missionary activities were blindly made and with little or no understanding of local conditions and local needs. Enthusiasts on the subject failed to consider the temper of the popular mind; in their opinion the chief difference between the white man and the negro was the enforced ignorance of the latter, a difference which could easily be removed. Note the following, taken from a pamphlet issued near the close of the war, by a Massachusetts minister: —

We have four millions of liberated slaves who should be educated. They ask it at our hands, and the world expects us to do it; because in the very act of emancipation there is the sacred promise to educate. Slavery has kept the word education out of our national constitution. Now four millions of starved minds implore its introduction. . . . Their former masters will not take the trouble to educate them, and would generally refuse to pay a local tax for the purpose. Since the Christian era there has not been such an opportunity for such a country to do such work; the noblest work man can do. . . . The old slave States are to be new missionary grounds for the national schoolmaster. . . .

Others believed that

when the combat was over and the "Yankee" schoolma'ams followed in the train of Northern armies, the business of educating the negroes was a continuation of hostilities against the vanquished South and so regarded, to a considerable extent, on both sides.[1]

---

[1] Alice M. Bacon, in *Occasional Papers of the Slater Fund Trustees*, no. 7.

From such an early beginning, therefore, it is not astonishing that inaccurate notions concerning Southern educational conditions should have developed and persisted even until recent years. In his *Autobiography*, General Oliver O. Howard, of the Freedmen's Bureau, said of the State which had the most creditable school system to be found in the entire South before 1860: —

It is a wonderful thing to recall that North Carolina had never had before that time a free-school system even for white pupils, and there was then no publication in the State devoted to popular education. The death of slavery unfolded the wings of knowledge for both black and white to brighten all the future of the "Old North State." [1]

The inaccuracy of such a statement is obvious. We have already traced the State's educational effort before the war and noted that during the years from 1852 to 1861, known as the period of "reorganization," a journal of education was begun and maintained and proved a valuable auxiliary agency in the promotion of popular education. Other statements equally inaccurate have also been developed and recorded by men who should, indeed, know better. One of these is found in *The Southern South*, where Professor Hart says —

... as for free public schools, not a single Southern State had organized and set in operation a system before the Civil War.[2]

From such inaccurate generalities there has grown up the constantly repeated statement that the schools which did exist in the South were altogether unlike those found elsewhere in the United States. A careful study of conditions in the other sections of the country shows a striking similarity to conditions in the Southern

[1] Page 338. [2] Pages 289, 290.

States. The laws, reports of the administrative officers, school statistics, complaints against the inefficiency of teachers and other school officials, found in the legislative documents and the messages of the governors of the various States, all bear testimony that in origin, organization, and comparative results, there was a striking likeness between educational conditions in North Carolina, Virginia, or Alabama, and those of the more advanced States of New York, Pennsylvania, or Connecticut. Indeed, one does not have to search far for evidence that conditions in one section of the country were more or less similar to those in another section, and that the history of public education is much the same in the United States, whether it be the history of one part of it or of another. This does not necessarily mean that educational conditions in any two sections, or in any two States of the same section, are at any one time the same. Sentiment in favor of public schools for all the people may be stronger in one State or section than in another; or opposition to progressive educational policies may weaken or grow strong as the economic, political, or social conditions vary.

Most of the state school systems in this country have passed through what may be called the "storm and stress period" in their development. In most States there have been great educational landmarks, made, perhaps, by long periods of educational agitation and the resulting growth of unusual sentiment for schools. The so-called early educational revival in North Carolina, from the establishment of the literary fund in 1825 to the passage of the first school law fourteen years later, is practically paralleled by the educational campaign in Pennsylvania, in defense of whose school system and school law Stevens made his famous speech in the Legislature of that State in 1835.[1] The work of Horace Mann in Massachusetts and of Henry Barnard in Connecticut for public education, was not unlike that of Calvin H. Wiley in North Carolina at a somewhat later date. Early school legislation in Virginia and North Carolina was framed on a theory not unlike that on which similar legislation in New York was framed: that the income from the literary fund and a small tax were sufficient for educational purposes. The theory on which schools in Georgia were established and operated was more or less similar to the theory on which early schools in Pennsylvania rested; and the administrative machinery of the school system in Alabama and South Carolina and other Southern States was practically the same as that for other sections of the country. Except for details of administration, perhaps, educational custom in the United States before 1860 was very similar in every section of the country.

The successful application of the democratic theory of government to public education is the essential ideal of the origin and growth of our state school systems. This is abundantly illustrated by a study of the growth of our public education immediately prior to and just following the Civil War. And it is none the less true of one section than of another. When the story of this educational development is properly told, without the usual rhetorical embellishments which characterize the telling of a popular tale, this ideal will reveal itself as a characteristic of all earnest effort at sound educational progress. It is a long way from the payment by the State of tuition for the majority of its scholastic population for three or

[1] Wickersham, *History of Education in Pennsylvania*, p. 369.

four months in the year to the theory that the State should not only do this, but should even provide medical and dental attention for its young citizens while they are in school. And some socialistic educational theorists go further and believe that the State should provide free meals, in some cases clothe the children, and in rarer cases, perhaps, pay the parents for the time their children are in school. The theory, however, is always the same.

The theory that the school is for all the people, the well-to-do and the poor, has developed slowly. This slowness has been due to the varying social, political, and economic conditions, as well as to the fact that education is marked by a conservatism equaled only by that in religion. That this theory has developed more rapidly and thoroughly in some sections of the country than in others, no one now questions; that in most sections its periods of growth have often been followed by corresponding periods of retardation is also generally accepted. It is also agreed that the Southern States passed tardily through the so-called experimental stage in their educational growth. Hurried comparisons have been made of conditions in the various sections prior to 1860 in an effort to show a diversity of educational theory and practice and that out of the war and reconstruction were born the free public-school systems of the South. That certain differences did exist, and that remarkable changes in constitutional and legislative provisions for education appeared after the war, no one will undertake to deny. But these changes were not confined to the Southern States; and a careful study of conditions before and after 1860 shows that it is not the differences but rather the similarities in the essential features of public education in this country which are, after all, most pronounced.

General opinions formed from such hurried comparisons of conditions have led to the more definite question, "What influence did the Reconstruction or 'carpetbag' régime have on education in the South?" Obviously a satisfactory answer to the question can be found only by a detailed and careful comparison of *ante-bellum* with reconstruction and *post-bellum* conditions. This comparison requires a clear differentiation both of the periods between 1865 and 1876 and the plans proposed for restoring the South, and of the classes of men who took part in the formal restoration of the seceding States and in the work which followed.

Of the two plans proposed the presidential plan of Reconstruction, from 1865 to 1867, marks an attempt to enlist the coöperation of the native white citizens in restoring civil order in the South. Under the congressional plan, however, from 1867 to 1876, three classes instead of one, as in the presidential plan, participated in political affairs: the native whites, the negro freedmen, and men from the North. The native whites were sharply divided into two classes, the conservatives and the radicals or "scalawags." The negroes were the most homogeneous, usually of the same mind and easily influenced; while the men from the North, commonly known as "carpetbaggers," were, from the point of view of the South, predominantly radical. The Reconstruction conventions and legislative bodies from 1867 to 1876 were composed largely of negroes, carpetbaggers, and scalawags, the conservatives in most cases being in the minority.

The presidential plan of Reconstruction began in

North Carolina in May, 1865, when President Johnson appointed W. W. Holden provisional governor of the State. Holden was instructed to call a convention for the purpose of altering the state constitution in such a way that relations with the federal government could be reëstablished. Only those who had been granted amnesty by taking the oath prescribed in the proclamation of the President, May 29, 1865, could qualify as electors or as members of the Constitutional Convention. Fourteen classes of people were exempted from the benefits of the amnesty proclamation, but hope of executive clemency was held out to those exempted, through application to the President for pardon. A large number of persons were pardoned through this means. The election of delegates to the Convention was held and the Convention met October 2, 1865. The body was very largely composed of men who had not favored secession. "Most of them were old Whigs, who, while opposed to secession, had submitted to the will of the majority. With these were many members of the peace party during the war. The delegates were unanimous in their desire to restore the State to normal relations with the federal government, and this was constantly shown as the session progressed."[1] The convention abolished slavery, repudiated the war debt, and declared the ordinances of secession null and void.

The election of state officers and of members of the General Assembly was held November 9, 1865, and that body met November 27. But little is known of the former political affiliation of most of its members. The uncertainty of the legality of its actions prevented the Assembly from concerning itself with general legislation,

[1] Hamilton, *Reconstruction in North Carolina*, p. 121.

and after a short session it adjourned until February. This session continued until the middle of March, giving attention also primarily to private legislation. The only act of educational significance was one to abolish the office of superintendent of public instruction and the office of treasurer of the literary fund.

This law, which was passed March 9, 1866, allowed the justices of the county courts to lay and collect taxes at their discretion for common-school support; and county school communities were given discretionary powers to grant aid, "to the extent they may be authorized by the court, to subscription schools, the teachers of which have qualifications prescribed for teachers of the common schools, and to allow such schools to be carried on in the schoolrooms of their districts." The arguments made in the discussions of the bill when it was proposed throw light on the actual condition of the time. The literary fund was indeed inadequate to maintain a system of public schools, a large part of that previous source of support having been lost. Moreover, the people of the State were impoverished as a result of the war. To certain members of the Legislature it appeared inexpedient and well-nigh impossible to support a system of schools; to others the great service rendered by the school system before the war now made the necessity for its revival and support appear the more imperative. Efforts were made by the friends of the schools to get appropriations from the state treasury, or by borrowing money, in order that they might continue. Finally the House passed a bill, by a vote of 49 to 40, authorizing an annual appropriation of $75,000 to assist the schools, but it was killed in the Senate by a vote of 23 to 14. It does not appear that there was outright legislative hostility to the system, however. At the same session the Assembly appropriated $7000 to relieve the state university of temporary embarrassment. Many of those who voted for this resolution also voted for the bill to abolish the office of state superintendent of schools. They did so, however, because there was no well-defined and adequate plan by which the schools could be continued except by taxation, and this method could hardly have been afforded at a time when the people of the State were pathetically poverty-stricken.

There did appear some objection to Mr. Wiley, the superintendent of schools, however; and in all the debates on the bill nothing was quite so strangely severe as certain remarks made against him. In one of his recent reports on certain swamp lands in the eastern part of the State, which were the property of the literary fund, that officer had urged that the lands be properly surveyed and drained so as to make them profitable for the school fund. There was a mild suggestion of gross negligence in the administration of this property. It appeared that members of the Legislature from that part of the State where the lands were situated were offended, and the remarks of one member were particularly bitter. In his opinion the office of superintendent was an unnecessary expense; a salary had been paid that officer for years and he had been of no use on "God Almighty's earth, and the State was unable to pay a salary to a man who merely wrote long essays and drew interminable bills." This objection to Wiley seems to have been interpreted by some of those who really favored the schools as objections to the schools themselves. It was suggested that this opposition originated with the Finance Committee who wished to divert the literary fund to other purposes. There were those also who saw in the condition of the state treasury a ready use for the remainder of the literary fund.[1] And this bankrupt condition of the State may help to explain the strange conduct of the Legislature in abolishing the office of superintendent.

Whatever the explanation, however, this legislative action was highly inconsistent with the former policies of the lawmaking bodies of the State. There was, to be sure, a feeling of uncertainty, a lack of funds, and an absence of a plan which seemed to be feasible for maintaining a school system. The financial condition of the government was deplorable. But it was unexpected that the State which claimed *ante-bellum* educational leadership in the entire South should, in a time of uncertainty, deliberately abandon its schools, transferring all the assets of the school fund to the general treasury of the State, and leave all matters of educational concern in local hands, whose powers were permissive and discretionary.

At the meeting of the Legislature of 1866–67, however, which was composed largely of Whigs, two acts of educational importance were passed which tended to make amends for the strange conduct of its predecessor. The first of these was an act authorizing towns and cities to establish public-school systems "to be supported by the taxes collected or authorized to be collected for corporation purposes." Provision was made for local trustees, for a local board of education, and for other features of a modern school system. All towns which established public schools under the provisions of this law were required to set apart for educational purposes all the funds which could be spared from other purposes;

[1] The State had borrowed $128,000 from this source in 1863.

"and in addition to the powers of taxation, with which they are already invested, they shall be authorized to levy and collect a poll-tax on every white male inhabitant of the corporation, over twenty-one years old, of not more than two dollars, to be wholly appropriated to the use of the public schools." Provision was to be made "first, for primary schools for all the children who need them, and if, after such provision, there be other funds, they may be used for schools of higher grade. . . . "

On the same day that the law described above was ratified, another act was passed "to protect certain interests of the common schools." By this law the county courts were required to appoint county superintendents, similar to those in service before the war, and to serve under the same rules and regulations. Local trustees were to be appointed as in *ante-bellum* times, whose duties were practically the same as those of the *ante-bellum* officers. Now that there was no superintendent, all official returns from the counties were to be made to the literary board, however. The law was an attempt to revive the former system of schools.

It should be remembered that these acts were passed by the native white citizenship of the State at a time of great confusion and uncertainty, and when it was known that Congress would replace with military governments the state governments as organized by the presidential plan. In view of these conditions the acts are of great importance. They are evidence of an interest in education which was rarely seen in other things, and of a determination to protect the schools at whatever cost. But for the plan of congressional Reconstruction, which set in immediately, the history of education in North Carolina would be a different story.

Jonathan Worth, who had defeated Holden in the fall election of 1865, was reëlected governor by a large majority in 1866. The state government was not recognized by the federal government, however, and political, economic, and social conditions were constantly growing worse.[1] The agitation of the "rebel question" in Congress, the congressional investigations which looked to a safe plan to pursue in dealing with the Southern States, and the passage of certain Reconstruction legislation, each had its peculiar influence. The presidential plan of restoring the States which had seceded had failed. Enough of the Southern States had rejected the Fourteenth Amendment when Congress met in December, 1866, to indicate the prevailing opinion in that section; and when the Congressmen from the South presented themselves, a resolution was introduced by Thaddeus Stevens and passed by both houses of Congress, which forbade the admission of members from the eleven Southern States until Congress had decided on their eligibility to membership. Nothing could be done until the political and civil status of the various States had been formally determined upon. So confusing was the condition of the time that little thought or attention could be given to matters of local educational concern. In February, 1867, it became known that the state governments as organized by the presidential plan of Reconstruction would be superseded by military governments and that the suffrage would be extended to the negroes. For the purpose of administration North Carolina was put in the Second Military District with South Carolina, in command of General David E. Sickles, who was later succeeded by General E. R. S. Canby.

[1] See Hamilton, *op. cit.*, chap. IV.

In November, 1867, a Convention was called for the purpose of revising the constitution of the State in accordance with the congressional plan of Reconstruction. In spite of conservative opposition the Convention was voted and met January 14, 1868. The composition of this body, which was unlike anything ever before seen in North Carolina, consisted of one hundred and twenty radicals and only thirteen conservative members. Eighteen of the radicals were "carpetbaggers," or men from the North, and fifteen were negroes. Not a few of the former had been officers in the Union army and were more or less prominent. Among the more intelligent ones were Albion W. Tourgée, who was a native of Ohio and a graduate of Rochester University; General Byron Laflin, of Massachusetts; Major H. L. Grant, of Rhode Island; the Reverend S. S. Ashley, of Massachusetts, who became the first superintendent of public instruction under the Reconstruction régime; and John R. French, of New Hampshire. Of the negroes, James H. Harris, J. W. Wood, and A. H. Galloway were men of some ability. The conservative minority contained no members of political importance, and only two of them, Plato Durham and John W. Graham, both of whom were "Confederate soldiers and men of education," took any prominent part in the work of the Convention.

On the same day that the Convention met the *Raleigh Sentinel* said: —

> The pillars of the capitol should be hung in mourning to-day for the murdered sovereignty of North Carolina. In the hall where have been collected, in days gone by, the wisdom, the patriotism, the virtue of the State, there assembles this morning a body convened by an order of Congress, in violation of the Constitution of the United States and in utter disregard of the Constitution of North Carolina, a body which, in no

228   THE PUBLIC SCHOOL IN NORTH CAROLINA

sense, as a whole, represents the true people of the State, which has not been elected according to our laws nor chosen by those to whom those laws have committed the right of suffrage. In the seats which have been filled by some of the best and truest sons of North Carolina will be found a number of negroes, a still larger number of men who have no interests or sentiments in common with our people, but who were left in our midst by the receding tide of war, and yet others who have proven false to their mother and leagued with her enemies.[1]

The Committee on Education, appointed soon after the Convention was organized, consisted of two conservatives and eleven radicals. The radicals consisted of seven carpetbaggers, two of whom were negroes, and four scalawags. The chairman of the committee was the Reverend S. S. Ashley. From time to time resolutions in reference to the schools or school funds, introduced by various members, were referred to the Committee on Education, which made its first report on March 6. The report was signed by all the members of the committee except the two conservatives, and passed the first reading with but little discussion. But it contained no provision for separate schools, and Plato Durham, conservative, offered the following as an additional section: —

The General Assembly shall provide separate and distinct schools, for the black children of the State, from those provided for white children.

Ashley immediately offered the following as an amendment to Durham's proposed section: —

It being understood that this section is not offered in sincerity, or because there is any necessity for it, and that it is proposed for the sole purpose of breeding prejudice and bringing about a political re-enslavement of the colored race.

After some discussion the previous question was called

[1] Hamilton, *op. cit.*, p. 256.

and sustained, Ashley's amendment was adopted, and Durham's proposed section as amended was rejected by a vote of 86 to 11.

Later, when the Convention was considering section eighteen, J. W. Graham sought to secure provision for separate schools. The section read: —

The General Assembly is hereby empowered to enact that every child of sufficient mental and physical ability shall attend the public schools during the period between the ages of six and eighteen years, for a term of not less than sixteen months, unless educated by other means.

Graham's amendment to this section was: —

Provided, That there shall be separate and distinct schools and colleges for the white and colored races.

Tourgée, carpetbagger, immediately offered the following as a substitute: —

Provided, That in all cases where distinct schools shall be established, there shall be as ample, sufficient, and complete facilities afforded for the one class as for others, and entirely adequate for all, and in all districts where schools are divided, the apportionment to each shall be equal.

Both the amendment and the substitute were rejected and the section adopted. The entire report, with the few slight verbal changes which had been made, passed the Convention by a vote of 88 to 12, and became Article IX of the constitution. The constitution was finally adopted by the Convention, all the conservative members voting against it, however. The election on its ratification by the people of the State was held April 21, 22, and 23, 1868. The number registering for the election was 117,428 whites and 79,444 negroes, and the vote was 93,084 for the constitution and 74,015 against it. More than 29,000 registered voters neglected to vote.

At the same time W. W. Holden was elected governor of the State.

The new constitution provided that the General Assembly, in its first session, should "provide by taxation or otherwise for a general and uniform system of public schools, wherein tuition shall be free of charge to all the children of the State between the ages of six and twenty-one years." The counties were to be divided into convenient districts, "in which one or more public schools shall be maintained, at least four months in every year," and the county commissioners who failed to comply with this requirement were "liable to indictment." The governor, lieutenant-governor, secretary of state, treasurer, auditor, superintendent of public works, superintendent of public instruction, and attorney-general constituted the state board of education to replace the *ante-bellum* literary board. Section sixteen provided: —

As soon as practicable after the adoption of this constitution, the General Assembly shall establish and maintain, in connection with the university, a department of agriculture, of mechanics, of mining, and of normal instruction.

Practically no changes were made in the matter of the literary fund, the section dealing with that subject being a copy of the *ante-bellum* law on the same subject. The final section empowered the Legislature to enact

that every child of sufficient mental and physical ability shall attend the public schools during the period between the ages of six and eighteen years, for a term of not less than sixteen months, unless educated by other means.

The State now had very ample constitutional provision for schools, more mandatory and thorough than at any previous time.

THE BEGINNINGS OF RECONSTRUCTION 231

The Legislature elected in 1868 contained thirty-eight radicals in the Senate and eighty in the House. The conservatives numbered twelve in the Senate and forty in the House. At the special session of the body in July but little work of an educational importance was undertaken except the introduction of a few resolutions which concerned the literary fund and certain other features of a school system. These were promptly referred to the Committees on Education which were appointed early in the session. The House Committee consisted of one conservative and ten radicals, one of whom was a negro, and the Senate Committee was composed of seven radicals, one of whom was a negro. Each committee contained members who had been in the Constitutional Convention.

The committees did not become active until January of the regular session which met in November, 1868. The message of Governor Holden, which was read to the Assembly November 17, recommended the immediate establishment of a general and uniform system of public free schools. The executive also urged provision for separate schools for the two races, "but in other respects there should be no difference in the character of the schools, or in the provision made to support them." The constitution was silent on the subject of mixed schools, though the carpetbaggers seem to have planned such a system, and had given the matter some consideration in the Convention. The failure finally to incorporate in the constitution a provision either for mixed schools or against them created such an uncertain condition as to bring about harmful results later, even though the first school law provided for separate schools for the children of the two races. As for school support the constitution made provision for the expenditure of three fourths of the entire capitation tax for educational purposes.

On January 27, the chairman of the Senate Committee on Education, G. W. Welker, a minister from Pennsylvania, introduced a bill providing for a school system, which was read and referred to the committee. On February 12, after having been reported favorably in the House, it was reported back with certain amendments. On February 23, after several sections of the bill had been adopted in the Senate with but little significant discussion, J. W. Graham, conservative, who had been a member of the Committee on Education in the Constitutional Convention, sought to secure a provision in the bill for separate schools, and his amendment prevailed by a vote of 24 to 6. The six opposing votes were cast by radical members. Numerous attempts were made at this time to secure amendments dealing with the racial question. One member endeavored to have inserted in the bill a provision to prevent the teaching of "the doctrine of secession and of the lost cause," but the amendment was rejected by a vote of 34 to 5. Other amendments suggested that "textbooks and all publications prescribed and used in the public schools should be free from sectarian and denominational and partisan bias in religion and politics," and that instruction should be given with a view to creating that sentiment which would foster a love for the perpetual union of the States. One member sought to secure an amendment to prevent the teaching of "the sentiments embodied in that well-known song, 'John Brown's Soul is Marching Along.'" The president ruled this out of order, however, and when the member appealed from the chair the latter was sustained by a vote of 38 to 1. Later the same member, Love, of Jackson County, offered as an amendment that the school "committee shall never employ any colored teacher, male or female, to serve as such, in any school wherein white children are to be instructed." Another member immediately moved to amend this proposed amendment by adding, "or employ white teachers to serve in any school wherein colored children are to be instructed." The amendment to the amendment was adopted by a vote of 28 to 11. Thereupon still another member moved to amend by adding, "That no white Democrat should teach any colored girl," but this the chair ruled out of order. And then the original amendment as amended was rejected by a vote of 21 to 19.

Later the senator from Jackson was before the body again and on the same subject. This time his suggested amendment was that "No colored tutor or tutoress shall ever be engaged in any school wherein white children are to be taught." Moore, senator from Carteret County, though not a native of the State, offered to amend Love's amendment by adding, "nor any white tutor or tutoress wherein colored children are to be taught." The amendment to the amendment was adopted by a vote of 19 to 15, after which the original amendment was rejected by the same vote. A few days later Welker, chairman of the committee, showed signs of displeasure and moved the indefinite postponement of the entire bill, but the motion was lost by a large majority. Finally the bill came to its third reading; but when the Senate came to vote on a substitute which Welker offered for a portion of the proposed legislation, Love and another conservative refused to vote. Later, when they were allowed to explain their action, Moore, who had already

234 THE PUBLIC SCHOOL IN NORTH CAROLINA

opposed Love many times in discussions of the education bill, arose to a point of order and complained that Love was not confining his remarks to an explanation. Love remarked that the gentleman from Carteret (Moore) knew nothing of the affairs of North Carolinians, was not interested in them, and besides, he was a carpetbagger. Moore replied that the gentleman from Jackson was a liar. The gentleman from Jackson remarked that the gentleman from Carteret was not an ordinary liar, but a damned liar, and a final epithet was even more unbecoming a gentleman of senatorial rank. The encounter grew so fierce that the chairman rebuked the senators and a committee was appointed to investigate the case. No report was made, however, and the records do not show which of the "gentlemen" was correct in his contention.[1]

The bill finally passed the Senate by a vote of 30 to 10, March 17, 1869. Three days later it was received in the regular order of business in the House where some minor verbal changes were suggested, and was finally ratified, as amended, by joint conference April 12. The law was almost entirely the work of the Senate.[2]

North Carolina now had a thoroughgoing and definite school law, and, with reference to school support, more mandatory and less discretionary than previous acts on the subject. The law provided for a state board of education and prescribed its duties. The net annual income of the public-school fund (the remainder of the *antebellum* literary fund) was to be distributed among the counties of the State in proportion to their scholastic population, whenever the state board should direct. County commissioners were to order a tax for sites and

[1] Senate Journal, p. 432. [2] Senate and House Journals, *passim*.

THE BEGINNINGS OF RECONSTRUCTION 235

for building or renting schoolhouses, to be assessed and collected in the same manner as other county taxes. Local township committees were to "establish and maintain, for at least four months in every year, a sufficient number of schools at convenient localities, which shall be for the education of all children between the ages of six and twenty-one years residing therein." The duties usually belonging to such officers were described: to provide a schoolhouse and its furniture; to employ and dismiss teachers; to maintain all the schools "for an equal length of time during the year, with equal rights and privileges"; to require the exclusive use of the textbooks adopted by the state board; to visit the schools; to gather and report school statistics; and to attend to the details of the administration of the local schools. A county examiner was to be appointed by the county commissioners. His duties were to examine the teachers, to issue certificates, and to assist in enforcing the prescribed course of study and the rules and regulations governing the schools. The certificate granted by the examiner was to be valid only in the county where issued, and no person could teach without it. Separate schools were to be established for the children of the two races; "and such school or schools shall be supported, regulated, and instructed in the same manner and to the same extent as any other public school or schools of the same grade."

The course of study prescribed by the new law consisted of reading, writing, spelling, arithmetic, geography, and English grammar, and "such other studies as may be deemed necessary." Seventy-five per cent of the state and county capitation taxes were to be applied to public-school support; and in addition to this source of support, "in order that the schools may be continued for a term of four months," the Legislature appropriated the sum of $100,000 "out of any moneys in the treasury not appropriated otherwise." All school funds were to be apportioned on the basis of the school census.

In case any township failed at its annual meeting "to provide for schools to be taught at least four months for that year, and to provide for fuel, and to make any other provisions necessary for the efficiency and success of the schools, the school committee shall immediately forward to the county commissioners an estimate of the necessary expenses, and a tax equal to the amount of such estimate shall be levied on the township by the county commissioners at the same time that the county taxes are levied, and the school committee, under the direction of the county commissioners, shall provide whatever shall be necessary for the schools for four months, and pay all expenses for the same out of the funds raised by the tax" thus levied. We shall have occasion to refer further to this provision later.

In most respects the law of 1869 was practically the same as the *ante-bellum* educational legislation of the State, except for a definitely prescribed school term, and provision for a general school tax, and for the education of the freedmen. With these three exceptions the Reconstruction law was, to all intents and purposes, practically a copy of the law of 1839 and its subsequent revisions; and the system created in 1869 was, in its essential features, manifestly an adaptation of the system in operation in the State before the war. Concerning the educational changes produced by the war and Reconstruction more will be said in the next chapter.

REFERENCES

Constitution of 1868; Journals of the House and Senate; Public Laws of North Carolina; Legislative Documents; Weeks, *Calvin Henderson Wiley and the Organization of the Common Schools of North Carolina;* Smith, *History of Education in North Carolina;* Fleming, *Documentary History of Reconstruction;* Hamilton, *Reconstruction in North Carolina;* Hart, *The Southern South;* Dunning, *Reconstruction Political and Economic;* Murphy, *The Present South;* Knight, "The Influence of Reconstruction on Education in the South;" and "Some Fallacies concerning the History of Public Education in the South," in *South Atlantic Quarterly*, October, 1914.

SUGGESTIONS FOR FURTHER STUDY

1. What was the difference between the presidential plan of Reconstruction and the congressional plan?
2. How widespread was the belief that *ante-bellum* educational conditions in the South were responsible for the war?
3. What influence did slavery have on public education in the South before 1860.
4. What efforts were made in North Carolina between 1865 and 1868 to provide educational facilities adapted to the changed conditions? What was done in other Southern States during this time?
5. Why was the office of state superintendent of schools abolished in 1866?
6. Compare the composition of the Legislature of 1866 with that of 1868. Compare the work of the two bodies.
7. Compare the *ante-bellum* constitutional provisions for education with those made by the convention of 1868. In what respect were the latter provisions more advanced than the former?
8. Compare the *ante-bellum* school law with the law enacted by the Legislature of 1868. In what ways was the Reconstruction act more thorough and advanced than previous school legislation?

CHAPTER XII
EDUCATION DURING RECONSTRUCTION

THE elaborate constitutional and legislative provisions for education, enacted in 1868 and 1869, served well as the framework of a school system adequate for both races. In this respect the work of the Convention and of the Legislature had been well done. But elaborate educational statutes were not alone sufficient to begin and maintain a system of schools. Moreover, education was now confronted by new and peculiar obstacles. There was a feeling of uncertainty and insecurity, caused by the changed conditions of the time and by the poverty of the State; the inexperience, ignorance, and prejudice that came from the new order of things produced discouraging circumstances; and, although the opinion was gaining that schools and education were to be universal, there was an apparent lack of genuine educational interest. The new status of the negro also complicated an already difficult condition. He had suddenly been given a place in politics without any preparation for it; the Freedmen's Bureau and other organizations were disbursing their funds recklessly for his education; school officials were often foreign in their sympathies and, guided by questionable motives or by visionary missionary zeal, hoped to raise him to a place of universal brotherhood, politically and socially. A new power had been transferred to him under the new régime. Moreover, the possibility, under the constitution, of forcing mixed schools on the people produced a constant dread,

— though it was not so well founded in North Carolina as in some of the other Southern States, — and doubtless strengthened a natural prejudice against such a system. And this was a consideration of much weight, not only in North Carolina, but in the entire South.

S. S. Ashley, a minister and carpetbagger from Massachusetts, was elected the first superintendent of schools under the new régime. Though an earnest man and of some ability, he was narrow and possessed of pronounced prejudices which made him imprudent and reckless. His interest in a system of mixed schools which he wished to see established in the South, and his tendency to habits of his kind, together with the fact that he was said to be of negro descent, made him "one of the most unpleasant carpetbaggers in the State."

Ashley's first report was dated November 10, 1868, and appeared before the new school law had been enacted. The educational system had been only partially organized and the report was necessarily very brief, but it contained a few interesting educational facts. The total amount of income from all sources for educational purposes was shown to be about $32,000. This included the annual tax on auctioneers, entries from vacant lands, taxes on retailers, and a slight income from the old literary fund. Comparing this condition with the liberal fund for school support before the war, the superintendent said: —

A sad diminution! Prior to 1861, hundreds of thousands of dollars found their way into this treasury, and were distributed over the State, conferring upon not less than one hundred thousand white children the blessings of the free school.

Instead of a great fund for the support of public schools, henceforth for a long time the people of the State must be taxed for this purpose. In the aggregate the tax may appear large and onerous. But, scanned in detail, *per capita*, it will be seen to be small. But, whether large or small, ignorance is a far heavier tax than education. A State can afford to be poor, but cannot afford to be ignorant.

At a meeting of the state board of education in September, 1868, it was ordered that the county school officials appointed under the act of February 28, 1867,[1] immediately assume their duties under the new constitution, and make the usual report to the state superintendent. By this means the new school system was able to begin work on the organization of the system as revived by the law of 1867. This action was practically all that the superintendent was able to report in November, 1868. The condition and needs of the university were noted, and the need for normal schools discussed. In this connection the superintendent said: —

> Within four years the free schools of this State will require at least four thousand teachers — good teachers. Unless means for training these teachers are immediately instituted, whence will come the supply? . . . To within a recent period, the provision made by this State for free public Schools was not only generous, but munificent. All circumstances considered, scarcely any sister State of the Union surpassed North Carolina in this regard. A new era has now dawned, and it is hoped that the future care of the Commonwealth for her free public schools will not be less liberal or less noble than the past.

In August, 1869, the superintendent believed that a few schools would be in operation by the following October and that many communities would be supplied with schools by January, 1870. School taxes were to be collected, some communities had to build new schoolhouses, and the school machinery set in operation generally. It was believed that the available public-school

[1] See p. 224.

fund would be $300,000, and that aid from the Peabody Board, which was being solicited for towns and cities, would not only furnish immediate material assistance, but would also serve as an educational stimulus by increasing the schools and lengthening their terms. In less than a month, however, the superintendent had changed his opinion, and in September advised the agent of that fund to withhold appropriations to any towns in the State until the townships had fulfilled the requirements of the law in establishing schools. Moreover, the superintendent was discouraged because the taxes were coming in slowly. An exhibition of the several sources of the educational fund for the fiscal year ending September 30, 1869, showed no taxes whatever.

Ashley's second report dealt with conditions in the State during the year ending September, 1869. The school law had been in operation only a few months and the system was not in full operation. However, all the counties except Onslow and Edgecombe had reported a few facts to the superintendent. The school population for that year was 330,581. Of this number 223,815 were white and 106,766 were colored. The whole number of schoolhouses reported was 1906, and 685 of these were described as in bad condition. The sum of $165,290.50 was apportioned among the counties, on the basis of the school population, an amount which would have allowed about fifty cents to each census child. But the superintendent "apportioned" this sum on the assumption that the legislative appropriation of $100,000 would be available and that at least an equal sum would be derived from the capitation taxes. But the appropriation turned out to be only a paper appropriation and was not paid. And this continued to be the case throughout this period. In fact, not until 1899 did the public schools of the State receive any legislative appropriation from the general treasury. As for the capitation taxes, on which the superintendent was also depending for his apportionment to the counties, but little money was realized from that source. This condition also continued for several years. For the year ending September 30, 1870, the total amount of taxes collected for public schools was $136,076.92, and only $38,981.86 of that sum seems to have actually gone for educational purposes.

Several outside educational agencies were at work in the State, however, and rendered excellent service during the early years of Reconstruction. The Baltimore Association of Friends during 1869 established for white children forty-four schools with sixty-five teachers and an enrollment of more than three thousand pupils. These schools were located in Guilford, Yadkin, Iredell, Randolph, Alamance, Orange, Wayne, Northampton, and Perquimans Counties, and had an average term of more than six months. Between 1865 and 1869 this association built thirty-two new schoolhouses in the State. The Soldiers' Memorial Society of Boston, the American Unitarian Association, and the Peabody Board, which had begun its work in 1867, were also rendering aid to a number of schools in the larger towns of the State.[1]

The education of the freedmen was also receiving attention from a number of sources. Numerous charitable and religious organizations early began work in the State and furnished needed facilities for negro education. Among these societies were the New England Freedmen's Relief Association, New York National Freed-

---

[1] See chap. XIII for a discussion of the work of the Peabody Board in North Carolina.

men's Relief Association, American Missionary Association, Friends' Freedmen's Aid Association, Freedmen's Commission, the Protestant Episcopal Church, and the Presbyterian General Assembly.[1] Practically all these societies were also at work in South Carolina and in other Southern States at the same time.

Through the Freedmen's Bureau, established by Congress March 3, 1865, the education of the negro was further aided. By the act creating the Bureau no provision for education was made, but soon it turned attention to this work as one of its important functions. The Reverend F. A. Fiske, of Massachusetts, was appointed superintendent of this part of the Bureau's work and launched an extensive educational campaign, and large numbers of negro schools were established and carried on with zeal and effectiveness. By 1869 there were 431 such schools in the State with 439 teachers and more than 20,000 pupils. Most of the teachers were white and practically all came from the North. Many of them were earnest, courageous, and devoted, and untiring in their efforts, but frequently they lacked tact and a thorough knowledge of the actual condition and needs of the class for whom they labored. Indiscreet criticisms of the South and of the Southern people tended to antagonize the negroes against the whites, and to arouse among the latter bitter prejudice against the Bureau's teachers and their work. Moreover, failure to enlist the sympathy and coöperation of the influential white people of the State created an unfortunate attitude toward the education of the negro which persisted for many years after the work of the Bureau concluded.

The state board of education also gave special

[1] Hamilton, *op. cit.*, p. 314, note.

attention to the education of the negro by creating the office of assistant superintendent of public instruction. This action was taken, however, without any constitutional or legislative authority. The place seems to have been made for the Reverend J. W. Hood, a negro carpetbagger of rather unsavory reputation, who had served on the Committee on Education in the Constitutional Convention of 1868. He immediately began his duties of superintending the work of negro education, and his report for the year 1869 showed numerous negro schools in operation, supported by church and charitable societies and organizations. More than 150 schools, with 224 teachers and an enrollment of 11,826, were reported in the State in that year. Some of the more important of these were conducted by the Friends. The report said:—

> In educating the freedmen, the Friends are doing a work of praiseworthy benevolence. Without expectation of fee or reward; without attempting to teach the peculiar tenets of their faith; without any apparent desire to advance the interest of their own denomination, they are laboring to dispel the mist of ignorance which has so long hung over the colored people of the South. The Bible is introduced into all of their schools, but is read without comment. The teachers are selected without regard to sex, sect, section, nativity or complexion. They are particular, however, respecting the moral character of the teachers.

In 1869 the Friends were maintaining thirty-seven schools in North Carolina with an enrollment of nearly twenty-five hundred pupils. Facilities for the education of the negro were unexpectedly extensive. Nearly all the towns contained one or more schools for the freedmen, and private schools and Sunday schools were also assisting in their education. Hood's report stated that there were but few counties east of the Blue Ridge that did not have schools in which negroes were receiving instruction.

Ashley's report for the year ending September 30, 1870, showed that the State at that time had 1,071,361 inhabitants of whom 391,650 were negroes. The total number of public schools reported as maintained in the State was 1398; the estimated number was 1415. Schools were kept in seventy-four of the ninety counties. The whole number of children reported attending the public schools was 31,093; the estimated number was 49,000. The school population was about 229,000 white and 113,000 colored. The negro schools reported by Assistant Superintendent Hood numbered 347, with 372 teachers and 23,419 pupils. The whole number of teachers employed was placed at 1400 with an average monthly salary of $20.21. The number of schoolhouses reported was 709; of these 309 were frame buildings and 358 were log. The total amount of revenue available for school support was $152,281.82, but only $42,862.40 had been expended for schools. The Peabody Board was aiding the better regulated schools of the towns and was rapidly stimulating interest in education. In the main the school system was as successful as could have been expected during times of bitter party strife and violence. But the uncertainty of future legislation, together with other unfortunate conditions, had created numerous obstacles for the friends of public schools. Moreover, there were many inherent defects from which the system suffered. Teachers were scarce and incompetent, the school law was defective, there was a lack of school funds, school officials were careless and negligent, and textbooks were scarce. It is interesting to note here, however, that the series of textbooks which the board of education adopted for use in the schools contained the same readers and arithmetics which were recommended by Wiley and used in the State before the war.[1]

Lack of funds was one of the greatest weaknesses of the system. The income from the literary fund was small, the legislative appropriation could not be paid, and capitation taxes, seventy-five per cent of which was designed for educational purposes, were poorly collected. In March, 1870, a small tax of one twelfth of one per cent was authorized to be levied on the taxable property of the State in order to provide means of paying the legislative appropriation of April, 1869, but the tax was neither properly levied nor properly collected. Less than $23,000 was derived from this source the first year. Only a small part of the apportionments made to the counties could be paid, and this condition continued for several years. In 1871 there was no additional legislative provision for schools, and, what was even worse, county officials were accused of applying to other purposes the school funds derived from state and county capitation taxes.

A new and unexpected cause for discouragement appeared in 1870, in a decision of the supreme court which held that the law of 1869, so far as it provided for local taxes for education, was unconstitutional and could not be enforced. The constitution and the school law definitely prescribed the manner by which "a general and uniform system of schools" should be maintained for four months in the year. The law provided that local school committees should annually estimate the amount of money necessary for the support of schools during the prescribed term, and report the estimate to the township

[1] Leg. Doc., Session 1870–71, no. 6.

trustees and to the county commissioners ten days before the annual township meeting. In case the township failed to make provision for the necessary funds a local tax was to be levied for the amount of the estimate. On account of scarcity of funds for school purposes it was obvious that a considerable tax would be required on each district to maintain a school four months each year. It was also obvious that the straitened financial condition of the State made the people unwilling to be taxed further. The result was that the local officials failed to make the estimate or report to the county officials, and, as a rule, the taxes were not levied. Moreover, whenever the question of levying a tax was submitted to a vote of a community, "the people, without regard to party, voted against the tax almost unanimously."

The question soon arose as to whether the county commissioners could levy the tax after it had been defeated by a vote of the people. Section seven, article seven, of the constitution said: —

> No county, city, town, or other municipal corporation shall contract any debt, pledge its faith, or loan its credit, nor shall any tax be levied or collected by any officers of the same, except for the necessary expenses thereof, unless by a vote of the majority of the qualified voters therein.

If funds for the support of the public schools were necessary expenses, a tax for such funds could have been levied without or even against a vote of the people. If schools were not a public necessity, funds for their support could have been levied only by a vote of the qualified voters in the community.

Craven County furnished a test case. The school officials of a certain district in 1870 estimated the expenses necessary to provide a four months' school and reported the estimate to the trustees of the township. The question was submitted to a vote of the people and a majority voted against the tax. However, the county commissioners proceeded to levy a tax on the property of the township to secure funds for maintaining the school. Complaint was filed that the commissioners had violated the constitution in that the levy had not been authorized by a vote of the people, and also in that in levying the tax the constitutional equation of taxation had not been observed. The judge ordered a temporary injunction to be issued until the defendants could appear and show cause why an injunction should not be issued to restrain the collection of the levy. The defendants answered that in making the levy they had obeyed the constitution and the school law, and that the tax did not require a vote of the people because it was levied for *necessary expenses*. On November 12, 1870, the injunction was dissolved. The case was appealed to the supreme court, however, and in the following January decision was given in favor of the plaintiffs, thus reversing the order of the lower court. The opinion of the court concerned two points. In the first place, it was held that the tax was not a necessary expense, within the meaning of the constitution. The second point concerned the equation of taxation. The constitutional limitation of state and county taxation was sixty-six and two thirds cents on the hundred dollars' valuation and a capitation tax of two dollars, and the court held that this equation had not been observed.[1]

The effect of this decision tended to be destructive to the school system. One clause in the constitution

[1] 65 N. C. 153.

required the county commissioners to maintain schools in every township for four months in every year, while another clause made it impossible to do so legally. With popular opinion against levying taxes for educational purposes the school law was practically ineffective and the continuance of schools seemed doubtful unless provision could be made for them by correcting the defective legislation of 1869.

When the Reform Legislature met in the fall of 1870 there was evidence that some relief would be afforded. This body had thirty-six conservatives in the Senate and seventy-five in the House; the radicals had fourteen in the Senate and forty-two in the House. Among the radicals there were three negroes and two carpetbaggers in the Senate and nineteen negroes and two carpetbaggers in the House. Thomas J. Jarvis, of Tyrrell County, who had been a prominent conservative in the preceding Legislature, was chosen Speaker of the House, and E. J. Warren, a conservative member from Beaufort County, was chosen President of the Senate. With the exception of two acts, one reducing the salaries of state officers, and the other looking to "the better protection of the literary fund," no legislation of educational importance was passed at the first session of this Legislature, which concerned itself almost entirely with the impeachment of Governor Holden. The first of these acts was passed in pursuance of a policy of economy, and both laws showed the conservative reaction to the radical régime. The salary of the superintendent of public instruction was reduced from $2400 to $1500, the clerical force of his office was removed, and no money was allowed him for traveling expenses. Similar reductions of expenses were made in other state offices. The law looking to a better protection of the literary fund made it unlawful for the state board of education to lend any amount of public funds under their control except by legislative direction.

At the second session, begun in the fall of 1871, a new school law was passed which looked to an improvement in conditions. The law differed from the law of April, 1869, which it repealed, by making more liberal provisions for school support and by providing a plan by which institutes for the training of teachers could be held. A levy of six and two thirds cents on the hundred dollars' valuation was made on all the taxable property and credits in the State, to be collected by the sheriffs under the same rules, regulations, and penalties prescribed for the collection of all other county taxes. A special capitation tax of twenty cents was also levied for school purposes.[1] At the next session of the Legislature, which was likewise conservative, an annual tax of eight and one third cents on the hundred dollars' valuation was levied on all the taxable property in the State, and the special capitation tax was raised to twenty-five cents. As before, seventy-five per cent of the state and county capitation taxes was applied to educational support. The law also gave authority to the commissioners of each county to levy an additional tax on the property and polls of the county for school support, but the levy had to be authorized by a majority of the qualified voters. The defect of this law was the same as that of previous educational legislation in the State: the right of local taxation was granted to the counties, which would often vote against it, and was withheld from the districts, some of which would have taxed them-

[1] *Laws* of 1871-72, chap. 189.

selves to maintain free schools. This had been one of the chief defects of the *ante-bellum* school law.

In September, 1871, after his salary had been reduced, Ashley resigned his position as superintendent of schools and accepted a position in a school for negroes in New Orleans. To fill the vacancy Governor Caldwell appointed Alexander McIver, a professor in the state university. He had been considered for the nomination as the Republican candidate for the position in April, 1872, but was defeated by James Reid, a retired minister of advanced years. Reid died before he was installed and before McIver left the office to which he had received the governor's appointment. The governor was then urged to appoint G. W. Welker to the position, but he refused to do so, and instead appointed Kemp P. Battle, who accepted the place. McIver refused to surrender the position, however, and, being sustained by the supreme court in his contention that there was no vacancy because no successor had legally qualified, he continued to hold the position until the next election.[1]

McIver's report for the year ending September, 1872, showed that the total amount of state funds expended for school support in the State was $155,393.96. The sum of $35,675.52 was received from property taxes in seventy-six counties during the year, and about $108,000 was derived from capitation taxes. Certain donations and a few items from other sources brought the total school fund up to about $332,000. The school population reported was 267,938, of which number 182,698 were white and 85,240 colored children. The enrollment in the public schools showed 34,294 white and 16,387 colored children. The number of teachers examined and

[1] Hamilton, *op. cit.*, p. 616.

approved was 2132, as follows: white males, 1261, females, 413; colored males, 317, females, 141.

Incomplete reports from the counties make a fair view of educational conditions during that year almost impossible. The number of schools in operation could not be ascertained or safely estimated, and the average school term and teachers' salaries also failed to be noted. As for the proportionate distribution of the school funds between the two races, it appeared that the sum of $71,861.35 was paid for the education of the white children in forty-six counties, and $27,256.19 for the colored children in the same counties. Conditions in general showed but little improvement. One sign of interest and improvement appeared, however, in the organization and maintenance of teachers' institutes in 1872. This means of improving the teachers of the State was made possible by the law of February, 1872, which appropriated fifty dollars to each institute organized and held in the State, a sum which was supplemented by a like amount from the Peabody Board. As a result six institutes were held within a year after the law was passed: the Cape Fear Teachers' Institute, held at Wilmington; the Cherokee Teachers' Institute, held at Murphy; the Graham County Teachers' Institute, held at Fort Montgomery; the Lowell Normal Institute, held at Newbern; the Friends' Institute, held at Springfield; and the Ellendale Teachers' Institute, held in Alexander County. The institutes continued for four weeks, and the attendance on each varied from thirty-seven to fifty teachers.

In spite of an improvement in school legislation conditions continued far from satisfactory, and the general aspects of education were undergoing but few changes.

The principle of education by public taxation had been settled upon, but the application of that principle and the adjustment of the school system to the needs and conditions of the State proved more difficult tasks. The school law was defective, there was indifference on the part of the people, the local tax provision was proving vague and uncertain, and litigation was often resorted to by those who were opposed to it. Local taxes were frequently not levied or collected and the state taxes were often uncertain and tardy in becoming available for school purposes. The law which required the separation of the school funds from other public funds was not always observed, and unscrupulous officials were sometimes accused of using the school funds for other purposes. The schools languished or were suspended for want of efficient administration. Dr. Sears, the general agent of the Peabody Board, saw all these disorders in the State in 1872, and at the same time the superintendent complained of the same conditions. At no time since the war had the conservative political party, which was laboring for social, economic, and political reform, faced such a crisis. The popular mind was confused and confidence was generally shaken.

Nothing was more confusing and alarming to the people of the State than the fear of mixed schools. Although the school law provided for an educational separation of the races, the constitution was silent on the subject, and there was a constant dread that by some means mixed schools would be forced on the people. Local conditions were made even more alarming through the attitude of Congress and its agitation of the Civil Rights Bill which looked to securing to freedmen rights identical with whites in hotels, in public conveyances, in schools, churches, and theaters. The measure passed the United States Senate May 23, 1874, and provided that

> All citizens and persons within the jurisdiction of the United States shall be entitled to full and equal enjoyment of the advantages of the common schools and other institutions of learning and benevolence without distinction of race, color, or previous condition of servitude.

It had considerable support in the House of Representatives, but not enough to take it from the table out of its order, and the measure was not enacted. Its agitation, however, which was deplored by all friends of education, of both political parties, temporarily retarded educational progress in every Southern State. In North Carolina, as in the entire South, opposition to mixed schools was very strong. When the measure was pending in Congress, Senator Merrimon asked the state superintendent concerning the probable effect on the schools in North Carolina if the bill became a law. McIver replied: —

> No legislation in favor of mixed schools has ever been attempted in this State. Public sentiment on this subject is all one way. Opposition to mixed schools is so strong that if the people are free to choose between mixed schools and no schools, they will prefer the latter. The friends of education would therefore deprecate and most sincerely deplore any congressional legislation which might tend to force mixed schools upon the people.

This was also the opinion of the Peabody Trustees, who doubted the origin of certain petitions to Congress and did not believe that they represented the saner sentiments of the colored people. The conclusion of a special committee, to which was referred that part of Dr. Sears's report in 1874 which dealt with the subject, was unanimously adopted as a resolution. The resolution held that

the prospects and hopes of the public systems of education in the South will receive a serious, if not fatal blow, from any legislation which should make such systems of education maintainable only upon the scheme of "mixed schools" as the organization requisite for such public education.

The trustees maintained that justice, public duty, and the interests of both races demanded equality of opportunity, and that no such result could be promoted by a compulsory system of mixed schools. They also believed that such a system would not only be pernicious, but that the greater share of the disastrous influence would be visited on the negro whose wants had all the while been the subject of diligent inquiry and of anxiety to the Peabody Board.[1]

The effect of the proposed legislation was everywhere widely felt in the South. In North Carolina contracts for building new schoolhouses were held up, engagements with teachers were suspended, school officials resigned, and state legislation which looked to an improvement in the school system was delayed. The most conspicuous example of this was a bill which provided for the establishment of city school systems in the State. This bill was introduced in the Legislature of 1872–73 and for a time was favorably considered. It was finally dropped, however, under the apprehension that the Civil Rights Bill would become a law.[2]

For the year ending June 30, 1873, only sixty-three counties made official reports of educational conditions.

[1] *Proceedings*, Peabody Board Trustees, vol. i, p. 411.
[2] For the influence of the measure on education in Virginia see the author's discussion of the subject in the *South Atlantic Quarterly* for January and April, 1916.

From these it appeared that the school population of the State was 348,603, of which number 233,751 were white and 114,852 were colored. The enrollment of white children was 106,039, with an estimated daily average attendance of 70,872. The number of colored children enrolled was 40,428, with an estimated daily average attendance of 26,958. It was estimated that the number of public schools for white children was 2565, and the number for colored children, 746. The average school term was only ten weeks. The estimated number of white teachers examined and approved during the year was 2160; the number of colored teachers examined and approved was 530. The entire public school fund derived from all sources for the year was $408,830.67, and the total disbursements were $191,675.07. Of the disbursements the sum of $112,175.36 was expended for the salaries of white teachers, and $45,954.19 for the salaries of negro teachers. The sum of $25,100 was expended for building and repairing schoolhouses, the sum of $1520 was paid examiners, and $6025.52 was paid to the county treasurers as commissions for handling the school funds. A balance of $217,155.60 was still in the hands of the county treasurers June 30, 1873.

In spite of the discouraging conditions which surrounded the school system, one hopeful sign of educational interest appeared in the summer of 1873. In April of that year the state board of education called all the friends of the schools to an educational convention to be held in Raleigh in July. The call was cheerfully responded to and the convention attended by representative men of both "political parties, of all the leading religious denominations, and of the principal institutions of the State." The convention continued three days, during which time the educational conditions of the State were discussed and plans made for improvement. Addresses were made by Governor T. R. Caldwell, Calvin H. Wiley, President Braxton Craven of Trinity College, Professor W. C. Doub of Greensboro Female College, Principal Robert Bingham of the Bingham School, Professor W. G. Simmons of Wake Forest College, Judge William H. Battle, Senator A. S. Merrimon, and other prominent men of the State. Among the resolutions adopted by the convention were the following: —

That the general educational interests of this State are deplorable and alarming in a high degree, and are such as to require the noblest and most self-sacrificing efforts of every true son of North Carolina to relieve her from such serious embarrassment.

That this convention respectfully but earnestly request and urge every friend of the State, the people, and particularly the clergy, all public speakers and the press, to be zealous and constant in making efforts to arouse the whole people to a realizing sense of the paramount importance of education, and especially of common schools, to the rising and coming generations, and of the overruling necessity for universal, active and cordial coöperation of all, to avoid the blight and the disgrace of ignorance.

Reports were submitted on the subjects of compulsory education, agricultural education, normal schools, textbooks, educational journalism, school funds and taxation, higher education, improved methods of teaching, and other subjects of educational importance. A permanent organization was formed with Judge W. H. Battle as president; a resolution was adopted recommending the organization of permanent county associations; and, through the influence and efforts of Dr. Craven, a plan was begun for the publication of an educational journal.

The second annual meeting was held in Raleigh in

258 THE PUBLIC SCHOOL IN NORTH CAROLINA

July, 1874, and continued three days. In addition to addresses by Governor Caldwell and President Battle the following papers were read and discussed: —

"Hygiene in the Schools," by Dr. S. S. Satchwell.
"Normal Methods," by Superintendent H. B. Blake.
"Education in Congress," by Senator A. S. Merrimon.
"Education by the Public Press," by Rev. T. H. Pritchard, D.D.
"Examinations, Certificates, and Diplomas, Tests of Scholarship," by Dr. Braxton Craven.
"Higher Education in North Carolina," by Ralph H. Graves.
"History of Education in North Carolina," by Dr. Calvin H. Wiley.
"The Duty of the State to educate her Children," by W. N. H. Smith.
"Multiplicity of Studies," by Osborne Hunter, Jr.
"Graded Schools," by Superintendent J. B. Boone.
"Methods of Teaching," by Rev. Charles Phillips, D.D.
"Public Education," by Rev. Father J. V. McNamara.
"Education in Georgia," by Superintendent Martin V. Calvin, of Augusta, Georgia.

At this session plans were made for an educational campaign and for memorializing the Legislature for assistance in improving the public-school system. Considerable interest appeared in the work of the convention and in the activities which were proposed. Especially did it stimulate institute work in several sections of the State and encourage attention to the training of teachers. A few teachers' institutes were reported in 1873 and others the following year. Among those in operation in 1874 several were attracting wide attention and were producing creditable results. Ellendale Teachers' Institute, in Alexander County, had an enrollment of forty-four teachers and a library of "fifty volumes of standard normal and educational works, and about thirty others of general interest to teachers." Meetings were held twice a month when topics of educational interest were discussed. The Pinewoods Teachers' Institute, in Davidson County, held annual sessions of one month each. In 1874 forty-three were enrolled. "At each of these sessions lectures were given by prominent teachers and other distinguished gentlemen from abroad, and much interest was manifested by the popular gatherings to witness the exercises." In the Asheboro Normal School the enrollment was one hundred in 1873 and seventy-five in 1874. Much interest was being created in public education through the work of this school. The Lexington Normal School, organized by the Davidson County Board of Education, under a special act of the Legislature, had annual sessions of twenty-five days, and gave instructions to the teachers of both races. In 1874 the enrollment showed seventy-one teachers, thirty-six white and thirty-five colored, who were instructed separately. The Cape Fear Teachers' Association held annual sessions of one month, under the direction of the superintendent. This work began in 1872. "Superintendent Blake has since that time continued to meet the teachers of the public schools in different parts of the county on stated days, and instruct them in the modes of teaching, and has thus contributed much to public schools in New Hanover County." Most of these institutes were organized under the law of 1872, which was later repealed; but through encouragement and assistance given by the Peabody Board and the Educational Association, they were continuing their work with marked success.

Reports for the year ending June 30, 1874, showed some educational improvement in the State. Public school funds for the year amounted to $496,405.23, and the disbursements were as follows: —

To teachers of white schools	$182,646.53
To teachers of colored schools	77,615.25
For school houses	22,676.46
For services of county examiners	2,854.55
For commissions of county treasurers	11,802.06
Total	$297,594.85
Balance in the hands of the county treasurers	$198,810.38

Of the total school population of 369,960 the white children numbered 242,768 and the colored 127,192. There were 2820 schools for white children and 1200 for colored children, with enrollments of 119,083 and 55,000, respectively. The number of teachers examined during the year was 2875, as follows: white males, 1495, females, 613; colored males, 515, females, 252. The average school term was estimated at ten weeks. The superintendent made two recommendations to the Legislature: appointment of a county superintendent of schools in every county in the State, the positions to be filled by practical teachers of high qualifications, and provision for the training of teachers by county institutes or normal schools.

In that same year, 1874, the conservatives nominated Stephen D. Pool for superintendent of public instruction. McIver had rendered valuable service and should have been retained in office, but unfortunately for the schools the position was kept in politics, from which connection the cause of education suffered. Pool was elected and assumed the duties of the office January 1, 1875, serving until July of the following year. At that time he was charged with irregularities in the handling of funds appropriated to the State by the Peabody Board while he served as its agent in the State. The irregularities, which were so gross as to suggest intentional fraud, so incensed "his party, which had made official corruption the chief count of its indictment against the Republicans," that Pool was forced to resign. Governor Brogden appointed John Pool, a "discredited politician," to the position, which he held until January, 1877, when John C. Scarborough was inaugurated.[1]

The year 1876 is usually taken as the date which marked the overthrow of Reconstruction and the end of foreign rule in the Southern States. In that year the conservative element regained control of the state governments. In North Carolina the first step in the overthrow of the Reconstruction régime began with the impeachment and trial of Governor Holden by the Legislature of 1870–71; the concluding steps were taken by the Constitutional Convention of 1875 and the campaign which followed the next year. The work of the Convention was of great importance politically and socially, many changes being made which promised the promotion of peace and good government in the State. Educationally, also, the constitutional changes made it possible for the State to advance, for there was now no further fear of the possibility of mixed schools. Unlike the constitution of 1868, that of 1876 required separate schools for the children of the two races.

The first Legislature under the new constitution, which went into effect January 1, 1877, passed two acts of great educational significance. The first of these was the law establishing two normal schools, one for each

[1] Hamilton, *op. cit.*, pp. 617–18; *Proceedings*, Peabody Board Trustees, vol. II, pp. 65, 66, 74.

race, "for the purpose of teaching and training young men" for teachers in the common schools of the State. The sum of $2000 was annually appropriated and paid from the state treasury to support each school. These or larger sums continued thus to be appropriated and paid for that purpose for many years. The law required and expected all

of both races, who may be thus taught and trained for teachers of common schools, at the cost of the State, to apply themselves, as far as practicable, to the occupation of teaching, within the borders of this State, for a term of not less than three years after leaving school.[1]

The other significant piece of educational legislation enacted in 1877, as soon as the conservatives regained power in the State, was an act giving authority to townships of a certain population to levy taxes for the support of public graded schools. The law required a majority of the qualified voters of the township to favor the levy before the tax could be legal. When legally ordered, however, a property tax of one tenth of one per cent and a capitation tax of thirty cents could be collected for educational purposes. The former property tax of eight and one third cents and the capitation tax of twenty-five cents were continued for general school support. Dr. Sears, general agent of the Peabody Board, expressed delight at these advanced legislative steps, declaring: —

Public schools were now fairly put upon their own merits. There can, henceforth, be little question of their perpetuity, for the tide of public opinion has recently turned in their favor and it will not be easy to resist it.

---

[1] Laws of 1877, chap. 234; Laws of 1881, chap. 141; Laws of 1885, chap. 143; Laws of 1887, chaps. 400 and 408.

The doctrine of universal education, free and open alike to all classes, was now generally accepted by the people at large, and continued to be so accepted so long as they were "free to act without unwelcome influences from abroad."

From the facts given in this and the preceding chapter certain interesting conclusions are evident. We saw in Chapter XI, that the constitution of 1868 was much in advance of the *ante-bellum* constitutional provisions for education, in that it was more mandatory and thorough. We also saw that through the constitution and law of the Reconstruction régime at least three important educational changes appeared in North Carolina, as indeed in all Southern States. These were provisions for a general tax for educational purposes, for the education of the negro, and for a definitely prescribed school term.

The Reconstruction provision for school support was, in principle at least, a decided improvement over the *ante-bellum* method, although the combination of local taxation and the annual income from the literary fund proved a creditable means of supporting schools and well adapted to the conditions of the State before the war. The greatest merit of this method was in its service as a powerful stimulant to local effort in educational enterprises. The popularity and efficiency of the plan were beyond question. Shortly after the establishment of the system, in 1840, practically all the counties adopted the plan and levied and collected taxes to supplement the annual apportionment from the income of the permanent educational endowment. Moreover, expenditures for schools in 1840, the first year of the operation of the *ante-bellum* system, were practically as large as in 1870; and, in spite of the permissive and discretionary character of the method used for school support, more than $100,000 of local taxes was annually collected for school support in North Carolina during the last years of the *ante-bellum* period. The literary fund thus stimulated local initiative, and sentiment in favor of an increase in taxation was rapidly developing at the outbreak of the war. With the loss of this fund the incentive to local enterprise and community effort was practically destroyed, and the schools were forced to depend on a general tax which, during Reconstruction and for two decades afterward, proved both insufficient and uncertain. Moreover, local tax sentiment, which needed to be revived and extended, for many years proved difficult to restore.

The otherwise creditable school system in North Carolina before the war was defective in that taxation for education was not required either by the constitution or by legislation. But the constitution and law of Reconstruction tended to correct this permissive and discretionary character of the former system. Changes in the method of school support, therefore, were probably the most lasting and beneficial of all the contributions made by the period, not only to education in the South, but to American education in general. The general effect of emancipation and the belief that Southern educational ideals lay at the root of the war had a powerful influence on educational legislation in all sections of the country. After the war there appeared a marked expansion of educational statutes in practically all those States which had previously been satisfied to depend for school support on the income from a permanent public endowment combined with a small local tax or a part of the capitation tax for school purposes. This custom was prevalent, not only in the South, but in other parts of the United States. Even an advanced State like New York did not abandon the so-called "rate bills" for school support until 1867.

Provisions for the education of the negro appeared naturally as a logical result of emancipation. The act of freeing the negroes implied a certain promise to educate and to provide opportunity to fit them, as far as possible, for citizenship. The changed political status of the negro also had an effect in other places as well as in the South; and provisions for his education became at least nominally effective in all sections of the country alike and at about the same time. In the South an unfortunate attitude was often assumed toward the education of the negro, an attitude for which the Freedmen's Bureau was largely responsible. This represents another "part of the heritage of evil" left by Reconstruction. In North Carolina the education of the freedmen was viewed with cordiality and favor by the more representative citizens of the State and would never have been regarded otherwise by other classes but for an unwarranted outside interference and an exploitation of the negro race by men who were both foreign in sympathy and visionary in judgment. Their indiscreet criticisms of Southern life and their failure to conciliate and to enlist the coöperation of the influential leaders created an unfavorable condition for the education of the negro race, and this condition persisted for many years after the South was restored to home rule.

The other educational change which appeared with Reconstruction was a definitely prescribed school term, but the term prescribed was precisely the same as the actual average term before the war. Again an *ante-bellum* educational practice of the State was adopted by the Reconstruction régime and claimed as a distinct contribution by the latter period. It should be borne in mind, however, that the average school term in North Carolina in *post-bellum* times, even as late as 1900, scarcely reached the average *ante-bellum* term. Like the "paper" appropriations of the Reconstruction régime the prescription of a school term proved ineffective.

In other respects, also, the Reconstruction period suffers in comparison with *ante-bellum* practices in North Carolina. The average salary paid teachers before the war was higher than that paid during Reconstruction or until about 1900; a larger proportion of the school population was enrolled in 1860 than in any year between 1868 and 1876; and in the administrative organization of the school system, the *ante-bellum* provisions for the state, county, and local supervision, defective as those provisions may have been, were not improved by the law of 1869. The duties of the state superintendent and of the county and district officials were as clearly defined before 1860 as at the later period; and the administration of these officials appeared more efficient under the *ante-bellum* system than under that of Reconstruction. School statistics, for example, were more nearly complete in 1860 than at any time between 1868 and 1876, and this is no mean test of interest in public education and of the efficiency of its administration.

Finally, however, Reconstruction left other educational legacies than those of an advanced constitutional requirement for public education, and of provisions for a uniform system of taxation for school support, for the education of the negro, and for a definitely prescribed school term. First of all, the constitution itself was not only ill-suited to the needs of the people, but contained conflicting provisions which proved inconvenient and retarding to educational progress. One clause required the maintenance of schools in every township for four months in every year, while another clause in the same constitution made the performance of this requirement legally impossible. For many years after the war the valuation of property adopted throughout the State was so low that nearly all the taxes it was possible to levy were required to carry on the state and county government, leaving but a pittance for the schools. Under the constitution it was impossible to raise by taxation enough money to maintain creditable schools; and so defective did this part of the school system appear, as the years went by, that amendments were frequently suggested and urged by which the constitutional limitation of taxation would not apply to taxes levied for the support of the public schools. The State is to-day laboring under the burden imposed by this defect in the constitution of 1868.

The real educational benefits that did arise from emancipation and Reconstruction were further lessened by the folly and offense committed by the partisan plan of the period. The infamy of radical rule during the dark days of Reconstruction, and the incapacity and ignorance which the negro displayed in his early participation in political affairs, finally produced a reaction damaging alike to the education of the negro and to that of the white child. The effect of that period of political and financial license, when a multitude of passions and vices were riotously indulged, was naturally blighting to the enthusiasm which native conservatives and former leaders may have felt on the subject of education. The influence of politics on education during the period was direful and far-reaching. Fear of mixed schools and the poverty-stricken condition of the State perhaps combined to produce an educational indifference, if not outright hostility, which did not die with the death of Reconstruction. But local evils were intensified by the agitation in Congress of the Civil Rights Bill which threatened temporary destruction to education in the South generally, and produced an influence as deadly as it was persistent.

Just what would have been the result in North Carolina had there been no outside interference is now, in the light of the facts, hardly a matter for speculation. On the whole, the evidence indicates that had the native conservative element been free to act, without unwholesome influences from abroad, better educational policies would have been outlined than were made by the Reconstruction régime. Reference has already been made to the noticeable expansion of educational statutes and the improvement of school systems after 1865. This expansion and improvement were general; everywhere there appeared a popular feeling that educational facilities should be extended and educational opportunities made more adequate and safe. This feeling was shared by leaders in the South, as well as in other sections of the country, between the close of the war and the beginnings of Reconstruction; and during the confusion of these years there was a marked interest in improving provisions for education in several of the Southern States which were expecting to have their relations with the national government restored in accordance with the executive plan of Reconstruction.

In North Carolina, as we have seen, although the

office of superintendent of public instruction was abolished in 1866, that action was not due to legislative hostility, but to the bankrupt condition of the State and because there appeared no plan for which this part of the system could be continued. Moreover, the same Legislature which took this action appropriated money to relieve the state university and made other efforts to assist the public-school system. It will be recalled that at that time the House actually passed a bill to appropriate $75,000 annually for that purpose, but the measure was defeated in the Senate. It will also be recalled that at the next Legislature, at a time of great confusion and uncertainty, when the state governments of the South as organized by the presidential plan were about to be replaced with military governments, the native white citizenship of the State passed acts which authorized taxation for school support and attempted to revive and improve the former school system. But for the crime of Reconstruction, therefore, the educational historian would have a different but better tale to tell of education in North Carolina and the entire South since the Civil War.

REFERENCES

Constitutions of 1868 and of 1876; Journals of the House and Senate; Public Laws of North Carolina; Legislative Documents; *Reports* of the Superintendent of Public Instruction; Fleming, *Documentary History of Reconstruction;* Hamilton, *Reconstruction in North Carolina;* Hart, *The Southern South;* Dunning, *Reconstruction Political and Economic;* Knight, *The Influence of Reconstruction on Education in the South; Reports* of the Supreme Court of North Carolina; *Proceedings* of the Peabody Board Trustees.

SUGGESTIONS FOR FURTHER STUDY

1. What were some of the conditions which retarded educational growth in North Carolina between 1868 and 1876?
2. What conditions aided educational sentiment during those years?
3. What outside educational agencies operated in the State following the war?
4. Discuss the work of the Freedmen's Bureau during Reconstruction.
5. What was the chief defect of the State's educational system during Reconstruction?
6. Show how the defective legislation of the period retarded education.
7. What was the Civil Rights Bill? What effect did it have on education in North Carolina? In other Southern States?
8. What was done for training teachers in the State during Reconstruction?
9. What good effects did the war and Reconstruction have on education in North Carolina? In other Southern States? In other sections of the country?
10. What evils did the period bring to Southern education in general? To education in North Carolina?

CHAPTER XIII

THE WORK AND INFLUENCE OF THE PEABODY FUND

PERHAPS the most wholesome and beneficial influence affecting education in all the Southern States, especially during the dark days which followed the war, came through the work of the Peabody Fund. This endowment was created in 1867 by George Peabody, a native of Massachusetts, who spent the last thirty years of his life in London. There he accumulated a vast fortune, and at the close of the war he became especially interested in the encouragement of education in the destitute Southern States. Accordingly, in February, 1867, he created a trust fund of $1,000,000, to which in July, 1869, he added another million, to encourage and assist educational effort in "those portions of our beloved and common country which have suffered from the destructive ravages, and not less disastrous consequences, of civil war." These two millions constituted the bulk of the productive capital. Nearly a million and a half in Mississippi and Florida bonds proved unproductive, being among securities which those States repudiated. As a result Mississippi and Florida were omitted in the distribution of the income from the Peabody Fund, from 1886 to 1892, at which latter date, on motion of ex-President Hayes, and by unanimous vote of the trustees the two States were reinstated as beneficiaries.

Mr. Peabody named as trustees of this fund sixteen men of prominence and distinction: Robert C. Winthrop, of Massachusetts; Hamilton Fish, of New York; Bishop Charles P. McIlwaine, of Ohio; General Ulysses S. Grant, of the United States Army; Admiral D. G. Farragut, of the United States Navy; William C. Rives, of Virginia; John H. Clifford, of Massachusetts; William Aiken, of South Carolina; William M. Evarts, of New York; William A. Graham, of North Carolina; Charles Macalester, of Pennsylvania; George W. Riggs, of Washington; Samuel Wetmore, of New York; Edward A. Bradford, of Louisiana; George N. Eaton, of Maryland; and George Peabody Russell, of Massachusetts. In his letter, dated at Washington, February 7, 1867, creating the trust, he said: —

I feel most deeply, therefore, that it is the duty and privilege of the most favored and wealthy portions of our nation to assist those who are less fortunate; and with the wish to discharge, so far as I am able, my own responsibility in this matter, as well as to gratify my desire to aid those to whom I am bound by so many ties of attachment and regard, I give to you, gentlemen, most of whom have been my personal and especial friends, the sum of one million of dollars, to be by you and your successors held in trust and the income thereof used and applied in your discretion for the promotion and encouragement of intellectual, moral, or industrial education among the young of the more destitute portions of the Southern and Southwestern States of our Union; my purpose being, that the benefits intended shall be distributed among the entire population, without other distinction than their needs and the opportunities of usefulness to them.

The following resolutions, adopted March 19, 1867, embody the plan of the trustees: —

1. *Resolved*, That for the present the promotion of primary or common-school education, by such means or agencies as now exist, or may need to be created, be the leading object of the Board in the use of the fund placed at its disposal.

WORK AND INFLUENCE OF PEABODY FUND 273

2. *Resolved,* That in aid of the above general design, and as promotive of the same, the Board will have in view the furtherance of the normal school education for the preparation of teachers, as well by the endowment of scholarships in existing Southern institutions as by the establishing of normal schools, and the aiding of such normal schools as may now be in operation in the Southern and Southwestern States; including such measures as may be feasible, and as experience shall dictate to be expedient, for the promotion of education in the application of science to the industrial pursuits of human life.

A third resolution, provided for the appointment of a general agent, "of the highest qualifications," to whom was to be committed, with the advice of an executive committee, the entire charge of carrying out Mr. Peabody's designs. Under this resolution, Rev. Dr. Barnas Sears, president of Brown University, Providence, Rhode Island, was offered the appointment which he accepted March 30, 1867. It may well be questioned whether any other man could have brought more valuable training and experience and greater adaptability and resourcefulness to the delicate and difficult duties of the position. He soon fixed his residence in Staunton, Virginia, so as to be in close communication with the region for which he labored so wisely and so ably for thirteen years.[1]

The directions of Mr. Peabody were that the principal of the fund should remain intact for thirty years. It could not be expended, neither could it be increased by accruing interest; but the method of using the annual revenue, as well as the final disposition of the original endowment, was left entirely to the discretion of the trustees. The solution of this latter question was, by

[1] Dr. Sears died July 6, 1880, at Saratoga, New York.

common consent, left to future developments and the ripe wisdom of the self-perpetuating board of trustees. The immediate need was obviously in the field of elementary instruction for the masses of Southern youth, and the Board early determined to give assistance to public free schools. The policy of the trustees was to coöperate, whenever possible, with state authorities, so as to prevent disorder and to secure unity and strength of action. The funds were not to be distributed as a charity to the indigent; this had been a more or less prevalent *ante-bellum* educational practice in several of the Southern States, proving inadequate to any effectual relief, wasteful and inefficient, and productive of no permanent and valuable results. Moreover, the funds were not to be appropriated according to population or according to comparative community destitution, but on the sound principle of helping those communities which would help themselves. The invariable adherence of the Peabody Trustees to this principle, throughout the operation of the fund, was probably the greatest single educational blessing the South ever enjoyed.

The plan formulated for the promotion of educational enterprise was designed from the outset to stimulate and encourage local initiative and community effort. All schools aided by the fund were to have at least one hundred pupils each, with a teacher for every fifty, and an average term of ten months. The sum of $300 was usually given to a school with an enrollment of one hundred, $600 to one having an enrollment of two hundred, and $1000 to one having as many as three hundred pupils enrolled. A card similar to the following was frequently distributed in order to acquaint the people with the plan and method of the trustees: —

For well-regulated public free schools, containing ten months of the year, and having an enrollment of not less than

100 pupils,	averaging 85 per cent attendance,	the Peabody Board pays	$ 300
150 "	" 85 " "	" " " "	$ 450
200 "	" 85 " "	" " " "	$ 600
250 "	" 85 " "	" " " "	$ 800
300 "	" 85 " "	" " " "	$1000

The schools are expected to pay for current expenses two or three times as much as the Peabody Board appropriates, to be graded, and to have a teacher for every fifty pupils.

As a rule colored schools received two thirds of the above amounts. These amounts were always given on the condition that the town or community receiving the aid should raise by subscription or otherwise at least twice or three times as much as the Peabody Board appropriated to it. Moreover, an average standard attendance was required as a further qualification for participation in the bounty. The soundness of this principle of distribution is only one of the creditable features of the organization of the fund. In addition to confining its attention to public free schools, the fund was thoroughly committed to the following principles in promoting educational endeavor: —

1. Rendering aid to schools where large numbers of children could be gathered and where a model system of schools could be organized and maintained.
2. Giving preference to those places which showed promise of influencing the surrounding community.
3. Making a limited number of schools effective rather than undertaking the "multiplication of schools languishing for want of sufficient support."
4. Working for an improvement of state systems of education, — "to act through their organs, and to make use of their machinery whenever" such agencies were offered.
5. Favoring the establishment and maintenance of normal schools over normal departments in colleges and academies.

6. Giving special attention to the preparation of female teachers for primary schools, "rather than to general culture of young men in colleges, who will be likely to teach in the higher schools for the benefit of the few."

7. Encouraging colored students who were preparing to teach to attend regular normal schools.

8. Favoring the support of state supervision, the formulation of state teachers' associations, and the publication of educational periodicals.

The policy of the fund and its administration was thus outlined. "Free schools for the whole people" became its motto and aim. And the conditions on which every appropriation was to be made were just those needed to secure coöperation with and security for the plan. No other method could have created or assisted in creating a wholesome educational sentiment or could have had the effect of encouraging local taxation for public schools. The absence of any element of charity in the plan of distribution, as a means to temporary relief, is a living witness to the judgment which marked the entire administration of the trust.

The States aided by the fund were those which belonged to the Confederacy and West Virginia. North Carolina was one of the first to participate in the distribution. Only a few months after the creation of the trust, arrangements were nearly completed for aiding a school in Salisbury to the amount of $500; and at the same time efforts were made to secure an appropriation for Hillsboro. More work would have been undertaken that year but for the absence from the State of William A. Graham, the North Carolina trustee, who was very familiar with the State's educational needs, and for whose personal influence there was probably no substitute. The amounts received by the towns and communities of the State gradually increased so that by 1877 the sum of $87,600 had been appropriated to them from the Peabody Board. During the same time Virginia received $201,250; West Virginia, $107,710; Georgia, $71, 062; Arkansas, $60,600; Mississippi, $58,578; Louisiana, $55,850; Alabama, $55,450; Tennessee, $191,650; Florida, $48,450; South Carolina, $27,650; Texas, $18,600; making a total of $984,450.

The sum of $22,000 was available for the State of North Carolina in 1868. But on the advice of Calvin H. Wiley, former superintendent of public instruction, Mr. Sears visited only the larger towns, where arrangements to comply with the conditions of the Peabody appropriations were completed. Applications for aid also came from private academies and colleges in the western part of the State, seeking endowment, but these could not be considered. Wilmington was offered $1500 on condition that it would raise $3000; Newbern was promised $1000 if its citizens would raise $2500; and Raleigh and Charlotte were to receive $1000 each on the same condition. Offers were similarly made to Goldsboro, Greensboro, and Fayetteville. Through F. A. Fiske, superintendent of education for the colored people of the State, Mr. Sears learned that the colored schools were "in a precarious, staggering condition on account of extreme poverty. . . ." and the sum of $4000 was offered, on the usual conditions, to aid these schools. The sum of $500 was also given to aid a colored normal school in Raleigh.

In addition to these money appropriations, a few textbooks were distributed in the State in 1868. These were elementary texts, gifts of the A. S. Barnes Publishing Company, D. Appleton and Company, Cowperthwait and Company, and Sheldon and Company. More than fifty thousand copies of these books were distributed in the South from September, 1869, to September, 1870. Some of the books given by these publishing houses were: Webster's *Elementary Speller* (25,000 copies); Webster's *Elementary Reader* (25,000 copies); Cornell's *First Steps in Geography* (25,000 copies); Quackenbos's *Primary Arithmetic* (20,000 copies); Quackenbos's *First Book in Grammar* (5000 copies); Page's *Theory and Practice of Teaching* (500 copies); Welch's *Manual of Object Lessons* (500 copies); Davies's *Outlines of Mathematical Science* (500 copies); Holbrook's *Normal Methods of Teaching* (250 copies); Wells's *Graded Schools* (250 copies); Jewell's *School Government* (250 copies); Fowle's *Teacher's Institute* (250 copies); Bates's *Methods of Teacher's Institute* (250 copies); Mansfield's *American Education* (250 copies); Mayhew's *Universal Education* (250 copies); Northend's *Teacher's Assistant* (250 copies); Northend's *Teachers and Parents* (250 copies); Root's *School Amusements* (250 copies); Stone's *Teacher's Examiner* (250 copies); *National Second Reader* (5000 copies); Davies's *Written Arithmetic* (5000 copies); Monteith's *Second Book in Geography* (5000 copies); Beer's *Penmanship* (5000 copies); Monteith's *United States History* (3000 copies); *A First Book of Science* (500 copies); Jarvis's *Physiology and Health* (500 copies); Peck's Ganot's *Natural Philosophy* (500 copies); Smith and Martin's *Bookkeeping* (500 copies).

Only $2700 of appropriations from the fund seems to have reached the State in 1868. Considerable more than this had been available, but it was hardly an opportune time for educational enterprise. The popular mind was agitated over the ratification of the new constitution in April, the call for a special session of the Legislature in July, and the approach of the regular session of that body in the autumn. Few of the offers previously made to towns and cities had been formally complied with, and Mr. Sears did not visit the State between July, 1868, and the following January. But he arranged with the Reverend H. C. Vogell, government superintendent of colored schools in the State, to select, superintend, and aid from the Peabody Fund such colored schools as would "otherwise have failed wholly or in part."

By April, 1869, a new school law had been passed providing for the establishment and maintenance of schools for the education of all the children of the State. In August the superintendent of public instruction believed that some of the schools would be opened by October and many of them by January, 1870. State funds for educational purposes, amounting to about $300,000, would be available and would afford accommodations for about 75,000 children. The Peabody Board could now act as a great stimulant in inducing cities and towns to furnish funds supplementary to the aid appropriated by Mr. Sears, which in 1869 amounted to $6350.

Wilmington was maintaining free schools by voluntary subscriptions amounting to $7500 and $1500 received from the Peabody Board. Newbern had failed to comply with the offer made by the Board in 1868 and was providing for only half of its white children; but on urgent request of the city council, the original offer was renewed on condition that provision be made for the education of all the white children there. Later the Newbern Academy was opened as a public school to which all the white children of the town were admitted. The sum of $300 was given to Newport on the usual conditions, and the same amount offered to a charity school in Charlotte on condition that it be converted into a public school. Little River Academy received $300. This school had been made free in all the common English subjects, had helped to break down the "barriers of caste," and had assisted in uniting the entire community educationally. Smithville received $300, Hillsboro $500, and $300 was offered to Thomasville. The school in Salisbury had suspended, and Raleigh and some other towns, to which offers of aid had been previously made, had been unsuccessful in their efforts to comply with the conditions. In most of these cases Mr. Sears renewed his offers.

The public-school system established by the Legislature in 1868–69 had struggled through its first year with as much success as was expected in times of such violent party strife. Both coldness and opposition had confronted it. Moreover, taxes had been only imperfectly collected, the schools, therefore, poorly supported, and there was a lack of general educational interest, of competent teachers, and of competent officials. The school population of 1870 was about 344,000, and the total enrollment was slightly in excess of 50,000. But there was an encouraging growth of educational sentiment in towns and communities which were being stimulated to local effort by the Peabody Board. Wilmington assumed control and support of its schools, which had previously been maintained by private contribution, the city adopting them and making appropriations to their support, and the Peabody Board continuing its aid of $1000. Newbern was this year (1870) receiving

$300 from the fund. Fayetteville was promised $1000; the sum of $600 was appropriated to Washington to assist a white school and a colored school; Hillsboro received $500, Oak Ridge $150, and a colored school in Charlotte $200. In addition to these the following places had fulfilled the conditions which were attached to the Peabody appropriations and in 1870 received $300 each: Cottage Home, Gilmer's Store, Hayesville, Jamestown, Kenansville, Mars Hill College, Mount Gilead, Grassy Creek, Durham's Creek, Newport, Polletier's Mill, Roan Mountain, Smithville, Springfield and Thomasville.

The following year did not see very many encouraging signs of educational growth in North Carolina, and the public mind, in the matter of free schools, was not so well settled there as in most of the other Southern States. The supreme court had decided that the school law, so far as it provided for local school taxes, was unconstitutional and could not be enforced; the Legislature levied no school taxes for 1871, and the county commissioners were in many cases accused of using the capitation taxes for other than educational purposes. The general aspect of education was undergoing but few changes. The principle of general education by public support had been agreed upon as the correct principle; but its application, in North Carolina at least, proved a more difficult task. Educational legislation, though well intended, had been hurriedly framed by lawmakers of little experience; local tax legislation was vague and uncertain, and litigation was resorted to by those who were opposed to it; officials seemed to have but little interest in the schools, many of which languished for want of proper administration.

These were some of the conditions which Mr. Sears

faced in his work in North Carolina in 1871. But he continued his labors there discreetly and with caution. He assisted Wilmington and Newbern again with $1000 each. In Newbern he found that opposition was being rapidly overcome and that the "partisan private schools" there had "been compelled to succumb to the generous provisions we have been enabled to make for all" those who take advantage of them. About 400 pupils were being educated in Wilmington and over 300 in Newbern. Washington had a white school with 132 pupils and a colored school with 451, and Mr. Sears gave $300 to the former and $600 to the latter. Durham's Creek, with an enrollment of 142, received $300; Beaufort, with a school of 150 white pupils, was promised $450 if it continued ten months, and $400 for its colored school with 200 pupils on the same condition. Smithville received $450 for its white school of 170 pupils and three teachers, and $200 for its colored school of 100 pupils and two teachers. It was said that a hundred children were being taught in these two places to read and write, "who, but for these schools, never would have known a letter." Other towns and communities aided this year were: Hillsboro, $500; Newport, $450; Kenansville, Grassy Creek, Carthage, Edneyville, Township No. 9, Mars Hill College, Mount Olive, Westfield, Sandy Mush, Blue Ridge, Chocowinity, Cane Creek, and Bush Hill, $300 each. A negro school at Kinston received $300, one at Plymouth $200, and one at Charlotte $200. Eighteen other schools, three of which were for negroes, received amounts ranging from $200 to $500; and the sum of $1000 was offered to aid teachers' institutes.

For the next year, ending July, 1873, the general agent did not report educational conditions in the State any more promising than hitherto. Indifference among the common people and a lack of coöperation among public men were everywhere noticeable. "Nowhere," said Mr. Sears, "has it been more clearly demonstrated that half-measures in establishing and supporting public schools cannot be attended with great success." It was feared that in many, if not in most, of the counties no schools would open in the fall; systematic and energetic efforts were needed to enlighten the people so that they would demand of the Legislature a working system of schools. The popular mind was confused and disconcerted by the agitation in Congress of the famous Civil Rights Bill, which Charles Sumner labored to enact in 1871–72. No legislation in favor of mixed schools had ever been attempted in North Carolina, and public opinion there was unanimously hostile to it.

Only in cities and towns, and largely in those which were being aided by the Peabody Board, were any serious efforts being made to maintain free public schools during these stormy days. The wisdom of the original policy of the trustees was confirmed by their action in the face of the discouraging circumstances of the time. They early saw the necessity of giving "preference to places which will, by their example, exert the widest influence upon the surrounding country." Any other method would have been wasteful, inefficient, and probably injurious; an unwise distribution of their funds could easily have demoralized the very region whose common sense and practical effort needed to be aroused in favor of education. But the concentration of assistance on a few strategic educational points, which were sustained by an intelligent and wholesome public sentiment, served to conciliate opposition when men were violent in the bitter expression of their disgust and restlessness, to enlist community coöperation when all sense of personal responsibility was deadened, and to encourage when apprehension verged on despair. The wisdom of the plan, adhered to so strictly, yet so discreetly and with such astonishing success, was early confirmed in many communities, and has had its triumphant vindication in the subsequent movement in the South for local taxation for school purposes.

Wilmington furnished an early example of the influence of the policy in North Carolina. In the winter of 1873 the town became responsible for its schools, and the authorities levied a local tax to supplement the county and state school taxes, to make more adequate provision for its children who now numbered nearly 1000. "We flatter ourselves," wrote the chairman of the local school committee, "that the start now taken in Wilmington will, in time, extend to every part of the State." From June, 1872, to July, 1873, Wilmington and Newbern received $1000 each. Washington received $600, Hillsboro $500, and some of the other places aided this year were: Hayesville, Catawba Vale, and Waynesville, $450 each; Portsmouth, Leicester No. 1, Leicester No. 2, Lebanon, Hendersonville, Hunting Quarter, Charlotte, Linville, Walnut Creek, Grassy Creek, Old Fort Township, Dysartville, Otter Creek, Big Laurel, Sulphur Springs, Hominy Valley, Bridge Water, Belmont, Democrat, Locust Field, Morgan Hill, Qualla Town, Newport, $300 each; a negro school at Warrenton received $400, one at Fayetteville $300, and one at Oxford $300. The sum of $300 was appropriated to aid six teachers' institutes.

The noble design of the great philanthropist was being

followed with fidelity and jealous care. In the work of the school year ending June, 1874, the superintendent of public instruction noticed an improvement in both pupils and teachers, and consequently increased interest in public education; and the influence of the Peabody Board received credit from that officer for this change. The school law was still defective, however, in that it failed to provide for the education and training of teachers and for efficient county and district supervision, and no authority for local taxation. The superintendent declared: —

The people are not deficient in energy or public spirit, or in a due appreciation of popular education. Our great want is *statesmen* in our legislative halls — laws that will permit the people to establish and maintain public schools for the education of their children. The want of active county supervision has been very greatly felt in administering the Peabody Education Fund.

Mr. Sears, however, felt more hopeful for the future. He was now convinced that "nothing in the future is more certain than the acceptance of that principle, the doctrine of free schools by the people at large, if they are free to act without unwelcome influences from abroad." And to hasten such a time he distributed in 1874 more than $12,000 to thirty different schools, thus stimulating interest in educational development. Wilmington received $2000, Newbern received $1000, and Charlotte received $1050. Among the other places aided were: Franklin and South Hominy, $450 each; Mill Shoal, Flat Creek, Table Rock, Dick's Creek, Clear Creek, Enon, Warrenton, Thomasville, Asheville, Hayesville, Dysartville, Rice Hill, Beaufort, Washington, Morgan Hill, Marshall, Pigeon Valley, Buffalo, Montanis Institute, and Bethlehem, $300 each; Smyrna, $200; a negro school at Beaufort and one at Tarboro, $300 each; one at Fayetteville, $50; and the sum of $100 was given to teachers' institutes.

By 1875, the schools aided by the Peabody Board were numerous in the State and the appropriations were larger than for any other year. Interest in public education was gradually increasing, though the State was not yet making equal educational progress with Virginia. The superintendent of public instruction was spending four months of the year as local agent of the Peabody Board, visiting various places in the State, setting the subject of public school properly before them. The towns and communities receiving appropriations this year were: Charlotte and Newbern, $1000 each; Laurel Branch, Balsam Seminary, Pleasant Hill, Rocky Hill, Ivy Shoal, Flat Creek, Grantville Seminary, Webster School, Cowee School, Fleming's Chapel, Shoal Creek Seminary, Roan Mountain, Pisgah, Smyrna, Smithfield, McElrath Chapel, Waynesville, Mill Shoal, New Salem Church, Laurel Hill (White Rock), Antioch School, Rocky Point, Grassy Creek, Ream's Creek, Nebo Creek, Dick's Creek, Fork Mount, Hicksville, Oak Grove, Harrol Township, Laurel Fork, Lewisburg Township, Capernaum Institute, River Bend, Blue Ridge, Washington School, Laurel Hill (Clay County), Cheoah, and Warrenton, $300 each; Hillsboro, $250; *Journal of Education*, $200; a negro school at Charlotte, $600; one at Fayetteville and one at Tarboro, $450 each; and $500 was appropriated for the North Carolina agency.

The successful operation of such schools and the free discussion of education soon led to the conviction that public schools were a necessity. In general, however, no great changes in public sentiment appeared in August,

1876, though steady progress in that direction was seen in spite of new obstacles. The state superintendent was charged with irregularities in the management of funds and resigned, and a successor was tardily named in his place. The state tax for schools was slight. A local tax was hardly known, and the policy of appointing politicians to head the educational system had revealed its extreme weakness and danger. The general financial embarrassment, common to all the Southern States, and the maladministration in the handling of school funds added to an already discouraging condition. Educational legislation, prepared hastily by those who had no experience to guide them, was commonly defective. Offices had been needlessly multiplied and unwisely distributed, and the school system burdened with supernumeraries; responsibilities were divided, and chances of active official coöperation were greatly decreased. The unwarranted outside interference in educational matters which Mr. Sears viewed with apprehension complicated an already anomalous condition; but the work of Mr. Sears and his Board, and the sight of success in the schools aided from that source, helped to keep alive a certain educational spirit. And appropriations continued to be made.

From October, 1875, to the summer of 1876, the following towns and communities were aided: Wilmington (for two years), $2000; Newbern, $1000; Warrenton and Greensboro, $750 each; Smithfield, Smyrna, Dysartville, Nebo, Hillsboro, $300 each; a negro school at Fayetteville, and one at Charlotte, $450 each; a negro school at Tarboro and one at Raleigh, $300 each; the agency for North Carolina, $500; the *Journal of Education*, $200; and teachers' institutes, $100.

The return to "home rule" was made in North Carolina in 1876, when the conservatives regained the state government. The new constitution was adopted January 1, 1877, and the liability of having mixed schools, which had been a matter of great consideration, was now removed. Forward educational steps are at once in evidence. One of the evidences of the change is the immediate provision for two normal schools, one for each race, and for their equal support from the State. A crying need of the years of Reconstruction was for competent teachers, and the only safe, thorough, efficient, and permanent policy was state establishment and support of normal schools. The Legislature appropriated $2000 to each of these institutions. Authority was also granted towns of a certain size to levy an extra property tax for schools of as much as one tenth of one per cent and a capitation tax of twenty-five cents for educational purposes was continued. Mr. Sears seems encouraged:—

Public schools are now fairly put upon their own merits. There can henceforth be little question of their perpetuity, for the tide of public opinion has been recently turned and set so strong in their favor that it will not be easy to resist it.

From the summer of 1876 to the summer of 1877 the Peabody Board appropriated $1500 to Raleigh, $750 to Greensboro, $600 to Wilmington, $500 to normal schools, $950 to the delinquencies of the state superintendent, and nine other schools each received from $250 to $450. Among these were two negro schools, one at Fayetteville and one at Charlotte.

In 1878 the wise administration of the trustees, through their able agent, Dr. Sears, took account of the changing demands in the South and began to apply the aid of the fund to the preparation of teachers. This aid was extended by assisting teachers' institutes and also by granting scholarships to the Normal College at Nashville, Tennessee. Through these scholarships, which were awarded to promising young men and women of the Southern States, a large number of teachers were annually well trained and returned to their home States for public educational service. One of the immediate results of this distribution of the fund was the growing interest taken in normal schools and the training of teachers. Soon after the new plan was begun many encouraging signs appeared, and a new era for education began to dawn. The trustees also continued to aid educational journalism and to stimulate educational enterprise in as many ways as possible.

From 1878 until a final disposition was made of the fund, North Carolina continued to share in its distribution. In 1878 about $4500 was distributed to graded schools, normal schools, and to other educational work in the State; and until 1907, sums varying from $3000 to $7000 were annually appropriated to aid the educational interests of the State. A part of these amounts was for scholarships in the Normal College at Nashville, which were eagerly sought after and very highly prized.

Certain definite results of the influence of the fund appear. It aided in the stimulation of local enterprise and community patriotism and the gradual rise of city and town school systems; in encouragement to the final establishment of complete state systems of schools; in the gradual removal of hostility to educating the freedmen; and it had a tendency to aid in removing the bitter spirit of sectionalism.

We have already seen that as much as $87,600 was

appropriated to North Carolina during the first ten years of the operation of the fund. This means that communities raised by local taxation or otherwise between $262,000 and $350,000 for education in the State which would otherwise not have been available. This does not, however, represent the permanent value of the spirit of local effort which was thus stimulated and which gradually developed and spread throughout the State; it would be difficult to estimate that spirit. It is enough to indicate the manner in which the Peabody appropriations early aided in the development of sentiment for local taxation for school purposes. After 1874, by special permission of the Legislature, several towns and cities were given authority to place their schools on a more efficient and substantial basis, extending their terms, and increasing their equipments and teaching forces. This idea of improvement gradually grew until it reached most of the towns of the State.

The final establishment of complete state systems of public schools was also aided by the policy of the trustees and the personal efforts of the agents of the fund. Through public addresses, conferences with legislative committees, and consultations with public leaders, Mr. Sears helped to make education appear as a function of government, a theory which soon became generally secure in the public mind. A property tax for purposes of education soon came to be regarded as legitimate and essential, opposition to which had before this time been more traditional than rational. And the general movement for normal schools and teachers' institutes, supported and maintained by the State, is easily traceable in its development and growth to the influence and aid of this benefaction.

Hostility to, or prejudice against, the idea of furnishing educational facilities to the freedmen was probably somewhat diminished by the influence of the fund. To offer the children of the emancipated slaves educational advantages equal to those now afforded the children of their late masters, in opposition to all tradition and custom, required a courage and a liberality that few men were thought to possess. And while a few slowly and with feeling made the necessary adjustment, the general disposition on the part of representative Southern leaders to discriminate against the colored people was rarely seen. Cases of discrimination were the exception rather than the rule; most of the leaders felt kindly toward the colored people until foolish ideas of unworthy teachers and of visionary and impassioned zealots created mischief and alarm among those who labored to preserve the integrity of Southern life. In spite of the confusion of the times and the vicious conditions and influences which lent themselves in making more difficult and delicate the problem of sympathetic racial coöperation, the Southern States gave nearly $110,000,000 between 1870 and 1900 to help educate the negro. The apparent disparity in the number of schools for white and for colored children was due to the extreme difficulty and often impossibility of securing qualified teachers for the negro schools.

While the trust was established primarily to help "the educational needs of those portions of our beloved and common country which have suffered from the destructive ravages, and not less disastrous consequences of civil war," Mr. Peabody clearly had in mind the promotion of the common good. "This I give to the suffering South for the good of the whole country" was the sentiment which he expressed when he made his second great donation in July, 1869. This benefaction of a Northern man, the caution and tact of his trustees, and the activity of their efficient and able agents, and finally, the influence on the masses of the gradual growth of a wholesome educational sentiment, for developing which the fund had been so faithfully used, helped to remove much of the bitter sectionalism which was known generally to exist, and to establish and maintain a bond of fellowship between the two sections so lately at war. Mr. Winthrop, for so long chairman of the board of trustees, pronounced the gift "the earliest manifestation of a spirit of reconciliation toward those from whom we have been so unhappily alienated and against whom we of the North had been so recently arrayed in arms."

REFERENCES

Proceedings of the Peabody Board Trustees, annual after 1867; Ayres, L. P., *Seven Great Foundations; Report* of the United States Commissioner of Education, 1893, vol. I, pp. 739-71; *Annual Reports* of the Superintendent of Public Instruction of North Carolina, 1869-1904; Knight, "The Peabody Fund and its Early Operation in North Carolina," in *South Atlantic Quarterly*, vol. XIV, no. 2; Alderman and Gordon, *J. L. M. Curry, a Biography;* Curry, *History of the Peabody Fund.*

SUGGESTIONS FOR FURTHER STUDY

1. What was the purpose of the Peabody Fund?
2. Note the plan adopted for administering the fund. How did the plan stimulate educational interest and effort?
3. How did the endowment stimulate the rise of public high schools in North Carolina?
4. What schools did the fund aid in your county?
5. How did the fund stimulate local taxation in your community?
6. What aid was given to teachers' institutes in your county?
7. In what other way did it aid teacher training in your county?
8. How did the fund probably assist in decreasing prejudice to the education of the negro?
9. Compare the principle on which the fund was distributed to the principle on which the literary fund was distributed before 1860.

CHAPTER XIV

ATTEMPTS AT READJUSTMENT (1877-1900)

Not only was a great political and social change taking place in North Carolina and in the other Southern States in 1876, but educational changes appeared as well. These changes were apparent in both sentiment and action. Men of reflection had agreed that an ignorant and debased people could not contribute toward the resources of the South, and free public schools for all classes were accepted as the only remedy for a desolate condition. In most sections schools began to advance in almost every respect. Attendance increased, popular interest in education became more general, school management greatly improved, and proficiency in the teachers' art began to show growth. Teachers' institutes and normal schools were rapidly multiplying and developing in efficiency in almost every State. In North Carolina educational conditions appeared more hopeful than at any time since the war.

This sudden change in educational enterprises is no less astonishing than creditable. The rebuilding of a public-school system after the war was a more difficult problem in the South than in any other part of the Nation; and the question of educating all the people soon became more critically important to the Southern States than to any other section of the Union. The South emerged from the Civil War with a loss of fully one tenth of her white male population and practically all of her accumulated capital. Not only was it difficult to restore the material resources necessary for an efficient school system, but the crime of Reconstruction made the restoration of public confidence a difficult and tedious process. In fact, Reconstruction proved more destructive than the war. Not only did it rob the South of what the war had spared, but by looting treasuries, squandering school funds, imposing enormous taxes, practicing fraud and extravagance, and by piling up colossal bonded debts, it succeeded in running its corrupt and criminal fingers deep "into the pockets of posterity." In North Carolina Reconstruction left a debt of $38,000,000, and more than $300,000,000 in the South. Thus, by the greatest tragedy in modern history, — the war and its aftermath, — many of the richest portions of the South were wasted and shorn of their prosperity, industry was checked, idleness and fraud were widely encouraged, local justice thwarted and put in contempt, the people ruled by evil and corrupt officials, and tendencies to good government stifled. This experience explains why the South has been charged with educational backwardness since the Civil War, with a reputation for hating taxes and tax collectors, and with distrust of "public welfare" plans and movements. In this experience may also be found an explanation for the so-called devotion of the South to a sort of *laissez-faire* theory in education, and frequent extreme applications of the principle of local government in educational administration. Here, again, are still other "heritages" of Reconstruction.

In view of the experiences of that bitter period, it is indeed surprising that the South, during the past forty years, has finally very largely overcome the financial and political relapses of the war and Reconstruction, and has so rapidly outgrown the deadening indifference which was born of pitiable poverty and the burden of a great wrong. Gradually, however, the South turned her face toward the future and, for the sake of her children, endeavored to forget the past. The thoughtful men of the time knew that the fortunes and prosperity of the South could be restored only by school systems adapted to the changed conditions; they understood that the industrial development of the South and her religious and social development all depended on the general education of the people. The beginning had to be made in poverty and discouragement, and in the face of numerous difficulties which tested the hope of a people already threatened with despair. But recuperation gradually set in, and so rapidly has it gained that the economic and social changes of the past forty years can scarcely be matched in all human history. With homes burned, fields laid waste, the political, industrial, and social systems destroyed; with many of her leaders dead, and with a generation of widows and orphans to educate and care for, the South, poverty-stricken, undertook the maintenance of two systems of schools for the proper training of her youth. For many years progress was necessarily slow, and much even now remains to be done. But what has been achieved finds explanation in the remarkable bravery, heroism, and industry of the Southern people which made them unwilling to live under the shadow of a bitter past.

Signs of an awakening began to appear in North Carolina in 1876, when the return to "home rule" was made. The gospel of public education for all classes began to be preached again and with an enthusiasm that was as rare as it was remarkable. In November of that year Governor Brogden said to the new Legislature: —

> Education is of the greatest value and importance to the people, and it should receive the cordial approbation and encouragement of all. . . . The hope of our State rests with a more thorough system of common schools. The position which she will in the future hold in the Republic must greatly depend upon the correct instruction given to the people. Our children must be elevated in the scale of intelligence ere the perpetuity of the Republic can be well assured, and nothing should be permitted to swerve us from our efforts to popularize education.

He also called attention to the need of provisions for training teachers, urged support for the university, and recommended a college for the education of the negro, and the passage of laws by which towns and cities could tax themselves for free-school support.

Two months later, in January, 1877, Governor Vance urged legislative attention "to the great subject of education." With his message he sent a memorial of the Central North Carolina Teachers' Association which asked the Legislature for the consideration for education "which its importance demands." The memorialists believed that the general educational fund was liberal, but that the results accomplished were not commensurate with the provisions of the constitution and the school fund.

> The money is spent, and the children are not educated. The people are taxed to support the schools, but they derive very little benefit from them. . . . The true remedy is, to permit the people of each township and of each city and incorporated town in the State to tax themselves by a majority vote for school purposes. There is no sufficient reason why the people of North Carolina should not enjoy this right and privilege which is enjoyed in almost all the other States of this Union. Surely the people may be trusted in this, as in other States, to

take care of themselves, and provide for the education of their children.

The memorialists also asked for adequate provision for the education of teachers. Lack of this provision had been a crying need of Reconstruction and the defect was widely felt. It was believed that the defect could be partially remedied by authorizing an annual county appropriation for teachers' institutes. Moreover, need was also felt for a fully organized normal school in which prospective teachers, as well as those already in service, could be drilled in the subjects taught in the public schools and also given training in methods of teaching and school management. Continuing, the memorial said: —

The public schools are the nurseries of the future citizen. A very large majority of the people will begin and end their education in these schools. Hence, whatever is done by education to make them better citizens must be done here. A withholding here would tend only to poverty. We are an industrial people, and our prosperity must depend mainly upon the great industries of agriculture and the mechanic arts. We will prosper as these interests are developed; and decline, as they are neglected. The branches of learning which tend to develop these great interests are already provided for in the university. To place them within the reach of the people, they should be put into the public schools. To this end your memorialists would ask that you establish a thoroughly organized normal school in the university.

In transmitting the memorial Governor Vance said: —

It is impossible to have an effective public-school system without providing for the training of teachers. The blind cannot lead the blind. Mere literary attainments are not sufficient to make its possessor a successful teacher. There must be added ability to influence the young and to communicate knowledge. There must be a mastery of the best modes of conducting schools, and of bringing out the latent possibilities, intellectual and moral, of the pupil's nature. In some rare cases these qualities are inborn, but generally it is of vast advantage to teachers to be trained by those who have studied and mastered the methods which have been found by experience to be the most successful in dispelling ignorance and inculcating knowledge. The schools in which this training is conducted, called normal colleges, or normal schools, have been found by experience to be most efficient agents in raising up a body of teachers who infuse new life and vigor into the public schools. There is urgent need for one, at least, in North Carolina.

The constitution of the State, in Section 4, Article IX, requires the General Assembly, as soon as practicable, to establish and maintain, in connection with the university, a department of normal instruction. I respectfully submit that it is now practicable to make a beginning in carrying out this provision of the constitution.[1] There cannot possibly be found in the State competent teachers for our public schools. The records of the county examiners show that most of the applicants for the post of imparting knowledge to others are themselves deficient in the simplest elements of spelling, reading, arithmetic, and writing. The university is now in successful operation. If the General Assembly should appropriate an amount sufficient to establish one professorship for the purpose of instructing in the theory and art of teaching, I am persuaded the best results would follow. A school of a similar character should be established for the education of colored teachers, the want of which is more deeply felt by the black race even than the white. In addition to the fact that it is our plain duty to make no discrimination in the matter of public education, I

---

[1] This suggests the criticism which Dr. Ruffner, superintendent of public instruction in Virginia, was at about the same time making of the Legislature of that State in neglecting to provide facilities for training teachers. The constitution of Virginia likewise required the establishment of normal schools "as soon as practicable"; but with the exception of two normal schools for negroes, supported largely by contributions from the North, no provision was made for normal training in Virginia until after Reconstruction. See the author's study, "Reconstruction and Education in Virginia," in the *South Atlantic Quarterly* for January and April, 1916.

cannot too strongly urge upon you the importance of the consideration that whatever of education we may be able to give to the children of the State should be imparted under our own auspices, and with a thorough North Carolina spirit. Many philosophical reasons can be given in support of this proposition. I am conscious of few things more dangerous than for a State to suffer the education of an entire class of its citizens to drift into the hands of strangers, most of whom are not attached to our institutions, if not positively unfriendly to them.

There are in the State several very respectable institutions for the education of black people, and a small endowment to one of them would enable it to attach a normal school sufficient to answer the present needs of our black citizens. Their desire for education is an extremely creditable one, and should be gratified as far as our means will permit. In short, I regard it as an unmistakable policy to imbue these black people with a hearty North Carolina feeling, and make them cease to look abroad for the aids to their progress and civilization and the protection of their rights as they have been taught to do, and to teach them to look to their State instead; to convince them that their welfare is indissolubly linked with ours.

Governor Vance's recommendations were not without effect, for, as was pointed out in the preceding chapter, two important laws were passed by the Legislature early in 1877. One of these acts established two normal schools, one for each race, and the other gave to towns of a certain size authority to raise additional funds for school purposes.

The normal school for white teachers opened at the state university July 3, 1877, and continued six weeks, with an enrollment of 235, representing forty-two counties. The average daily attendance was 157. Both men and women were enrolled in the school, though the law contemplated training only for the men. Instruction was given by a faculty of six members, all of whom were trained in normal-school methods. Recitations and lectures were given in arithmetic, grammar, analysis, geography, reading, orthography, phonetics, penmanship, and practical instruction was given in such subjects as "school discipline, methods, organization, qualifications, legal relation of teacher, parent, and child." Daily drills in vocal music were also given, and in addition to the regular daily exercises of the school, frequent public lectures were delivered by eminent men who visited the school for that purpose. There was no charge for tuition, and the railroads granted half-fare to the students. The Peabody Board appropriated the sum of $500 to supplement the state appropriation of $2000 to aid the work of the school. Certain book companies made valuable gifts of books to be used by the students.

The normal school for colored teachers was established at Fayetteville and opened in September, 1877, with an enrollment of 40. In a short time the attendance numbered 58, 20 of whom were women, who were admitted on equal terms with the men. The work of the school continued eight months and was successful beyond the expectations of the state board. The students were given instruction in practically the same subjects which the teachers in the other normal pursued and were given some training in practice teaching and observation.

> Each student teaches one class, at one recitation, daily, under the eye of the principal, and thus has an opportunity to put in practice the instruction obtained in the normal class. Theory and practice thus go hand in hand. Evidence of skill and faithfulness on the part of the teachers, and of diligence and perseverance on the part of the scholars, was exhibited in every branch of study pursued during the term.

This school was also aided by the Peabody Board, and the students also agreed to teach in the public schools of the State at least three years after leaving the normal school. Robert Harris, whom Governor Vance described as "a native colored man of excellent character and capacity," was in charge of the institution.

In 1878 the attendance at the white normal increased to 402, of whom 190 were women, and had an average attendance of 329. Fifty-nine counties were represented in the enrollment. At this session the teachers organized a "North Carolina Teachers' Association" and took steps toward the formation of county associations throughout the counties of the State. Committees were also appointed to make a thorough study of the state school system and suggest remedies for its weaknesses, which were numerous. The colored normal likewise prospered, with an enrollment of 114. The work was carried on practically as it was the previous year.

Probably in 1877, but certainly by the summer of 1878, normal school work was resumed in Trinity College under the direction of its president, Dr. Braxton Craven, and continued for several summers, with an annual term of four weeks. In 1879 the enrollment was 184, more than 100 of whom were teachers in the common schools of the State. They received instruction in English grammar, arithmetic, geography, spelling, reading, writing, history, algebra, Latin, school government, and methods of teaching, and in "all other matters pertaining to the common schools." In that year certificates were given to 38 teachers "who were found qualified according to law."[1]

[1] From the unpublished correspondence of Braxton Craven; letter of July 5, 1880, to the commissioners of Randolph County. The au-

ATTEMPTS AT READJUSTMENT

For the year ending September 1, 1877, the total expenditures for public-school purposes in North Carolina were $289,213.32. The school population was 408,296: whites, 267,265, and colored 141,031. Only 128,289 white children and 73,170 colored children were enrolled. The average attendance of the white children was 62,628, and of the colored children, 41,535. The number of public schools for white children was 2885, and for colored children, 1550. The number of teachers examined and approved during the year was 2382: whites, 1569, and colored, 813.

In 1878 the total public funds for educational purposes in the State were $452,515.53, and the total amount expended was $324,287.10. The school population was 422,380: whites, 273,767, and colored, 148,613. The enrollment for the year was as follows: whites, 146,681, with an average attendance of 82,054; colored 81,411, with an average attendance of 50,499. The number of public schools taught during the year was, for white children, 3388; for colored children, 1761. The average school term for the State was nine weeks, and the average monthly salary paid teachers was

thor is informed by Professor William H. Pegram, of Trinity College, who was an instructor in this normal school, that it was among the first, if not the first, institution in the State to give instruction in kindergarten methods. Dr. Craven brought to the school Mrs. Louise Pollock and her daughter, Miss Susie Pollock, of Washington City, for the purpose of giving instruction in this work. President Battle, of the University of North Carolina, to which institution these teachers later went for similar work, said of them, in reporting the work of the normal school at Chapel Hill in 1880: "The kindergarten department was a valuable and attractive feature of the Normal School. Mrs. Louise Pollock and Miss Susie Pollock brought to the management of this department the best theoretical instruction to be had in America and Europe, assisted by long and varied experience as practical teachers." (See Leg. Doc. 1881.)

$23.18. The number of teachers examined and approved during the year was 3722: whites, 2486, and colored, 1236.

The public-school fund in 1879 was $473,201.34, and in 1880 it had increased to $523,555.22. The disbursements in 1879 were $326,040.85; in 1880 they were $352,882.65. The school population increased from 426,189 in 1879 to 459,325 the following year; but the enrollment decreased from 238,749 to 225,606, and the average attendance had fallen from 150,788 to 147,802 in the same time. The number of public schools taught in 1879 was 5503 and only 5312 the following year. The average school term increased from nine and one fourth weeks to ten weeks. The average monthly salary paid teachers was $22.14 in 1879 and only $21.91 in 1880. The number of public schoolhouses had increased during that time from 3457 to 3766.

When the Legislature met in January, 1881, the opinion was widespread in the State that, in spite of certain improvements in the school system since 1876, it was still very defective and that further improvements were necessary. A demand appeared for as thorough revision of the school law as was possible at the time. "The old system was pronounced to be worse than no system; and in truth there was but little system about it." This opinion of Superintendent Scarborough was shared by Governor Thomas J. Jarvis, who, addressing the Legislature, said: —

Education I regard as the great interest of the State, an interest too great to be disposed of by a few paragraphs in a message. But while I may avail myself of another occasion to address you on this subject, I cannot now dismiss it without pleading for more money for the children. In the discussions I have seen in the papers, the system has been mainly the topic. Very little has been said about the money to carry on the system. While one system may be better than another, the most perfect is not worth the paper on which it is written without money to build schoolhouses and pay teachers. Money is, and must be, the heart and life of every system. While I hope to see you make the system as perfect as possible, I beg that you will not forget to provide the money. This can be done only by taxation. Will you impose it? I think the people will approve it. The tax for schools is now only eight and a third cents on a hundred dollars' worth of property, and twenty-five cents on the poll. Three times that on each would not be burdensome but wise legislation. The salary of the superintendent of public instruction should be largely increased, and I trust you will do this before the time comes for the gentleman [1] elected to that position to qualify. Instead of degrading this very important office into a mere clerkship, as has been the case, it should be dignified and elevated to a rank so high that it will command at all times the best talent of the State.

The governor commended the work of the normal schools and recommended that the annual appropriation for their maintenance be continued. He also urged proper attention to the university, which was "resuming her wonted place of usefulness and renown."

Another evidence of a demand for improved educational conditions appeared in a memorial which the State Teachers' Association, at its meeting in July, 1880, adopted and forwarded to the Legislature. The memorial requested that body to increase the school tax for the entire State to an amount sufficient to maintain a school four months each year in every district in the State and to give local districts authority to raise additional taxes for school purposes. This authority had already been given to several towns of the State. "It is the very germ of a good system, and this right belongs to every school district." The memorial also asked the Legislature to authorize the county boards of education

[1] John C. Scarborough.

to appropriate money for county institutes for training teachers; to authorize only two grades of teachers' certificates; to provide for the introduction of industrial subjects into the public schools; to require local school officials to erect a suitable house in each school district; to provide for the selection of a better equipped and more competent body of county examiners; and to prescribe a series of books to be used in the schools.

The recommendations of the state superintendent at the same time were also significant. First of all he urged increased facilities for training teachers by continuing the annual appropriations to the two normal schools already in operation, and by the establishment of other similar schools, for both races, and also by making provision for county teachers' institutes. He also recommended the creation of the office of county superintendent, to take the place of the county examiner; to authorize the appointment of the district school committees by the county boards of education; and to increase the school revenues to a property tax of twenty-five cents on the hundred dollars' valuation and a capitation tax of seventy-five cents. The superintendent believed this amount to be necessary to meet the constitutional requirements. "Our school system is far better than the support it receives in money. Herein lies its chief defect." He also recommended that legislative authority be given for local taxation; that provision be made for improving the swamp lands which were the property of the school fund; that measures be taken looking to securing uniformity in textbooks; that the school laws be codified; and that provision be made for defraying the traveling expenses of the superintendent. At this time his salary was only $1500 a year and no appropriations for traveling expenses or office assistance were allowed.

The year 1881 marked another forward step in public education in North Carolina. The old school system had been in operation since 1872, with a few slight improvements made in 1877. But the schools were poor and the school law defective.

> The school taxes were collected and spent and no adequate return of benefits was made. The schoolhouses were in a state of decay and ruin. The incompetency of the public-school teachers, with few exceptions, was proverbial. The system was a failure and a farce, and the people paid taxes unwillingly for its support.

This was the superintendent's comment on conditions in 1881, when the Legislature met. That body knew the conditions, which were brought to its attention through the messages of the governor, the reports of the state superintendent, and the press of the State; and acting on the knowledge thus gained, it revised and greatly improved the school laws.

The principal legislative improvements made that year were an increase of taxes for school support, provisions for county superintendents, for county teachers' institutes, and for four additional normal schools for each race. The curriculum of the public schools was also prescribed and a standard of examination for public-school teachers fixed for the guidance of the new county officers.

Property taxes for school support were increased from eight and one third to twelve and one half cents on the hundred dollars' valuation, and the capitation taxes were raised from twenty-five to thirty-seven and one half cents. Though this was a substantial increase, it was by no means sufficient to maintain schools for the term required by the constitution. Both the governor and the superintendent continued to urge more liberal support of public schools. Governor Jarvis said in 1883: —

The system may be perfect, the superintendent able, the teachers ready, and the people anxious, but unless the General Assembly supplies the money, it will all be worthless. . . . It is idle to talk of educating 490,000 children on $550,000 a year! The best system of common schools ever devised would be a failure if dependent upon so small an amount of money. So it need not be a matter of wonder that our system has not met public expectation, and that you hear unfavorable comment upon it.

He pointed out that under the constitution it was impossible to raise by taxation enough money to make the school system what it should be. And both he and the superintendent urged an amendment by which the constitutional limitation of taxation should not apply to taxes levied for school support. On account of the low valuation of property adopted throughout the State nearly all the taxes that could be levied were required to support the county and state governments, and only a small amount was left for schools. This lack of funds proved a persistent educational problem in the State for many years.

This improvement in provision for school support, though insufficient, was due in no small measure to the efforts of Governor Jarvis. With him public education was always a subject of supremest importance, and his example of fidelity and labor for its promotion remains as a sacred heritage to the people of the State to-day. He was foremost in the movement to rebuild and restore the fortunes of the State at the close of the war and of Reconstruction. During the six years that he filled the executive office of the State,[1] and indeed throughout the remainder of his life, the "Grand Old Man," as he was affectionately referred to in his later years, worked for "North Carolina — the development of her resources and the education of her children," and with a stimulating earnestness and a profound faith which everywhere lent hope and encouragement. In his inaugural address, when he assumed the duties of governor, he declared this to be his purpose, and his messages and numerous public utterances were filled with the same promise. Addressing the Legislature in January, 1883, he said: —

I have tried to keep that promise. I have visited the schools in the different sections of the State, from the university to the common schools, and have addressed teachers, pupils, and people. If North Carolina does not occupy a higher position in the scale of education in the next census report than she does in the last, it shall be no fault of mine. But after all, the chief responsibility is with the General Assembly.[2]

In the last ten years of his life Governor Jarvis devoted his efforts to the establishment and maintenance of the East Carolina Teachers' Training School, which he fathered with a beautiful affection and with an enthusiastic pride which was actually contagious. It began and continued the primary object of his thought and labor and soon became the concrete realization of unselfish devotion to the noble purpose announced in his address when he was inaugurated as governor many years before. That purpose remained with him through-

[1] As lieutenant-governor he succeeded Governor Vance in March, 1879, when the latter was elected to the United States Senate. And in November, 1880, Governor Jarvis was elected for a term of four years, beginning January 1, 1881.
[2] Leg. Doc., no. 1, Session of 1883, p. 31.

out life. An excerpt from his will is a solemn admonition to the people he loved so jealously: —

Intelligence and virtue mark the standing of any people in the State and Nation, and I would therefore urge the people to press the education of their children far beyond anything heretofore attempted.[1]

The provision for county superintendents was also a decided improvement which the Legislature of 1881 made. They were to be elected by a joint meeting of the county boards of education and the county boards of magistrates, for a term of two years. The compensation of the superintendent was to be three dollars a day "for all days necessarily engaged in the discharge of the duties of his position"; but his salary could not exceed five per cent of the apportionment of the county school fund.[2] The need for more central authority in the county, which this office now furnished, may be seen from the following description which the superintendent declared was

a true picture, in the main, of hundreds of cases in the State, all because there was no one with a wise head charged with the special duty of visiting the people, advising conservative measures and unity of action in the interest of the schools:

About one half of the districts were without houses and with no money to build them. This resulted in continued controversy as to where the school should be taught. A, B, and C of any given district had an unoccupied house that would do. Each urged upon the committee the importance

---

[1] Connor, "Thomas Jordan Jarvis and the Rebuilding of North Carolina," in *Publications of the North Carolina Historical Commission*, Bulletin no. 20.

[2] In 1883 the Legislature reduced the compensation of the county superintendents and somewhat restricted their duties. Superintendent Scarborough regarded the action as unfortunate, and noticed a decrease in the number of institutes held and the number of teachers attending.

of having the school taught in *his* house. The committee was forced to choose between them and selected the house of A; it was the best they could do in their judgment. B and C objected, became enemies of the school, threw obstacles in the way of the teacher, advised their next neighbors against sending to the school, circulated petitions for the division of the district, and presented them to the next meeting of the county board of education and demanded immediate action. Said board, recognizing the right of petition, ordered the division demanded, and the result was that the district, already too small, was divided into two, neither one of which had funds enough to continue a school for a longer term than four weeks with a very ordinary teacher.

The educational administration of the counties tended to improve after the provision was made for county superintendents. Many of the counties were redistricted, the needs of the schools became more vitally felt, and the teachers began to show some improvement under the guidance of new officers. This improvement was made possible by the same law which provided for teachers' institutes in the various counties. Although this provision was permissive, more than 120 institutes were held in 58 counties in 1881 and 1882, in which 2260 white and 650 colored teachers were instructed. Teachers' associations were formed in many counties and became means of educational improvement, and educational journals were beginning to be read also. Perhaps the most noticeable educational improvement, due to the work of the county superintendents, was the increase in expenditures for building schoolhouses. In 1880 the total amount spent for buildings and supplies was less than $19,000; in 1882 it was nearly $90,000. Although the results in some counties were not so favorable as in others, the outlook for the future appeared more hopeful than hitherto.

Another distinctly advance step was taken by the same Legislature when eight additional normal schools were established in 1881, four for white teachers and a like number for colored teachers. Those for the white race were established at Elizabeth City, Wilson, Newton and Franklin, and those for the colored teachers at Newbern, Plymouth, Franklinton, and Salisbury. The Legislature appropriated $500, and the Peabody Board nearly half that amount, for the maintenance of each school. The sessions of the white schools continued for from four to six weeks, and those of the colored schools for as long terms as the funds appropriated would provide, usually from four to eight months. This was allowed because the colored teachers needed, more largely than the white teachers, more instruction in the subject-matter than in methods of teaching. The enrollment in the white schools the first year was 472; in the colored schools it was 295. Attendance on these schools continued to increase each year. The normal schools at the university and at Fayetteville, established in 1877, were also in a thrifty condition and well attended. In 1882 fully 950 white teachers and 370 colored teachers received instruction in the normal schools of the State.

Other significant provisions of the new law allowed the state superintendent $500 for traveling expenses and $600 for clerk hire; authorized the state treasurer to restore to the school fund, from the general fund, the money hitherto expended for the support of normal schools, and defined the grades of teachers' certificates. Provision was made for first, second, and third grade certificates, valid for only one year and in the county where issued. Teachers of the third grade could not

ATTEMPTS AT READJUSTMENT 313

receive a salary of more than $15 a month, those of the second grade not more than $25 a month, and those of the first grade "such sum as may be determined by the committee, subject to the approval of the county board of education." The law required the teachers to attend institutes, but the requirement was not always met. With such improvements in the laws opportunities for corresponding improvements in the school system were now afforded. Considerable impetus was thus given to education, and the work of the Legislature was far-reaching in its good effects.

One sign of educational growth appeared in the establishment of free public graded schools, which were generally meeting reasonable public expectation both in their management and in the work which they were doing. The first of these schools was established in Greensboro in 1875, and two years later one was established in Raleigh. Others were established as follows: Salisbury, 1880; Goldsboro, 1881; Durham, Charlotte, and Wilmington, 1882; and Winston, 1885. These schools were established by local tax levy or by support from the town government, and in most cases they received aid from the Peabody Board also.

For purposes of comparison the following statistics may be noted for 1884:[1]

> Total public school funds $765,032.16
> Total disbursements 535,205.03
>
> Total school population:
> White 314,293
> Colored..................... 189,988

---

[1] Reports from only ninety-two counties. There were ninety-six counties in the State at this time.

Total enrollment:
 White 167,059
 Colored 111,239
Average attendance:
 White 104,291
 Colored....................... 65,403
Public Schools taught:
 White 3,845
 Colored....................... 2,175
Average school terms (in weeks):
 White 11½
 Colored 11¾
Average monthly salaries of teachers:
 White $24.16
 Colored....................... 22.06
Teachers examined and approved during the year:
 White men —
  First grade 1,030
  Second grade 1,059
  Third grade 207

 White Women —
  First Grade 518
  Second Grade................ 530
  Third Grade................. 125
   Total..................... 3,469

 Colored men —
  First grade.................. 315
  Second grade................ 600
  Third grade 585

 Colored women —
  First grade.................. 109
  Second grade 327
  Third grade 295
   Total..................... 2,231

   Grand Total............... 5,700

Between 1885 and 1900 progress in education was decidedly slower than was promised by the legislative enlargement of the school work of the State in 1881. School funds, which had always been insufficient, increased but slowly and school terms were lengthened by only a few days. In 1885 the total expenditures for public schools was about $650,000, and in 1900 only $950,000, though the school population had increased from 530,127 in 1885 to 659,629 in 1900. In 1885 fifty-two per cent of the school population was enrolled; fifteen years later only fifty-eight per cent was enrolled. The school term had increased from about sixty days in 1885 to seventy days in 1900. Teachers' salaries showed no improvement. In 1885 the average monthly salary paid white teachers was about $25, and negro teachers received about $23. In 1900 the salaries of white teachers was practically the same as in 1885 and negro teachers received slightly less than in that year. Many of the teachers were reported poorly prepared, in spite of generous legislative provisions for normal schools and county teachers' institutes. In 1888 the superintendent said: "Many of our teachers are themselves schoolboys and schoolgirls, without sufficient knowledge in books, and especially without sufficient training in school government and management." In the same year a large number of the schoolhouses of the State were reported "unfit for use, being uncomfortable and unsafe to the health of the children."

The needs of the schools during these years were numerous. More money for longer school terms, better salaries, and improved school equipment was perhaps the most urgent need. From 1872 to 1881 the property tax for school support had been eight and one third cents on the hundred dollars' valuation, and the capitation tax thirty-seven and one half cents. In 1891 these taxes were raised to fifteen cents and forty-five cents, respectively. The regular *ad-valorem* taxes provided by the revenue law for school support showed a very slight increase during these years. But the superintendent in 1890 declared it "simply idle to expect satisfactory schools with an average annual term of sixty days, and with an expenditure of money amounting to ... only one dollar and twenty-two cents on each of the school population." The average school term in the South at that time was 101 days, and in the United States it was 135 days. The revenue available was insufficient to maintain schools for the term required by the constitution, and decisions of the supreme court made it difficult to secure more money for educational purposes.

We saw in Chapter XII that a decision of the supreme court in 1870 had a retarding influence on education in the State, by holding that schools were not a necessary expense. The defective character of the constitution and of the school laws of 1868 and 1869 was also noted; they contained defects which the Reform Legislature of 1871 failed to correct. Under the constitution [1] it was the duty of the county commissioners to levy a tax sufficient to maintain the schools for four months in each year, but in discharging this duty they were not allowed to disregard the limitation imposed by another section of the constitution as to the amount of tax to be levied. However, by the act of 1885,[2] the commissioners were allowed to exceed this limit.

In 1885, obeying the constitution and the statute, the commissioners of Sampson County levied a special tax

[1] Art. IX, sec. 3.   [2] Laws of 1885, chap. 174, sec. 23.

for supporting a four months' school. The commissioners were enjoined, and at the October, 1885 term of the superior court of the county there was a judgment for the plaintiffs, the court ruling that the tax levied under the act of 1885 overstepped the limits of the taxing power conferred and was not warranted by the constitution, and could not, therefore, be enforced. The defendants appealed and the supreme court affirmed the decision of the lower court, holding that the act of 1885 was unconstitutional and did not come within the provisions of the constitution which authorized a special tax for a special purpose with the approval of the General Assembly.[1]

Before 1885 the general attitude on the subject of local taxation for educational purposes had been more or less indifferent, though the influence of appropriations from the Peabody Board was rapidly improving that sentiment in many sections. The result was a slow but gradual increase in the establishment of graded schools by local taxation. That sentiment was spreading and proving of wholesome influence when the supreme court again appeared as an obstacle to educational progress by holding that the constitutional limitation of taxation could not be exceeded except for necessary expenses, and a four months' school term was not considered a necessary expense. However, the same court held that taxes for public streets, lights, and water works were necessary expenses for which a special tax could be levied in excess of the constitutional limitation. Therefore, the decision in the case cited above made it impossible to keep schools open for more than two or

[1] Barksdale *et al. vs.* Commissioners of Sampson County, 93 N.C. 472.

three months in the year. Several counties had already levied special taxes in order to maintain schools for the term required by the constitution, but they were now forced to abandon this plan of school support, and the development of local tax sentiment was thus retarded.[1]

Other decisions of the supreme court had an unwholesome effect during these years. By act of March 11, 1883, provision had been made for local assessment for school purposes.[2] Acting under the provisions of this act the commissioners of Gaston County ordered an election in one of the school districts for white children on the question of an additional tax of twenty cents on the property of white *owners* and an additional tax of sixty cents upon every taxable white poll, for furnishing increased public-school advantages to the white children of the district. Only white electors were allowed to vote. The election was carried, and officers proceeded to collect the assessment. Action was instituted perpetually to enjoin the commissioners from levying and collecting the taxes, but the restraining order was refused and the plaintiffs appealed. The supreme court found error and reversed the decision, holding the act of 1883 unconstitutional both because it did not provide for uniform and equal taxation on all property and because it made a race discrimination as to the application of the funds. The constitution required all taxes for whatever purposes to be uniform and allowed no discrimination in favor of any class, person, or interest, but required all property to be taxed equally and by uniform rule. Therefore, the court argued, a law which

[1] The decision of the court in 1885 held until 1907, when it was reversed. See 145 N.C. 170.
[2] Laws of 1883, chap. 148.

permitted a tax on the property and polls of one color to be applied exclusively to the education of children of that color was unconstitutional. The law was also considered discriminative and in conflict with the constitution which said: "There shall be no discrimination in favor of or to the prejudice of either race." However, Justice Merrimon, who did not concur in so much of the opinion of the court as declared the law of 1883 inoperative and unconstitutional, held that statute to authorize a local tax and not to prescribe a public tax within the meaning of the constitution.

In still another case the supreme court held that legislation which directed the tax raised from the polls and property of white persons to be devoted to sustaining schools for the children of the white persons, and that raised from the polls and property of colored persons to be used for supporting their schools, was unconstitutional. There were several graded schools in the State which were affected by this decision, because by provisions of the special acts under which they operated money derived by taxation from white persons was applied exclusively to white schools and that from colored persons to colored schools. Some of these schools were forced to discontinue, or to depend for support on private donations, while awaiting favorable legislative relief.[1]

More active and competent county supervision was also a serious need of the school system. Various changes were made in the law providing for county superintendents after its original enactment in 1881, but improvement in this part of the school system was slow. In 1883 the duties of the office were restricted and its pos-

[1] Rigsbee *vs.* the Town of Durham, 94 N.C. 800.

sibilities somewhat crippled. In 1895 the office was abolished and its duties placed in the hands of the clerk of the board of county commissioners. The same act [1] abolished the county board of education and the duties of that body were turned over to the county commissioners. In the same year provision was made for county examiners, but two years later that office was abolished and provision made for a county board of education and a county supervisor of schools with duties practically the same as those previously prescribed for county superintendents. Two years later the Legislature provided for the election of a county superintendent, who was required to be "a practical teacher" and to have had at the time of election at least two years' experience in teaching or in public-school work. He was to be paid a *per diem* for the number of days actually at work, provided the number did not exceed in any year the average length of the school term plus fifty per cent thereof. The average salary of the ninety-six county superintendents in 1890 was only $175, and in some counties it was only $50 or $60. As late as 1899 Wake County was paying its superintendent only $128, after deducting the small fees collected for private examinations. The counties of Durham, Mecklenburg, and Buncombe were paying slightly more than this, however. No man capable of becoming an efficient superintendent could afford to give much of his time for the small compensation which he received and from which he was forced to pay his expenses. Most of the superintendents had other occupations, and their educational labors consisted mainly of holding examinations for teachers and an occasional teachers'

[1] Laws of 1895, chap. 439.

institute. Their work as county superintendents was, until recent years, too often a secondary matter. In some cases the county board of education would not allow the superintendents to visit the schools because of the expense of such service.

Provision for normal instruction was gradually enlarging, though many of the teachers continued poorly prepared and inefficient. In addition to the normal schools established in 1877, four additional schools for each race were established by act of 1881. From that year until 1885 the sum of $4000 was annually appropriated to train the teachers of each race. In 1885 the normal school established at Chapel Hill in 1877 was discontinued and the appropriation used for similar work in schools established at Asheville, Boone, Washington, and Winston; but the sum of $4000 continued to be appropriated annually for the normal instruction of white teachers until 1889.[1]

About this time two young teachers, Charles D. McIver and Edwin A. Alderman, names which were soon to become closely identified with progressive educational policies, not only in their own State but in the entire South, began to attract wide attention by their interest and zeal in behalf of universal education. They appeared before the Legislature and pleaded for more efficient educational facilities for the youth of the State. Their earnestness attracted legislative attention. The numerous normal schools for white teachers were abolished [2] and McIver and Alderman were selected as

[1] In 1893 the Legislature appropriated $1500 to establish a normal department in connection with the Cullowhee High School, in Jackson County, and this or greater aid has been annually continued.

[2] Laws of 1889, chap. 200.

state institute conductors, to canvass the State, hold educational meetings, conduct teachers' institutes, and enlist the interest of the public on the subject of more and better education for all the children of both races. For two years they went up and down the State teaching teachers, organizing educational associations, holding mass meetings, and preaching the gospel of universal education, free and open alike to all classes. The influence of this work literally converted the Farmers' Alliance, which at that time was recognized as an organization of power and influence in the State. The Legislature of 1891 was in large measure controlled by this organization and showed some liberality toward public education. At this session the State Normal and Industrial College for the training of white teachers was established and the Agricultural and Mechanical College for negroes was also created.

Meantime, however, it appeared impossible to hold an annual institute in every county in the State, on the fund appropriated by the Legislature, and the Peabody Board, through its efficient agent, Dr. J. L. M. Curry, appropriated funds sufficient to employ several other institute conductors for the summer months. From July, 1889, to October, 1890, more than 135 institutes were held in the State, attended by 5775 teachers. In addition to these, 7 institutes for white and 21 for colored teachers were held under an act of 1881 which gave permission for county institutes.

Facilities for the normal instruction of the negro teachers of the State were also increasing, and from 1887 to 1895 the annual appropriations for that race were $8500. From 1895 to 1897 the appropriations for the same purpose were $10,500 annually. In 1897 the sum of $14,500 was appropriated for the professional preparation of the negro teachers of the State, and this continued to be appropriated annually for several years.

During these years there was a serious, steady growth of sentiment in favor of public education, and local taxation for schools of both races was gradually developing. By 1891 graded schools had been established in sixteen towns in the State and the city-school idea was growing in popularity. In 1887 Reidsville and Asheville voted local tax and established graded systems, and in 1891 similar schools were established in Concord, Statesville, Shelby, Tarboro, Wilson, and Murphy.[1]

This gradual development of wholesome educational sentiment was threatened with serious arrest in 1893, however. The financial stringency of that year forced the Farmers' Alliance into politics and created three political parties of unequal strength. In 1894 the negro held the balance of power and the Populists and Republicans, by fusing their interests, succeeded in controlling the Legislature. Two years later, by the same methods and a negro vote more than 120,000 strong, they got complete control of the state government as well as of many counties. The Legislature of 1895 resembled the lawmaking bodies of Reconstruction days.

By "an act to restore to the people of North Carolina local self-government," the system of county govern-

[1] High Point and Washington established graded schools in 1897, and two years later similar schools were established in Newbern, Waynesville, Selma, Kinston, Albemarle, Mount Airy, Gastonia, Marion, and Cherryville. By 1899 graded schools had been established in twenty-seven towns in North Carolina, and were being supported largely by local taxation or by aid from the town governments.

ment in use in the State at that time was completely overturned.

Whether so intended or not, the new system turned over to negro rule the chief city of the State, several important towns, and many of the eastern counties. Then the country saw repeated the scenes which have made the memory of Reconstruction a nightmare to the people of the South. Negro politicians, often illiterate, always ignorant, generally corrupt, presided over the inferior courts, dominated county school boards and district school committees, and served as county commissioners and city councilmen. They were found on the police force of the State's chief city, they were made city attorneys, and they were numbered among county coroners, deputy sheriffs, and registers of deeds. Lawlessness, violence, and corruption followed. In some of the counties the situation became unbearable, while in such towns as Wilmington, Newbern, and Greenville neither life nor property nor woman's honor was secure.[1]

More firearms were sold in the State in a year or two than had been sold for twenty years preceding. Rumors of race riots inflamed the passions of the people, property was burned, and men went armed day and night. The serious situation culminated in the disastrous riots of Wilmington in 1898, when the mayor and negro officers were driven from the city and the white men took possession by force. These alarming conditions threatened destruction to the school system and forced the thoughtful people of the State to seek a safe solution for one of the most difficult problems in its educational history. Until now the principle of special local taxation was slowly but gradually growing in public favor, but the bitter political experiences of those years caused a dangerous reaction, and educational sentiment cooled.

[1] Connor and Poe, *The Life and Speeches of Charles B. Aycock*, chap. v.

In one instance the local tax was voted out and the victory celebrated with bonfires and bands.

Notwithstanding the unfavorable conditions in the State the Legislature of 1897 passed one of the most advanced educational laws yet enacted, but it was short-lived and proved ineffective. The act [1] was intended to encourage local taxation for public schools, and provided for an election to be held on the question in every school district. In every district which failed to vote the tax in 1897 the county commissioners were required to order an election every two years until the tax was properly voted. The law further provided that every district voting the special tax should receive from the state board of education, annually for three years, a sum equal to the special school tax collected in the district each year, provided, however, that no district should receive from the state board more than $500 a year.

The elections were held in August, 1897, at a cost of more than $12,000, and eleven townships voted for the tax and raised the sum of $2260.07, which was duplicated by the State. The law also provided that, in case an amount should be raised by voluntary subscription or donation, an equal amount thus raised should be duplicated by the state board, and sixty-three communities raised in this manner $8596.63, which was likewise duplicated. These results were far from satisfactory and were indicative of gross indifference, and the act was repealed by the Legislature of 1899. The same Legislature, however, appropriated $100,000 to be apportioned to the counties on the basis of their school population — legislative liberality which gave renewed hope and encouragement to the friends of education.[2]

[1] Laws of 1897, chap. 421.   [2] Laws of 1899, chap. 637.

The trying days just described brought into prominence Charles B. Aycock, a brilliant young lawyer of Goldsboro, who caught the public ear at a time when real educational leadership was sorely needed, and he became the spokesman of North Carolina. He advocated a constitutional amendment which would deprive the negro of suffrage until by education and training he could be fitted for intelligent citizenship. Immediately the advocates of better educational facilities rallied to his support because he pleaded so earnestly for universal education for all classes and races. The entire State responded, and in 1900 Aycock was nominated for governor by acclamation on a platform which he had made popular by his earnestness and eloquence two years before. Sixty-six of the ninety-seven counties in the State gave majorities for the amendment to the constitution, which eliminated the ignorant negro from politics, and Aycock was elected governor by the largest majority ever given a man for that office in North Carolina. This bitterest political contest which the State had ever witnessed was momentous for popular education.

The two races had been arrayed in fearful antagonism and the elemental passions of both had been deeply stirred. The fires of race prejudice and bitterness still smouldered in the hearts of thousands and but the slightest breath was necessary to fan them into a conflagration of fearful consequences. It was a situation which required a leader with a cool head, a clear vision, and a judicious temperament. He must have an abundance of patience, wisdom, and charity. He must be a courageous man. It was no time for a time-server. He who would allay the apprehensions of the negroes and check the passions of the whites must be a statesman.[1]

---

[1] Connor and Poe, *op. cit.*, p. 90.

Happily for the cause of the public schools North Carolina now had such a leader in its new governor. There was, indeed, a great sociological problem yet to be solved, but faith, courage, and untiring industry promised success in its solution. A new and more hopeful day began to dawn for a State and a citizenship which had too long known the burden of a bitter wrong. The educational uplift of all classes of both races, and the public schools soon came to be regarded too sacred for any party to touch with unholy hands. This condition was made possible through the wise statesmanship of North Carolina's "educational governor."

REFERENCES

Journals of the House and Senate; Public Laws of North Carolina; *Reports* of the Superintendent of Public Instruction, 1876–1900; Boyd, "Some Phases of Educational History in the South since 1865," in *Studies in Southern History and Politics; Proceedings* of the Peabody Board Trustees; *Report* of the United States Commissioner of Education, 1904, vol. 1; Connor, "Thomas Jordan Jarvis and the Rebuilding of North Carolina," in *Publications of the North Carolina Historical Commission*, Bulletin no. 20; Connor and Poe, *The Life and Speeches of Charles B. Aycock.*

SUGGESTIONS FOR FURTHER STUDY

1. What political changes took place in the United States in 1876?
2. How did those changes affect educational conditions in the South?
3. What legislative changes affecting education were made about this time?
4. Why was the educational problem in the South such a difficult one after the war?
5. How did educational interest express itself after 1877?

6. Account for the slow educational progress in North Carolina between 1877 and 1900. What improvements were made during these years?
7. Why were facilities for normal instruction not provided before 1877? How does the experience of North Carolina in this respect compare with the experience of other Southern States?
8. What were the educational services of Thomas J. Jarvis?
9. Name the superintendents of public instruction in North Carolina since 1868 and discuss their educational services.
10. Account for the conditions between 1895 and 1900. What were some of the needs of the schools during these years?
11. How did the interpretations and decisions of the courts affect education in the State before 1900?
12. What was the actual condition of public education in your county in 1900?
13. What is the history of city or town high schools in your county?

CHAPTER XV
AYCOCK AND THE REVIVAL (1900–1910)

On a hundred platforms, to half the voters of the State, in the late campaign, I pledged the State, its strength, its heart, its wealth, to universal education. I promised the illiterate poor man, bound to a life of toil and struggle and poverty, that life should be brighter for his boy and girl than it had been for him and the partner of his sorrows and joys. I pledged the wealth of the State to the education of his children. Men of wealth, representatives of great corporations, applauded eagerly my declaration. I then realized that the strong desire which dominated me for the uplifting of the whole people moved not only my heart, but was likewise the hope and aspiration of those upon whom Fortune had smiled. . . . We are prospering as never before — our wealth increases, our industries multiply, our commerce extends, and among the owners of this wealth, this multiplying industry, this extending commerce, I have found no man who is unwilling to make the State stronger and better by liberal aid to the cause of education. Gentlemen of the Legislature, you will not have aught to fear when you make ample provision for the education of the whole people. . . . For my part I declare to you that it shall be my constant aim and effort, during the four years that I shall endeavor to serve the people of this State, to redeem this most solemn of all our pledges.

Thus spoke Charles B. Aycock when he was inaugurated governor of North Carolina in January, 1901. The platforms of all the political parties had declared in favor of a liberal policy toward popular education, and the platform of the Democratic Party in 1900 said: —

We heartily commend the action of the General Assembly of 1899 for appropriating one hundred thousand dollars for the benefit of the public schools of the State, and pledge ourselves to increase the school fund, so as to make at least a four months' term in every year in every school district in the State.

In the campaign conducted throughout the State with so much earnestness that platform was made the basis of all promises made to the people. And through the leadership of Aycock those promises were destined soon to be completely redeemed.

Until this time, as we have seen, there was much indifference on the subject of public education: —

Only thirty districts in the State, all urban, considered education of sufficient importance to levy a local tax for the support of schools. The average salary paid to county superintendents annually was less than one dollar a day, to public-school teachers, $91.25 for the term. This meant, of course, that the office of county superintendent was either a "political job," usually given to some struggling young attorney for local party service, or a public charity used to help support the growing family of some needy but deserving preacher; and, further, that there were no professional teachers in the public schools. Practically no interest was manifested in the building or equipment of schoolhouses. The children of more than 950 public school districts were altogether without schoolhouses, while those in 1132 districts sat on rough pine boards in log houses chinked with clay. Perhaps under all these circumstances it was well enough that the schools were kept open only seventy-three days in the year, and that less than one third of the children of school age attended them. . . . To complicate a situation already sufficiently difficult, the race issue injected its poison into the very vitals of the problem.[1]

Soon after taking the oath of office Governor Aycock and State Superintendent of Public Instruction Thomas F. Toon began a canvass of the entire State in behalf of its educational interests. It was known that if the people were to be convinced of the necessity for better

[1] Connor and Poe, *The Life and Speeches of Charles B. Aycock*, pp. 114, 115.

educational facilities, the question must be discussed with them. But there were serious obstacles in the way of a complete canvass of the State. North Carolina was large, had no centers of population, and eighty per cent of its people were engaged in agricultural pursuits, and were therefore widely scattered. Only a small part of the people could be reached except through a general campaign for which there were then no resources at hand. This problem was soon solved, however, through the liberality of the Southern Education Board, an organization composed of educational statesmen and philanthropists for the promotion of education in the Southern States. This organization offered $4000 annually for financing such an educational campaign as Aycock and the other friends of education believed to be necessary to bring relief to the poor school conditions of the State.

At the suggestion of Dr. Charles D. McIver, chairman of the campaign committee of the Southern Education Board, a convention was called to meet in Raleigh February 13, 1902. Invitations were sent to forty-three educational workers in the State, representing all the institutions of higher education, the normal schools, and county and city-school systems. Governor Aycock presided over the conference, which met in his office for the purpose of organizing a thoroughgoing educational campaign and of uniting all the educational forces of the State.

There was but one man in the State who could have brought together all these warring factions and accomplished this purpose. Him all, whatever their previous differences may have been, were willing to follow.[1]

---
[1] Connor and Poe, *op. cit.*, p. 119.

With this conference a new era in North Carolina's educational history began. "A Declaration against Illiteracy," in the form of an address to the people of the State, was adopted. The address gave a plain statement of educational conditions and urged all patriotic citizens to aid in promoting

> free public schools, open to all, supported by the taxes of all its citizens, where every child, regardless of condition in life, or circumstances of fortunes, may receive that opportunity for training into social service which the constitution of this and other great States and the age demand.
>
> We realize [continued the declaration] that our State has reached the constitutional limit of taxation for the rural schools, that she has made extra appropriations to lengthen the term of these schools to eighty days in the year. We realize, too, that the four months' term now provided is inadequate for the reason that more than 20,000,000 children of school age in the United States outside of North Carolina are now provided an average of 145 days of school out of every 365; that the teachers of these children are paid an average salary of $48 a month, while the teachers of the children of North Carolina are paid hardly $25 a month, thus securing for all the children of our sister States more efficient training for the duties of life. And we realize that, according to the latest census report and the report of the United States Commissioner of Education, for every man, woman, and child of its population, the country at large is spending $2.83 for the education of its children, while North Carolina is spending barely 67 cents; that the country at large is spending an average of $20.29 for every pupil enrolled in its public schools, while North Carolina is spending only $3 or $4, the smallest amount expended by any State in the Union. And still further do we realize that the average amount spent for the education of every child of school age in the United States is approximately $9.50, while North Carolina is spending $1.78.
>
> The facts should arouse our pride and our patriotism, and lead us to inquire whether the future will not hold this generation responsible for the perpetuation of conditions that have

resulted in the multiplicity of small school districts, inferior schoolhouses, poorly paid teachers, and necessarily poor teaching; in twenty white illiterates out of every one hundred white population over ten years of age; in generally poor and poorly paid supervision of the expenditure of our meager school funds and of the teaching done in our schools; and, finally, in that educational indifference which is the chief cause of the small average daily attendance of about fifty pupils out of every hundred enrolled in our public schools.

The plan of the campaign was outlined and "The Central Campaign Committee for the Promotion of Public Education in North Carolina" was created. The work of the committee, which was composed of Governor Aycock, Superintendent Toon, and Dr. McIver, was to plan systematic campaigns for local taxation, for the consolidation of school districts, for building and equipping better schoolhouses, and for longer school terms and larger salaries for teachers. Provision was also made for committees to collect, write, and distribute to every newspaper in the State weekly articles bearing on the matter of better schools, and to write to every minister in the State requesting him to preach a sermon on public education at least once a year. A few days later [1] Superintendent Toon died of an illness contracted while canvassing the State in behalf of improved educational facilities, and James Y. Joyner, Professor of English in the State Normal and Industrial College, was appointed as his successor. Dr. Joyner was eminently qualified by nature and training to direct the public-school system of the State, and its growth since 1902 has in great part been due to his wise leadership.

The following June the Central Committee opened headquarters in the state superintendent's office, and

February 19, 1902.

Superintendent Eugene C. Brooks, of the Monroe City Schools, was appointed executive secretary to conduct the campaign. Though a young man, Mr. Brooks was rapidly becoming recognized as a wise and progressive school man, and to his new work he brought rare industry, resourcefulness, sound judgment, and earnestness which were soon to place him in the foremost ranks of educational leadership in North Carolina. The campaign which was to lift the State from its low educational position was thus launched. Through the leadership and under the inspiration of Aycock, Joyner, McIver, and Brooks a genuine educational revival began which has continued even to the present. Men of every profession and business, of every political faith and religious belief, gladly volunteered their services in one of the most inspiring and effective educational campaigns ever witnessed in any State.

In open-air meetings, in courthouses, in churches, in schoolhouses, wherever the people could assemble, they gathered to hear the most effective orators and debaters in the State discuss educational problems and policies. For the first time in the history of North Carolina politics yielded first place in public interest to education.[1]

The first rally was held at Wentworth, in Rockingham County, with Thomas J. Jarvis and Dr. Charles D. McIver as speakers. More than one hundred school committeemen and every teacher in the county, besides hundreds of other citizens, were present. A press dispatch, after describing the interest manifested by the audience, said of the address of ex-Governor Jarvis: —

For two hours this most gifted and honored of all North Carolina's most illustrious sons held the large audience spell-

---

[1] Connor and Poe, *op. cit.*, p. 122.

bound. At times his plea was pathetic and few could resist it; at times his flight of eloquence was soul-stirring as he warmed to his subject and pleaded for the education of the children of the State: Few of those who heard him will ever forget this closing thought: that he was an old man, that his face was turned toward the setting sun, that never again would he solicit suffrage of the State for himself, that in all probability he would never again address a Rockingham audience, that he loved the State above the power of expression, that it had honored him more than he deserved, that he wanted his audience to know that his parting injunction was to keep the churches and schoolhouses open. Do this, and the future will be glorious; neglect it, and we go back to barbarism.

In the afternoon Dr. McIver spoke on local taxation and the consolidation of districts, in a practical, strong, and convincing manner. This first rally of the campaign was typical of scores of others held during the summer of 1902.

In March of the following year plans were made for another summer's work similar to but more extensive than the first. By June, seventy-eight of the ninety-seven counties of the State had planned educational rallies in connection with the township meetings which were legally required of the school officers. This almost universal response greatly impressed the people of the State. The press, already strong for educational progress, now became stronger and more earnest in its behalf. Public men of every calling again offered their services, many refusing to accept their traveling expenses. Superior court judges instructed grand juries to report on the condition of school-buildings. Never before had interest in public education in North Carolina so reflected itself. By the close of the campaign in the fall, when many of the teachers and college men who had been engaged in it were called back to their work, more than 350 rallies had been held in addition to the regular township meetings conducted by the county superintendents. Seventy-eight counties had been reached, local tax districts had increased from 56 to 181, more than 300 districts had been abolished by consolidation, and 676 new schoolhouses had been built.

The campaign was carried on without cessation by bulletins, through the press of the State, and by public speakers. The state officers used all the time they could spare from their duties for field work in behalf of the cause which had grown so strong in popular favor. There was a universal quickening of the public mind — the question of education for all the people seemed to revive everywhere. The Southern Education Board continued its generous aid of the campaign work and other agencies lent support to the great movement. "The Woman's Association for the Betterment of Public Schoolhouses and Grounds," an organization formed at the State Normal and Industrial College in 1902, after Dr. McIver had called the attention of the women of the State to the conditions of the schoolhouses, rendered especially valuable service in cultivating a wholesome public sentiment toward their improvement.

These public campaigns between 1902 and 1904 stimulated an even more powerful though quieter campaign which has continued uninterrupted. Said Superintendent Joyner in December, 1904: —

I weigh my words when I declare it to be my deliberate conviction that the great masses of the people in North Carolina are interested as never before in this question of the education of their children, that they are talking about it among themselves more than ever before, and that a deep-seated conviction and a quiet determination that their children shall be educated are finding surer lodgment in the minds and hearts

AYCOCK AND THE REVIVAL

of the people than ever before. This is, to my mind, one of the most significant evidences of progress. Mighty revolutions are always noiseless and must be wrought first in the minds and hearts and wills of the masses. I believe that such a revolution upon this question of the education of all the people is well under way in North Carolina.

A growth in sentiment for public education and in confidence in the public schools was everywhere noticeable. Moreover, there was a marked increase during the first decade of the century in the enrollment in the institutions of higher education and in the private schools and academies of the State.

Legislative action during this period is another evidence of the revival that was taking place in education in the State when many forward educational steps were taken. The annual legislative appropriations, which were first made in 1899, when $100,000 was distributed to the counties of the State in order to lengthen the school term, have been liberally continued. From 1901 to 1908 these sums amounted to $200,000 annually. Since that time they have gradually increased until they now amount to $250,000 annually. Since 1901 the Legislature has also made liberal provision for establishing rural libraries, and there are now nearly 4000 such libraries in the State. More than half the districts, both white and colored, are now provided with them, and they are constantly being established in others. During the biennial period closing June 30, 1914, more than 500 new and 347 supplemental libraries were established, at a cost of more than $20,000, and containing an average of nearly one hundred volumes of well-selected books.[1]

[1] Statistics given in this chapter are of the biennial period closing June 30, 1914, unless otherwise stated.

In 1901 the Legislature set apart one day in each year, to be known as "North Carolina Day," for the consideration of the history of the State by the public schools. Through the aid of members of the State Literary and Historical Association and other patriotic citizens of the State, the department of education has been able to prepare and issue in attractive pamphlet form interesting programs dealing with the history of North Carolina. The articles thus prepared and distributed have dealt with the past history of various sections of the State, the lives of noteworthy leaders, the present resources of the State, and other subjects which tend to awaken in the present generation an interest and pride in the history of North Carolina, and to inspire confidence in its future. The annual celebrating of "North Carolina Day," when children, patrons, teachers, and school officers gather at the schoolhouse, has helped to stimulate a literary and historical spirit among the people of the State.

The reorganization of the old literary fund in 1903, when $200,000 was set aside as a permanent fund to be known as the "State Literary Fund," and to be used as a loan fund for building and improving schoolhouses, was another forward legislative step. The fund has gradually grown and has been the means of greatly improving the physical equipment of more than one fifth of the schools in the State. Since its establishment sums amounting in the aggregate to more than one million dollars have been lent to communities in practically every county for the purpose of building new or improving old schoolhouses. Seventy-nine counties were aided by the fund during the biennial period closing June 30, 1914; and the total value of houses built or improved by this aid during that time was nearly $800,000.[1]

Legislative attention to the state department of education has also been a significant means of increasing the efficiency of public education in North Carolina. Until 1903 the superintendency of public education in North Carolina was little more than a poorly paid clerkship, and had been so since the early seventies. This unfortunate condition was produced by the reaction to fraud and extravagance practiced in the name of education during the Reconstruction period. But in 1903 the salary of the superintendent was increased and appropriations were made to make his department equal in dignity and equipment to the other departments of the state government. Unlimited authority was given the superintendent to issue at public expense bulletins on educational topics, such as local taxation, consolidation of districts, improvement of schoolhouses, and like subjects. These bulletins have been distributed in large quantities and sent into every district in the State, and have rendered incalculable educational service.

In 1905 the State Association of County Superintendents was legalized and the counties required to pay the expenses of the superintendents while in attendance. The school term was equalized throughout the several counties and state aid was withdrawn from any counties which were careless in levying the authorized school taxes. The state board of education was empowered to consolidate into five the seven normal schools for negro teachers, and Mr. Charles L. Coon, one of the foremost school men of the State, was engaged to superintend their work.

[1] See chap. VII.

During the period under discussion the Appalachian Training School was established at Boone, and the East Carolina Teachers' Training School at Greenville, and liberal legislative appropriations were made for their maintenance. Improvement was also made in provisions for institutes, and other means of training public-school teachers while in service. Improvement has likewise been made in the compulsory-school law and in child-labor legislation, though there is at both of these points room for more improvement. In 1907 the Legislature authorized the establishment of rural high schools and appropriated $45,000 annually for their maintenance. This appropriation was increased to $50,000 in 1909 and to $75,000 annually two years later. The development of rural secondary education in North Carolina since that time has been rapid. Between 1907 and 1911 more than two hundred rural high schools were established in ninety-three counties, supported by local taxation, state appropriation, county apportionment, and private donations. Many of these schools had a four-year course.

Progress in rural elementary education for the decade from 1901 to 1910 was also conspicuous. During that time the annual expenditures for this part of the school system increased from $1,018,000 to more than $2,126,000; the average term was increased nearly a school month; the value of rural school property was increased from $1,146,000 to $3,094,000; more than 3450 new schoolhouses were built between 1902 and 1910, an average of more than one a day for every day in the year; expenditures for teachers' salaries doubled; enrollment increased 22 per cent, and the average daily attendance 41 per cent. The expenditures for the salaries of county superintendents increased from $23,000 to

$78,000, and the average annual salary paid these officers increased from $243 to $796. The number of special local tax districts increased from 18 to 1167; rural teachers increased from 7971 to 9440, and rural libraries increased from 472 to 2272. These libraries contained 265,000 volumes costing nearly $100,000. The number of schools having more than one teacher also annually increased. There was likewise noticeable progress in school equipment; in 1910 more than 2000 schoolhouses were equipped with modern furniture.

Through the generosity of the Peabody Board and the Southern Education Board, there was added to the state department of education a supervisor of rural elementary schools, who gave his entire time to assisting teachers, county superintendents, and local officers in further improvement of the country schools. A supervisor of teacher-training was also added to the department, to give directions to county institutes, county teachers' associations, and teachers' reading-circles. In this way the professional training of teachers while in service was greatly improved. There was also a marked improvement in the efficiency of the normal schools, and corresponding progress in high-school work, both city and rural, during these years. The number of towns and cities establishing schools between 1901 and 1910 increased from 42 to 118; and city school property in 1910 was double the value of the total school property of the State ten years before.

During the decade here considered illiteracy was greatly reduced. The percentage of illiteracy among the white population above ten years of age was reduced from 19.4 to 12.3, and among the negroes from 47.6 to 31.9. Among both races it was decreased from 28.7 to

18.5. Other Southern States showed a greater reduction of illiteracy among the negroes during these years, but no State in the Union surpassed North Carolina in the reduction of white illiteracy.[1]

This great change in concrete educational results and, what is even more important, in public sentiment for improved educational conditions, was due in large measure to the momentum given the cause by Aycock and his devoted and tireless co-laborers, Joyner, McIver, and Brooks. Aycock's modesty would not allow him to lay claim to his just share of the credit of the marvelous educational awakening which the State experienced during the early years of the present century. But it must be remembered that while the revival was gaining force "he was the leader of the State which was itself the leader of the South." This leadership gave him a wide reputation, and his services as an educational campaigner were sought from "Maine to Alabama, from North Carolina to Oklahoma." He made a tour of Maine in 1904, on the invitation of the superintendent of public instruction of that State; and he was delivering his famous speech on "Universal Education" to a large and enthusiastic audience in Birmingham, Alabama, April 4, 1914, when he fell dead.

Aycock's philosophy of education was simple: he believed in "educating everybody and educating everything." This creed made him the negro's best and most active educational advocate, although he labored to disfranchise the black man until the latter could qualify for intelligent participation in political affairs. A conspicuous illustration of his sense of right and justice on the question of negro education was his firm stand

[1] Connor and Poe, *op. cit.*, p. 138.

against, and final defeat of, a movement to amend the constitution so as to make provision for distributing school taxes to each race in proportion to the amounts paid by each. He regarded such an amendment both unjust and dangerous and a gross violation of his solemn pledge that all the people of both races should be given improved educational facilities. Like another great apostle of democracy and education, Aycock had great faith in the mass of the people; and like Jefferson he believed that they meant well and would act well whenever they understood. His labor in their behalf will continue an inspiration and a blessing to the future generations of the State for whose advancement he gave such noble and unstinted service.

REFERENCES

Public Laws of North Carolina, 1899 to 1911; *Biennial Reports* of the State Superintendent of Public Instruction, 1898 to 1912; *Annual Reports* of the United States Commissioner of Education, 1898–1912; *North Carolina Education* (E. C. Brooks, editor), vols. i to x; Connor and Poe, *The Life and Speeches of Charles B. Aycock;* Brooks, "The Development of Public Education in North Carolina" (unpublished manuscript); Murphy, *The Present South;* Boyd, "Some Phases of Educational History in the South since 1865," in *Studies in Southern History and Politics.*

SUGGESTIONS FOR FURTHER STUDY

1. Compare educational conditions in North Carolina in 1860 and in 1900.
2. What were the obstacles in the way of educational improvement in the State in 1900?
3. In what way was Aycock the leader in the revival between 1900 and 1904?
4. What other forces were at work during those years? How did the movement continue?
5. Account for educational indifference in the State at that time.
6. What educational progress did the State make between 1900 and 1910?
7. What improvements were made in your county during that decade?
8. Compare this period with the period under Wiley's leadership before the war.
9. Read Aycock's speech on "Universal Education" and note the educational philosophy which it contains.

CHAPTER XVI

THE PRESENT SYSTEM: ITS TASKS AND TENDENCIES

THE momentum given educational development in North Carolina through the campaigns described in the preceding chapter has continued uninterrupted. The questions of local taxation, the consolidation of schools, and of improvement in teachers, continue to be agitated through bulletins issued by the state department of education, through the press, and through numerous other effective means. Much of the state superintendent's time, as well as the time of members of his staff, is given to field work and to educational campaign work throughout the State. And in many counties enthusiastic and energetic county superintendents carry on continuously active and effective campaigns for school improvement. Their work, which is also assisted by the more enterprising and devoted teachers and public-spirited citizens, is promoted by public addresses, community meetings, circular letters, bulletins, and by numerous other means; and, to quote Superintendent Joyner, "the most effective part of this campaign is that carried on from year's end to year's end, without blare of trumpets, in the county, under the direction of efficient county superintendents of common sense and consecration." Indeed, the county is now the strategic point in the State's educational system.

Present educational growth appears in improved legislative action, in an increase in available funds and expenditures for public-school support, in an increase of public-school property, of local tax districts and funds raised by local taxation, and an increase in the school term and in attendance. There has also been considerable improvement in teachers' institutes and in other facilities for the professional training of teachers while in service. Improvement likewise appears in county supervision, and in the adaptation of the work of the country school to the everyday needs of the country people.

Through some important educational legislation, enacted in the State in recent years, means have been created for increasing the efficiency of the public-school system of the State. One of the most important pieces of recent legislation is the act of March, 1913, which provides for a six months' school term. By the provisions of this act the "state equalizing fund" was created by setting aside "annually five cents of the annual *ad-valorem* tax levied and collected for state purposes on every one hundred dollars' value of real and personal property in this State." The fund thus derived is used exclusively to pay the salaries of teachers, to lengthen the school term, and to bring the term in every school district of the State to an equal length of a minimum of six months or as near thereto as the increased funds will provide. In appropriating the equalizing fund no account is taken of local tax funds in the county; and in order to participate in its distribution a county must first provide, with its own funds, a school term of at least four months, and is required, in order to provide this minimum term, to levy a special property tax of as much as fifteen cents on the hundred dollars' valuation and a capitation tax of forty-five cents. When a county has complied with these requirements it is entitled to receive appropriations from the equalizing fund. The additional tax levied by this act has made it possible to appropriate the sum of $250,000 annually to be distributed *per capita* to the public schools of the State.

The same Legislature passed an improved compulsory-attendance act. All children between eight and twelve years of age are required by this law to attend school at least four months each year. Parents are required to send their children to school and are subject to punishment for violating the provisions of the act. Attendance officers are appointed by the county board of education, and teachers are required to coöperate with them in the enforcement of the law. The county board of education is given power "to make such rules and regulations as they may deem best to secure the attendance of all children between the ages of eight and twelve years upon schools of the county." The act exempts children whose physical or mental condition renders their "attendance impracticable or inexpedient"; those who reside "two and one half miles or more" from the schoolhouse; those whose services, "because of extreme poverty," are needed for their own support or the support of their parents; and those who are without the necessary books and clothes for attending school and are unable to provide them.

Another act of great educational importance passed in 1913 is the "act to regulate and restrict labor in manufacturing establishments." By the provisions of this act no child under twelve years of age can be employed in any factory except in the capacity of an apprentice, "and only then after having attended school four months in the preceding twelve months." The employment of persons under sixteen years of age "in any mill, factory, or manufacturing establishment," between 9 P. M. and 6 A. M., is also forbidden.

Another advanced legislative step was the act providing for the establishment of farm-life schools. This step was first taken in 1911, when the Legislature passed an act to promote the teaching of agriculture and domestic science in the public high schools of Guilford County. Two years later the law was made to apply to any county in the State which complied with its provisions. Any county which provides the required equipment and an annual maintenance fund equal to the amount appropriated from the State, receives from the State an annual appropriation not to exceed $2500 for instruction in agricultural subjects, sewing, cooking, household economics, and other similar subjects, in connection with one or more of its rural high schools.[1]

Any school which applies for the benefit of this provision must first provide a building with suitable recitation rooms, laboratories, and apparatus necessary for efficient instruction in the subjects prescribed and such dormitory facilities as the county board of education may require. A farm of "not less than ten acres of good arable land," situated near the school, must also be provided, and both the site and the equipment must be approved by the state superintendent of public instruction. No part of the funds for the annual maintenance or equipment of these schools is allowed to come from the regular school funds of the county until such funds are sufficient to maintain a minimum school term of six

[1] This type of school is discussed more fully below in connection with a discussion of public high schools.

months in the county. The coöperation and often the sacrifice of the communities in which such schools are established are significant evidence of widespread interest in the movement which looks to furnishing a more adequate training for the country youth, "and of the faith of the country people in a sort of education and school that can and will provide better preparation for more profitable, more comfortable, more healthful, more joyous, and more contented living in the country." The courses of study of such schools are subject to the approval of the state superintendent, and the teachers must show "satisfactory evidence of a liberal English education, and in addition thereto special preparation and fitness for the specific branches to be taught," and they must also hold a high-school teacher's certificate in all required subjects except Greek, Latin, and modern languages.

An act to permit counties, townships, and certain school districts to issue bonds to build schoolhouses; an act to authorize the aldermen or other governing officials of towns and cities to issue bonds, upon approval by a vote of the people, for purchasing sites and erecting buildings for school purposes; an act allowing women to serve on school committees under the same conditions and restrictions as are now imposed on men; and an act to provide for the establishment of county farm-life schools, are among other advanced legislative steps taken in recent years to promote the educational development of the State.

As a result of new and improved legislation, and of interest and enthusiasm which began during the Aycock campaigns, notable progress has been made in the development of education in North Carolina in recent years. This progress appears in numerous ways. Nearly $6,000,000 was spent for public-school education in the State during the scholastic year ending June 30, 1914, an increase of more than $1,000,000 over the previous year. Of this amount about $4,000,000 was for rural and $2,000,000 for urban schools. The total amount raised by county and local district taxation for public schools in 1914 was more than $4,000,000, an increase of more than $600,000 over 1912. During the biennial period ending June 30, 1914, nearly 200 local tax districts were established by voluntary vote of the people in villages and rural communities, an average of nearly two a week during the two years. On June 30, 1914, there were 1629 such districts in the State. All the counties of the State now (1916) have from one to sixty local tax districts, and more than twenty-two per cent of the entire school fund is raised in this manner.

Progress in the building, improving, and equipping schoolhouses has also continued. During the biennial period ending June 30, 1914, more than 800 new rural schoolhouses were built at a cost of more than $800,000, an average of more than one schoolhouse for every day, a rate of building which has been maintained for more than twelve years. These houses were built according to modern plans prepared by expert architects and approved by the state superintendent of public instruction. Three fifths of all the schoolhouses in North Carolina have been built anew or rebuilt since 1902. Along with this improvement in schoolhouses there has gone a corresponding improvement in school furniture and equipment. During the biennial period ending June 30, 1914, more than $313,000 was spent for furniture and equipment in rural schools. At the close of that period more than 3400 rural schoolhouses were equipped with modern furniture. There were reported at that time, however, about 165 log schoolhouses and more than 3000 rural schoolhouses were reported furnished with home-made desks. The total value of the public-school property of the State in 1914 was more than $9,000,000; rural school property was valued at more than $5,000,000 and city school property at more than $4,000,000. This was an increase over 1912 of more than $1,600,000.

Largely as a result of the equalizing fund and the compulsory-attendance act, marked improvement has recently appeared in enrollment, average attendance, and in the length of the school term. The school population in 1914 was 525,000 white and 253,000 colored. The enrollment for the same year was 409,000 white and 189,000 colored, which was 75,000 more than in 1912, — white children 38,000 and colored children 37,000. The school population increased during these years only 16,000. The increase in average daily attendance during this biennial period was 75,000, — white children about 46,000, and colored children about 29,000. During this period there was an increase in the average term of the rural white schools of 17.8 days and of the rural colored schools of 19.3 days. The average public-school term of the entire State in 1914 was about 122 days. There has been a notable increase in the number of rural teachers and in their average annual salary. The total number of white teachers in the rural schools of the State in 1914 was 8344. Of this number 6357 held first-grade certificates, and 1884 and 103 held second- and third-grade certificates, respectively. More than 3500 had normal training, and more than 1250 held college diplomas. In the same year 2650 colored teachers were employed in rural schools. Of this number 888 held first-grade certificates, and 1706 and 56 held second- and third-grade certificates, respectively. More than 1300 had normal training, and 366 held college diplomas. The average monthly salary paid rural white teachers in 1914 was $40.74, and colored teachers received $24.69. The average monthly salary paid all public-school teachers in the State in that year was $39.81.

The State also has numerous agencies for the preparation of teachers and for their professional training while in service. The State Normal and Industrial College at Greensboro, established in 1891, and the East Carolina Teachers' Training School at Greenville, established in 1907, are the largest institutions supported by the State for the normal instruction of white teachers. The Cullowhee Normal School at Cullowhee has, since 1893, been receiving state support for the training of young men and women for teaching in the rural and village elementary schools. In 1903 the Legislature established, for the counties of Alleghany, Ashe, Watauga, Mitchell, Yancey, Caldwell, and Wilkes, a school for the training of public-school teachers and has made liberal appropriations for its maintenance since that time.[1] All of these institutions have rendered noteworthy service in promoting the educational development of the State. The Peabody School of Education of the state university is doing highly creditable work, a school of education has been maintained at Trinity College since 1910, and practically all other private institutions of collegiate rank in the State are giving courses for the preparation of teachers.

There are three normal schools for negroes in the

[1] See pp. 339, 340.

State — the State Colored Normal School at Elizabeth City, the State Colored Normal School at Fayetteville, and the Slater Industrial and State Normal School at Winston-Salem. These institutions are supported by state and local funds and appropriations from the Slater Fund, which fund has been of great service to negro education in the State, and are doing commendable work. Especially efficient work is done in these schools in the industrial and manual subjects. Courses in teacher-training are also given during the summer term of the Negro Agricultural and Technical College at Greensboro, which was established in 1891. The Indian Normal School, at Pembroke, in Robeson County, was established by the Legislature in 1887 to train teachers for the Croatan schools of that county, and is supported by state funds. The work of the negro and Indian normal schools is supervised by a special superintendent, on the staff of the state department of public instruction.[1]

Improvement in facilities for training teachers while in service has also been made in recent years. By amendments to the school law, enacted in 1909, a teachers' institute, to continue two weeks every two years, was made mandatory for every county in the State. These institutes are conducted by competent and well-trained men and women and are of much service to the

[1] Separate schools are provided for the education of "persons residing in Robeson, Sampson, and Richmond counties, supposed to be descendants of a friendly tribe once residing in the eastern portion of the State, known as Croatan Indians, and their descendants." In 1914 there were 2498 such persons of school age in these counties, with 1854 enrolled in 28 schools, which had an average term of nearly 103 days. With the exception of the provisions for separate schools the general public-school law is applicable to the education of these children. Laws of 1885, chap. 51, sec. 2; 1889, chap. 60, sec. 1; 1911, chap. 215.

public-school teachers of the State. Through the state supervisor of teacher-training, an office created in 1909, this work has been systematized and greatly improved. In 1914 teachers' institutes were held in sixty-four counties. Special arrangements are allowed in Chowan, Durham, Guilford, Orange, Pitt, Wake, and Watauga Counties for the training of teachers through special work in summer schools or otherwise. Teachers' associations have been organized in practically every county in the State with regular monthly meetings of the teachers; and reading-circles, for pursuing the professional course of study prescribed by the state department of public instruction, are also organized in many communities. In all of these agencies, and especially in that of the professional improvement of teachers, *North Carolina Education*, the official state teachers' journal, is heartily coöperating and rendering most valuable service.[1]

Encouraging progress continues also in the development of rural secondary education.[2] Since the passage of the public high-school law in 1907 there has been a gradual increase in the number of schools and their equipment, and in teaching force, enrollment, and length of school term. The report of the state inspector of high schools for 1915 showed that there were 214 of these schools in the State in that year, and that the number was gradually increasing. At that time only five counties

[1] See p. 363.
[2] The author is indebted to Professor N. W. Walker, state inspector of high schools, for practically all the material contained in the following discussion of secondary education. The material is included here practically as he prepared it. This discussion pertains primarily to rural public high schools. The city schools of North Carolina operate under special charters and are not affected by the public high-school law.

THE PRESENT SYSTEM

in the State were without these institutions — Chowan, New Hanover, Pasquotank, Perquimans, and Watauga. Eighty-nine of these schools had four-year courses, eighty-seven had three-year courses, and thirty-eight had two-year courses. The enrollment in 1915 was 8986 and the average daily attendance was 6773. The number of teachers employed in these schools at that time was 434. More than $260,000 was expended for rural secondary education in the State in that year, and the average school term was about 156 days. Considerable progress was being made in the construction of new and better buildings, in improving dormitory facilities, and in the improvement of equipment and apparatus. Since the beginning of this system of state-aided public high schools new buildings and equipment costing $2,000,000 have been provided for them and for the elementary grades operated in connection with them. Forty of these schools have provided dormitories. The accompanying table indicates the material progress that was made in this part of the educational system of the State between 1908 and 1915: —

	1908	1915
Schools in operation	145	214
Schools reporting four-year courses	2	89
Schools reporting three year courses	43	87
Schools reporting two-year courses	100	38
Number of teachers in these schools	215	434
Number of full-time teachers	173	340
Number of students enrolled	3,949	8,986
Number of fourth-year students enrolled	70	609
Amount of high-school funds raised by local taxation for maintenance	$27,474.48	$81,267.62

Amount of high-school funds contributed by the counties for maintenance...................... $21,943.65 $75,348.92
Amount spent for maintenance. .. $91,415.99 $247,253.59

In the rural high-school development of the State standardization has not been made a fetish. The chief emphasis has been on laying safe and sane foundations for a state-wide system of secondary schools which may be standardized later according to rational standards. When begun, a few years ago, these schools were engrafted upon some of the best rural elementary schools in such a way as to insure their development from the elementary school upward rather than from the college downward. This does not mean that in the effort to build up high schools for the country districts standards have been forgotten or neglected. Along with the increase in popular interest in public secondary schools, and with their increase in numbers, in financial support, teaching force, and material equipment, there have come better organization, correlation and system, and better standards of work. The school officials have come to a better understanding and appreciation of the scope and purpose of the secondary school, and realize that as an institution it has peculiar problems and unusual obligations and opportunities. The tendency now is to put into practice principles which were long ago accepted only in theory — to adapt the high school, through properly differentiated courses of instruction, to the needs of the individual pupil, and to relate it more closely to community life. This tendency is especially pronounced in the farm-life school departments.

The farm-life school in the State is in every case, except Vanceboro in Craven County and Clemmons in

Forsyth County, a department of the state-aided public high school, in which department special provision is made for affording the boys of the country districts an opportunity to study agriculture and certain allied subjects, and for affording the girls an opportunity to study home economics and certain related subjects. The funds for operating the departments of agriculture and home economics are contributed by the county and the State, and these funds are in addition to all others contributed from these sources. This type of school, known in most States as the "agricultural high school," has been given the local name of "farm-life school" in North Carolina because its primary purpose is to fit boys and girls for happier and more profitable living on the farm. Instruction in farm-life subjects in these schools is not confined, however, to pupils of the high-school grades; the farm-life department is open also to pupils of the intermediate and grammar grades. Moreover, certain kinds of extension work are carried on in the community and throughout the county, not only during the regular session, but also during vacation time.

At this time (1916) there are in operation in the State nineteen of these farm-life departments, and provision has been made for opening others. The present value of these nineteen high-school plants, in connection with which these departments are operated, is about $420,000. Improvements made during the year 1914–15 amounted to more than $178,000. The school buildings proper are worth about $240,000, and the dormitories connected with them are worth nearly $100,000. These schools own 698 acres of land worth $44,000, and barns, stock, and equipment worth nearly $20,000. For the year

1914–15 there was spent for the maintenance of these special departments the sum of $39,000, and for the year 1915–16 more than $60,000 was spent for the same purpose.

All public high schools receiving state aid are, of course, under state supervision. Their courses of study must be approved by the state superintendent of public instruction; their teachers must be examined and certificated by the state board of examiners; and their buildings and equipment must be adequate for the work which they undertake to do. The state inspector of high schools, who is appointed by the state superintendent of public instruction, gives practically all of his time to the supervision and direction of all high schools which are aided by the State.[1] Speaking of this part of the educational system of the State, Professor Walker says: —

The outlook for the larger development of this system of schools is indeed encouraging, and the remarkable progress already made is prophetic of greater expansion and growth in the near future. The present policy and ideal of those charged with the direction of educational affairs in North Carolina look to providing a system of public secondary education adequate enough to meet the State's needs for high-school training — the needs for college preparation, for cultural training, and partially, at least, the needs for vocational training. It will, of course, be some time before this system of schools will be developed to such a degree of efficiency, but the progress already made is highly encouraging for the future. For the present the effort is to develop from one to four state-aided high schools in each county, at least one of which shall be fully and adequately equipped for giving a standard four-year program of study, with courses properly differentiated

---

[1] The state inspector of high schools is also Professor of Secondary Education in the University of North Carolina.

to meet varying individual and community needs. A safe foundation has been laid, and the public high schools of the State are rapidly becoming enabled to meet any reasonable demands made upon them in the matter of preparing young people for college and for the duties of citizenship and life.

Attention should also be called to the rapidly developing city and town public high schools. These schools are not operated under the special high-school law, but under special charters. For the year 1914–15 seventy-one such schools reported to the state department of education. Forty-five of these reported four-year courses, and twenty-six reported three-year courses. In these schools 339 teachers were engaged in instructing nearly 8000 pupils. These schools are rapidly becoming standardized, and are reorganizing their work so as to meet the demands of the colleges for more advanced preparation for entrance and the demands for vocational and industrial training that come from the communities supporting them.

An increase in the number of well-trained county superintendents who are giving their entire time to the work of supervising the country school is another sign of continued educational progress. In 1914 seventy-one superintendents were devoting their entire time to this important work, an increase of twenty over 1912. These officers are organized into state and district associations, and hold annual meetings for a study of their common problems and for making improvement at this vital point. More intelligent and expert supervision is now one of the most persistent needs of rural education in North Carolina.

To promote improvement in this part of the public-school system two state agents for rural elementary schools, one for the white and one for the colored schools, give practically all their time to field work, in making a first-hand study of the needs and conditions of rural education. Their work has revealed the need for more adequate school supervision, and many county boards of education have appropriated funds for employing competent women to assist in this work. Seven counties were employing rural supervisors for white schools in 1914, and supervisors for the colored schools were employed in nineteen counties in the same year. Of these latter fifteen were employed by county funds and appropriations from the Jeanes Fund, and four received their compensation from the counties and the Slater Fund. The Peabody Rural Supervision Fund aids in the work among the white schools. Through the work of the supervisors among the negro schools improvements have been made in buildings and grounds, in sanitary conditions, and in the efficiency of the teaching. They aid the regular teachers in teaching the usual subjects, and in addition teach cooking, sewing, house-cleaning, shuck mat-making, chair-caning, basketry, and other forms of industry. They have also helped to organize "Home-Makers Clubs" among the girls and women, the purpose of which corresponds to the "Tomato Club" and "Corn Club" work carried on among the white people.

The first great educational problem [in North Carolina to-day, says Dr. J. Y. Joyner, state superintendent of public instruction] is the adaptation of the work of the rural school to the needs of rural life, to the everyday needs of the country people, that constitute more than eight tenths of our population. We must prepare country boys and girls to make the most, and to get the most, out of all that is about them — soil, plant, and animal, the three great sources of wealth in the world; and to use what they make and get in the best ways to enrich, sweeten, beautify, and uplift country life, socially, morally, intellectually, spiritually, making it the ideal life that God intended it to be, which men will seek and love to live. This includes and necessitates the development of a type of country school, by reasonable consolidation of small districts and by local taxation in larger territories, that shall not have less than three teachers and shall be adequately equipped in all respects to give such preparation, vocational and cultural, to the country boys and girls, and to become the social, intellectual, industrial, and civic center of the whole community.[1]

To the successful solution of this problem many agencies are contributing, and encouraging signs of success are rapidly appearing. The establishment of farm-life schools and of rural high schools, and special attention to the preparation of teachers for instruction and training in rural-life subjects, all show promise of almost unlimited development for "the preservation, prosperity and happiness of our rural population, for the protection and progress of our urban population and for the prevention of the decay of our whole civilization." Other hopeful and stimulating means for rural uplift are "Community Service Week," which was inaugurated in 1914 to improve the schools, roads, and social, economic, moral, and health conditions of the State, "North Carolina Day," and county commencements. County commencements mark one of the most significant forward educational steps taken in the State in recent years. In 1914 forty-one counties held commencements in which 75,000 children participated,[2] and 2500 children received certificates for the completion of

[1] *News and Observer* (Educational Edition), July, 1915.
[2] The first county commencement in North Carolina was held in Wayne County in 1910. For "North Carolina Day" see chap. xv.

the seventh grade of school work. These occasions are proving very effective means for cultivating local pride and community patriotism and sentiment for general educational improvement. In all of this work many agencies are helping: the state department of education, educational institutions, the state department of agriculture, the Farmers' Union, and the state board of health. Practical instruction in public health and hygiene is another forward step toward improvement of rural conditions, and wholesome sentiment is rapidly gaining that such instruction should be more extensively emphasized through educational agencies.

Effective means for promoting practical instruction and of connecting the work of the school with the life of the people have also appeared in the development of boys' corn clubs, girls' tomato clubs, and other forms of community organization. Through the aid of the national department of agriculture, the state department of agriculture and experiment station, the Agricultural and Mechanical College, the state department of education, coöperating with teachers, supervisors, and county superintendents, an increased interest in this work continues to develop.

In the general movement for educational improvement the North Carolina Teachers' Assembly and *North Carolina Education*, the official state teachers' journal, continue to lend invaluable aid. The state teachers' organization, which had a creditable *ante-bellum* career,[1] was revived in 1884, and since that time has been one of the most helpful agencies in educational progress and in the professional improvement and inspiration of the teachers of the State. The meetings, which are

[1] See chap. IX.

held annually during Thanksgiving week and usually in Raleigh, are largely attended by all the educational forces of the State. Numerous organizations are allied with the assembly and hold their annual meetings at the same time. Among these are the Association of Kindergarten Teachers, the Association of Primary Teachers, the Association of Grammar Grade Teachers, the State Association of County Superintendents, the Association of City School Superintendents and Principals, the Association of Music Teachers, and the Association of High School Teachers and Principals. President Robert H. Wright, of the East Carolina Teachers' Training School, is president of the assembly for 1916.

North Carolina Education, now for many years the official teachers' journal of the State, is devoted to "education, rural progress, and civic betterment." The magazine is edited by Professor E. C. Brooks, of the Trinity College School of Education, and published by Mr. W. F. Marshall, of Raleigh. It is published monthly except July and August, and since its establishment under the present editorship in September, 1906, has been of immediate help to all movements that looked to promoting educational advancement in the State, and has rendered especially valuable service in stimulating a professional spirit among the teachers of North Carolina.

The *North Carolina High-School Bulletin*, edited by State Inspector of High Schools N. W. Walker, began publication in 1910. This magazine is published quarterly by the University of North Carolina and is sent free of cost to all superintendents and high-school principals in the State. It is devoted to the improvement of the high schools, its articles dealing in the main with

364 THE PUBLIC SCHOOL IN NORTH CAROLINA

the various phases of secondary educational work, and in this field it is rendering a high order of service.[1]

Another important task facing the State to-day is the elimination of adult illiteracy. According to the federal census of 1910 fully twelve per cent of the total white population of North Carolina above ten years of age, and fourteen per cent of the white male adults, are unable to read and write. The number of white female adults who are unable to read and write is probably as large, though statistics are lacking on the subject. In 1910 the census showed that, with the exception of Louisiana and New Mexico, North Carolina had the largest number of native-born white illiterates in the United States. These conditions are arousing the people of the State to action. Through the coöperation of the North Carolina Farmers' Union and the state board of agriculture, funds have been provided for the

[1] Since the war educational journalism in North Carolina has had numerous careers. Stephen D. Pool edited the *North Carolina Journal of Education* at Raleigh in 1874 and 1875; J. F. Heitman edited the *North Carolina Educational Journal* at Chapel Hill from 1881 to 1883 and at Trinity College from 1883 to 1885; Eugene Harrell edited the *North Carolina Teacher* at Raleigh from 1883 to 1895, a magazine intended largely for graded-school teachers; W. A. Blair and J. F. Tomlinson were joint editors of the *School Teacher*, published at Winston-Salem from January to November, 1887, when Blair became sole editor and proprietor. After that time the magazine appeared for several years at Winston-Salem and Baltimore. The *Southern Educator* was edited by Edwin S. Shepp at Durham from 1890 to 1893. The *Western North Carolina Journal of Education* was published by D. L. Ellis at Fair View Collegiate Institute from August, 1891, to 1892. P. P. Claxton and Logan D. Howell began editing and managing the *North Carolina Journal of Education* at Greensboro in August, 1897, where it appeared monthly for three years. It was suspended for six months, but resumed publication in February, 1901. In July of that year it became the *Atlantic Educational Journal*, published at Richmond, Dallas, and St. Louis, with P. P. Claxton as editor.

THE PRESENT SYSTEM

employment of a secretary who is devoting his attention to the organization of a movement to reduce illiteracy. Other civic, social, educational, and benevolent organizations, and the press of the State, are lending their assistance also; and through the means of the "moonlight school," which has been found effective in Kentucky and other States and successfully used in several counties of North Carolina in 1914, rapid progress is being made in solving this problem, which is giving concern to all thoughtful people of the State.[1]

Other tendencies and tasks than those of increasing the material equipment of the schools; of improving, professionalizing, and protecting the teachers;[2] of adapting the work of the school to the life of the people; of emphasizing agricultural, industrial, and vocational training, and of eliminating adult illiteracy, are also present in education in North Carolina. The complex business life of the time has produced a condition which calls for more attention to moral instruction in the schools, in favor of which sentiment is gradually growing. The education and training of defectives is also claiming increased attention, and development in this direction will likely continue. The State School for the Blind, at Raleigh; the State School for the Deaf, at

[1] The "moonlight school" is a school conducted in the public-school building at night by volunteer teachers. For the convenience of the country people the school is conducted preferably on moonlight nights. The first of these schools for illiterate adults was established in Harnett County by J. D. Ezzell, the late superintendent of schools of that county.

[2] The State has never undertaken a pension system for its teachers, though the matter has been frequently agitated locally, and a teachers' mutual aid society was formed by the public-school teachers of Raleigh in January, 1915. This is the first step taken in North Carolina toward teachers' pensions.

Morganton; the Stonewall Jackson Training School, at Concord, for moral defectives; and the Caswell Training School, at Kinston, for mental defectives, are liberally supported by the State and are doing creditable educational work. The tendency of the State to care for its mentally deficient children and the universal growth of the humane spirit have given impetus to a rather widespread movement to secure a better organization of education and a more rational grading of school work. This movement is rapidly appearing in the larger and better regulated city systems and will perhaps eventually receive attention generally. The application of more scientific methods to educational problems is likewise a significant tendency in the State at the present time, and gives evidence of a broadening conception of educational enterprise.

THE PRESENT SYSTEM

REFERENCES

Public Laws of North Carolina; *Report* of the State Superintendent of Public Instruction for 1912–14; *North Carolina Education*, vols. i to x; *Reports* of the State Inspector of Public High Schools, 1907–08 to 1914–15; *Report* of the Supervisor of Teacher-Training, 1912–14; *Reports* of the State Agents of Rural Schools, 1914.

SUGGESTIONS FOR FURTHER STUDY

1. What improvements in supervision are being made in your county?
2. How did your county observe "North Carolina Day" last year? How did it observe "Community Service Week"?
3. How does the compulsory-attendance law work in your community? What are the difficulties of enforcing the law?
4. How many rural high schools in your county? How many farm-life schools?
5. What is being done in your school to give instruction and training in domestic science and industrial work?
6. How have the qualifications of the teachers improved in your county in recent years?
7. What is being done to promote the professional development of the teachers in your county?
8. What is the most difficult educational problem in your community?
9. What is your most difficult problem as a teacher?
10. How many commencements has your county held? What has been the value of such occasions to your community?
11. What is your community doing to reduce adult illiteracy?
12. How many moonlight schools were conducted in your county last year? How many this year? What has been the result of this work?

CHAPTER XVII [1]

WHAT OF THE FUTURE?

THE history of education in North Carolina is an inspiring story of the heroic struggle of the common man for equality of opportunity in education that he and his might have equality of opportunity in life. It is a story of a struggle first against the hindering hand of inherited aristocracy, tradition, and prejudice, reaching out from a revered but dead past, and later against the ruin, poverty, and demoralization of a devastating civil war. This story has been well told in the preceding pages, and the author has rendered a valuable service to this and subsequent generations of North Carolinians.

The names of Murphey and Wiley, of McIver and Aycock, and of other great leaders in this glorious struggle, shall shine on the pages of North Carolina's history and be cherished in the hearts of her people until time shall be no more. But in a democracy the burden of every battle for better education must be borne at last by the multitudes and the victory finally won by them. Let us not forget, then, the common man and the common woman, — common in numbers, uncommon in character and consecration, — in shop and field and office, in home and schoolroom and market-place, through whose quiet labor and unheralded sacrifice, through whose dauntless courage and deep conviction, so many of the dreams of these great leaders and prophets of

[1] The author is indebted to Dr. James Y. Joyner, state superintendent of public instruction, for this chapter.

WHAT OF THE FUTURE? 369

education have been turned into splendid realities and so many of their hopes into happy fulfillment. May this story of our educational struggle and achievement in past and present serve to inspire all who read it with a larger hope for the future, to quicken their zeal and strengthen their arm for the larger educational tasks that lie before us.

For what has been done let us thank God and from it take courage. But, after all, looked at in the large, how small indeed does seem the little done, how great the much to be done, and how little the time to do it.

With 13,255 teachers employed in the white and colored schools of North Carolina, only about one fifth of whom have college diplomas, less than one half of whom have had any special professional training, but little more than one half of whom have had as much as four years' experience in teaching, there is still much to be done. More money must be spent, more legislation must be enacted, and more must be accomplished for elevating, standardizing, and improving the profession of teaching and for guaranteeing to it, the children, and the public the protection which they deserve.

With an average annual school term for the United States of 158.1 days, an average annual school term in many States of 180 days, and with an average annual school term of only 121.98 days in North Carolina, much remains to be done to increase school funds by state appropriation, by county and district taxation, and otherwise, so as to lengthen the school term of the State to eight or ten months.

Of the 7565 rural white and colored schools in the State, nearly seventy per cent of them are still one-teacher schools in which seven grades of work are required. These schools are wholly inadequate for the task of properly preparing country boys and girls for citizenship and for the other duties of country life. Here also much work remains to be done. By conservative consolidation and by transportation and otherwise, these schools must be made into community-center schools, with more and better teachers and better equipment, so that they will more adequately perform the true mission of the country school in ministering to the social, intellectual, moral, industrial, and agricultural needs of the country community.

With 12.3 per cent of the total white population of North Carolina over ten years of age, 14 per cent of the total white voting population, and 31.9 per cent of the negro population, unable to read and write, according to the United States census of 1910, a great task and a great duty confront us for the reduction and elimination of this menacing illiteracy.

With only seventy-six of the one hundred counties of the State employing whole-time superintendents and only sixteen counties employing assistant superintendents and supervisors for the rural schools, much remains to be done for the adequate supervision and direction of these schools.

With the average monthly salary of rural white teachers in North Carolina only $40.74, and the average annual salary of the same teachers only $235.27; with the, average monthly salary of colored teachers only $24.69, and the average annual salary of the same teachers only $128.42, much more money is needed. Funds must be supplied to increase their compensation, so as to command and retain for this most delicate and difficult work the type of men and women needed for it, in order

WHAT OF THE FUTURE?

to justify them in the long and expensive preparation necessary for professional and masterful teaching.

With a total school population of 778,283 from six to twenty-one years of age, only 77.2 per cent of which is enrolled, and only about 53 per cent of which is in continuous daily attendance in the public schools, much work still remains to be done. Through the enforcement, enlargement, and improvement of our compulsory attendance laws and through the cultivation of educational sentiment and interest, this multitude of children must be brought into the schools and kept there long enough to give them at least a mastery of the rudiments of education.

With only 214 regularly established rural high schools, enrolling only 8,986 country boys and girls and only 19 farm-life schools, there still remains great need for more money and more work. The number of these schools must be increased and the development of the work of those already established must be enlarged for the preparation of a larger number of country boys and girls for college and for life through adequate high-school and vocational training.

Such are some of the hard but glorious educational tasks and duties that lie before our people. What a splendid opportunity for constructive educational work and development the future holds for patriotic citizens of the State! What a joyous privilege to every son and daughter of the State to have a part in such a work!

From the evidence of our recent progress, indicating on the part of our people an aroused public sentiment, a determination to make adequate provision for the education of their children as rapidly as their means will permit, a sacrifice in time, convenience, and money, beautiful and sometimes touching to behold, are we not justified in predicting the rapid development of a public-school system in North Carolina that shall be adequate to the demands of this age of universal education and to the stupendous task of training for citizenship and service, according to their various capacities, all of her children white and black?

Within the next quarter of a century or less we confidently expect to see within reasonable reach of every country and city child in the State a complete system of public education. This system will include elementary and high schools adequately equipped with comfortable houses, ample grounds, and trained teachers. The schools will be efficiently supervised by competent superintendents, maintained for eight or ten months in the year by state, county, and district taxation. Every child will be required to secure at home in the elementary school a mastery, at least, of the rudiments of learning that constitute the foundation of all education and of all preparation for intelligent citizenship and efficient service. Every child who has the desire and capacity will be afforded opportunity to secure near home, in county and township high schools, fuller preparation for college or for life, through courses of study shaped to meet the needs and natural adaptations of all for literary, professional, commercial, and industrial life.

These elementary and high schools, planted in the rural districts within reach of the rural population, will become the centers of a new social, intellectual, civic, industrial, and agricultural life. They will be the effective means of breaking up the isolation, the loneliness, and the colorlessness of rural life. They will elevate to a higher plane of intelligence, labor, and service the

WHAT OF THE FUTURE? 373

great masses of the country people and prevent the degeneration of this biggest and best part of our population into an Old-World peasantry. Through the dissemination of intelligence and special training for their work, adapted to their environment, among the masses of the country folks, our farms will become more productive; our waste lands will be reclaimed; our roads will be improved; modern conveniences that increased wealth can command will be brought to the farmers' doors, and rural life will be made more livable.

Such a system of schools do we foresee in the near future for the Old North State, extending its educational ladder, without a missing rung, from the doorstep of the humblest cottage in the remotest rural district to the doorway of the highest university or college of State or of Nation. This is the lever that shall uplift the State and roll it in another course.

For such a system of schools the foundations, deep and broad, have been completed. Most of the constructive work still lies before us, but we shall do it in another generation. We must do it largely by ourselves. By sympathetic coöperation others can help us to help ourselves, but we cannot successfully engraft the work of others upon our foundations. An effective educational system must ever be an organic growth; so must ours grow out of our own life and heart and be shaped largely by our own needs and the spirit and genius of our own people, embodying in itself the best ideals of our past, but ever broadening to comprehend also the safest educational ideals of the present and of the future in all the world.

Let all who love the State and believe in the splendid possibilities of her children, and in her wonderful material resources, rally to the standard of the schools and labor without ceasing for their improvement until every child in North Carolina shall have as good a chance, through as good a school, as any other child in all the world for the highest development of every power within him and of every resource about him.

INDEX

"A. B." articles on education by, 80.
Academy movement, 44–62; decline of, 54.
Academies, early, 37–43; number chartered from 1785 to 1825, 49–53; curricula of, 54–56; physical equipment of, 56; tuition charges in, 56, 57; salaries of teachers in, 56, 58; teachers in, 58; methods of teaching in, 58, 59; jealous of the public school system, 150.
Act to encourage local taxation, 325.
Adams, Rev. James, missionary, 6, 9.
Adult illiteracy, 364.
Agents of rural schools, 359, 360.
Agricultural and Mechanical College for Negroes, 322.
Agricultural education, 257.
Alamance County, educational conditions in, in 1857, 204, 205.
Alderman, Edwin A., 321, 322.
Alexander, Rev. Joseph, 40.
Allen, Miss Mariah, 58.
American education, periods of, 138, 139.
American Missionary Association, 243.
American Unitarian Association, 242.
Ante-bellum educational practice, 192–211.
Antioch College, 184, note.
Appalachian Training School, 339, 340, 352.
Apprenticeship system, 12, 14–30.
Appropriations for schools, 35, 326, 337.
Archibald, Rev. Robert, 41.

Arguments against schools, 118, 119.
Arithmetics used before the war, 197.
Ashe, S. P., 79.
Asheboro Normal School, 259.
Ashley, Rev. S. S., 227, 228, 239, 251; reports of, 239 *ff*.
Association of City School Superintendents and Principals, 363.
Association of Grammar Grade Teachers, 363.
Association of High School Teachers, and Principals, 363.
Association of Kindergarten Teachers, 363.
Association of Music Teachers, 363.
Atlantic Educational Journal, 364, note.
Attempts at readjustment (1877–1900), 294–328.
Attempts to preserve the schools during the war, 184.
Avery, Waightstill, library of, 11.
Aycock, Charles B., educational services of, 326, 327, 333, 342, 343, 368; and the revival, 329–44; inaugural message of, 329; philosophy of, 342, 343.

Bacon, Alice M., quoted, 215.
Bacon's Rebellion, 1.
Baltimore Association of Friends, 242.
Baptists, 4.
Barksdale Case, 316, 317.
Barnard, Henry, 158, 161, 218.
Barr, Rev. John, library of, 11.
Bath, library at, 7–9.
Battle, Kemp P., 251, 303, note.
Battle, Judge W. H., 257.

INDEX

Beaufort County, petition from, 81.
Beginnings of Reconstruction, 212-37.
Benbury, Thomas, 45.
Berkeley, Governor of Virginia, 1.
Bingham, Robert, 257.
Blackboards, 59, 60, 209, 210; scarce in "old field" schools, 152.
Blair, W. A., 364, note.
Blake, H. B., 259.
Blakely Gazette, 77.
Blind, State school for, 365.
Bray, Rev. Thomas, aided establishment of libraries, 7.
Brooks, Eugene C., 334, 342, 363; quoted, 172.
Burgwin, John, library of, 11.
Burke County, educational conditions in, in 1857, 200-04.
Burrington, George, Governor, instructions to, 4, 5.

Caldwell, Dr. David, library of, 11; educational influence of, 39; "Log College" of, 39.
Caldwell, Dr. Joseph, 116, 117; letters on education by, 120-29.
Caldwell, Governor T. R., 251, 257.
Campbell, J. D., 177.
Canby, General E. R. S., 226.
Cape Fear Teachers' Association, 259.
Carolina Watchman, 144.
Caswell, Richard, 45.
Caswell Training School, for mental defectives, 366.
Cathcart, William, library of, 11.
Central North Carolina Teachers' Association, memorial of, 297.
Charity, element of, in the school system, 66.
Charlotte Democrat, 184.
Child labor law, 347, 348.
Chowan Precinct Court, records of, 21, 22.
Church wardens, duties of, 16, 17, 25.

City school systems, 268, 283, 341.
Civil Rights Bill, 253, 254; effect of, in North Carolina, 255; in Virginia, 255, note.
Civil War, attempts to preserve the schools during, 184.
Classical schools, 38-41.
Classics, in academies, 54-56.
Claxton, P. P., 364, note.
Clio's Nursery and Science Hall, 39, 40.
Colonial period, slow educational growth during, 1, 2.
Community Service Week, 361.
Comparison of reconstruction and *ante-bellum* conditions, 263-69.
Compulsory education, 257.
Compulsory school, law, 347.
Confederate securities, 185.
Congressional plan of Reconstruction, 213, 220, 225, 227.
Connor, R. D. W., quoted, 324, 326, 327, 330, 334.
Consolidation of schools, 370.
Constitutional convention (1865), 221; (1868), 186; composition of, 227; committee on education in, 228; work of, ratified, 229; educational provisions of, 230; (1875), 261.
Constitutional provision for schools, 81.
Coon, Charles L., 339.
Corn Club work, 360, 362.
Counties released from levying school taxes during the war, 103.
Counties, adopting the first school system, 145.
County commencements, 361, and note.
County superintendents, salaries of, in 1890, 320; improvement in, 359.
Course of study in 1869, 235.
Court records of educational importance, 19, 20, 21, 22.
Craven, Braxton, established the first state normal school in North Carolina, 171-73; educa-

INDEX

tional philosophy of, 173; interest in educational journalism, 173, note; normal school work after the war, 302, and note, 303, note.
Crowfield Academy, 39.
Cullowhee Training School, 321, 352.
Cumberland College, 48.
Curriculum of academies, 54–56; of the early school system, 147; of the "old field" schools, 151, 152; before the war, 192, 193.
Curry, J. L. M., 322.

Davidson Academy, 48.
Davidson College, 39.
Deaf, State school for, 365.
Debts left by Reconstruction, 295.
"Declaration against Illiteracy," 332, 333.
Defect of the early school system, 148.
Dickinson, Matthew, 57.
Difficulties in the way of education, 121–24.
Doherty, W. H., 184, note.
Drummund, William, first "governor of Albemarle," 2.
Durham, Plato, 227, 228.

East Carolina Teachers' Training School, 309, 340, 352.
Edenton, library in, 9, 10; act to build schoolhouse in, 34, 35; attempts to establish a school in, 37.
Edgecombe County, educational meeting in, 80.
Education, under lords proprietors, 1–13; under royal rule, 32–43; first public expenditures for, 36; first legislative committee on, 69; held in low estimation, 128; of the freedmen advocated by Calvin H. Wiley, 188.
Educational Association, formation of, 176, 259.

Educational convention, (1873), 256, 257; (1874), 258; program of, 258; (1902), 331.
Educational Journal, 180, 257.
Educational journalism, need for, 174, note; since the war, 364, note.
Educational practice before the war, 192–211.
Educational sentiment, growth of, 113–37; conditions in 1836, 136; campaign of 1839, 144; in 1840, 146; during the Civil War, 181, 182, 186; during Reconstruction, 239 ff.; between 1885 and 1900, 315–28; in 1900, 330; in 1902, 332, 333.
Edward VI, suppression of monasteries by, 15.
Elizabeth, poor-relief enactments of, 15, 16.
Ellendale Teachers' Institute, 258.
Ellis, D. L., 364, note.
Emigration, problem of, 129, 130; evils of, 131.
England, educational philosophy of, in the seventeenth century, 3; boys sent to, for educational advantages, 32; argument of, against public schools, 69, note.
English Church, encouraged intellectual growth, 5.
English Schism Act, enforced in the colony, 5; reproduction of, 5; influence of, 12.
Enrollment, in 1914, 371.
Equalizing fund, 346.
Established Church, 12; and the Schism Act, 37. See also English Church, State Church.
European influences, 14.
Evergreen, 174, note.
Ezzell, J. D., 365, note.

Fair View Collegiate Institute, 364, note.
Family Lyceum, 133.
Farmers' Alliance, 322, 323.
Farmers' Union, 362, 364.

Farm Life Schools, 348, 349, 356, 357, 358.
Fayetteville, memorial by citizens of, 135.
First public school law, 96, 140–44.
Fiske, Rev. F. A., 243, 277.
Flinn, Andrew, 58.
Fourteenth Amendment, 226.
Free school, bill to establish, 35.
Free-school idea, growth of, 84–85.
Freedmen, education of, 242, 243.
Freedmen's Bureau, work of, 243; mistakes of, 243, 265.
Freedmen's Commission, 243.
French, John R., 227.
Friends, Baltimore Association of, 242; education work of, 244, 245. See Quakers.
Friends' Freedmen's Aid Association, 243.
Fusion Legislature of 1895, 323, 324.
Future of the schools, outlook for, 368–74.

General statements concerning education in the South, 212–14.
Geography, methods of teaching, 59; late in entering the curriculum, 197; textbooks in, used before the war, 197–98.
Germans, educational influence of, 38.
Gordon, Rev. William, missionary, 9.
Graded schools, early movement for, 183; 313, 323.
Graham, John W., 227, 229, 232.
Graham, Joseph, library of, 12.
Graham, William A., 94.
Grammar, early textbooks on, 198, 199; variety of texts before the war, 199.
Grant, Major H. L., 227.
Granville Hall, 45.
Greensboro Patriot, 188, note.
Griffin, Charles, first professional teacher in North Carolina, 6.

Hall, Dr. James, library of, 11; school of, 39, 40.

Harrell, Eugene, 364, note.
Harris, Robert, 302.
Hart, Albert Bushnell, quoted, 216.
Haywood, John, 80.
Heath, Robert, charter to, 3.
Heitman, J. F., 364, note.
Henry VIII, suppression of monasteries by, 15.
Hill, Charles A., plan for a school fund, 79, 82.
Hill, J. A., resolution of, 78.
History, late in entering the curriculum, 199, 200; textbooks on, before the war, 199, 200.
Hodgson, John, library of, 11.
Holden, W. W., 221, 226, 230, 231, 249, 261.
Holmes, Gabriel, interest in agricultural education, 77.
"Home geography," 198.
"Home-Makers' Clubs," 360.
Hood, Rev. J. W., assistant superintendent of schools, 244, 245.
Hooper, William, library of, 11.
Howard, General Oliver O., quoted, 216.
Howell, Logan D., 364, note.

Illiteracy, 341, 342, 370; "Declaration against," 332, 333.
Immigration encouraged, 1, 2; slight, before 1728, 2.
Indians, schools for, 353, and note; normal school for, 353.
Influence of Reconstruction on education, 263–69.
Innes, James, library of, 11; will of, 46, 47.
Innes Academy, in Wilmington, 46, 47.
Institutes, 322, 323.
Internal improvements, committee on, in 1833, 130; slow progress of, 132.
Iredell, James, library of, 11.

Jarvis, Thomas J., 249, 304, 305, 308, 310, 334, 335; quoted, 304, 305, 308, 334, 335; excerpt from will of, 310.

INDEX

Jeanes Fund, 350.
Jefferson, Thomas, 343.
Johnston, Samuel, library of, 10, 11.
Johnston, Gabriel, library of, 10, 11; message of 33, 34; Assembly's reply to, 34, 35.
Jones, Willie, library of, 11.
Joyner, James Y., 333, 334, 342, 360, 361, 368; quoted, 108, 336, 337, 360, 361; chapter by, 368–74.
Journal of Education, aided by the Peabody Board, 286, 287.

Kenney, Charles R., plan of, for schools, 115.
Ker, Rev. David, 57; his school near Fayetteville, 41.
Kindergarten work, beginnings of, 303, note.

Lack of qualified teachers, 126, 127.
Laflin, General Byron, 227.
Lancaster, Joseph, 73; school system of, 60, 61.
Lancasterian schools, 73; method of, 75.
Land values, decrease of, 129.
Latin Grammar School, 44.
Law, first, of educational importance in the colony, 36, 37; first, for public schools, 96, 140–44; of 1869 compared with *antebellum* legislation, 236; of 1869, provisions of, 234–36.
Laws, first printed collection of, 32.
Lay readers, the first teachers in the colony, 3.
Legislative appropriations, made but not paid, 241, 242.
Legislature, expense of, 117, note; of 1868, composition of, 231.
Letter against schools, 118, 119.
Lexington Normal School, 259.
Liberty Hall Academy, 41, 45, 48.
Libraries, early, 7–12; circulating, 12; in academies, 56.

Library associations, need for, 165, 174, note.
Liquors, import duty on, for education, 37.
Literary Board, report of, in 1838, 96.
Literary Fund, created, 65, 88; 84–112; sources of, 88; early growth of, 89, 90; idle and unproductive, 90; poorly managed 91, 92; increased by surplus revenue, 93; first appropriations from, 97, 98; income of and disbursements from, 98; threatened by the war, 101, 102; effort to protect during the war, 102, 103, 104; losses of, 100, 101, 104, 105; not used for war purposes, 185; condition of, in 1869, 105; provision for, in 1868, 105; in 1876, 105, 106; from 1870 to 1903, 106, 107; reorganization of, in 1903, 107–08; operation of, since 1903, 108–10; schoolhouses built by, 108–10; income from, small, 246.
Local taxation, beginning of, 97; first in the State, 145; in 1859, 180; in 1860, 186; act to encourage, 325.
"Log College" of Dr. Caldwell, 39.
Log schoolhouses, in 1914, 351.
Lord Bishop of London, license of, required of teachers, 4, 5.
Lords proprietors, education under, 1–13; charters to, provided for State Church, 3.
Lottery, privilege of, allowed, 45.

Maclaine, Archibald, library of, 11.
Mann, Horace, 158, 161, 184, note, 188, 218.
Maps, used in academies, 55, 56.
Marshall, W. F., 363.
Martin Academy, 48.
Martin, William, bill by, 76.
Mashburn, early teacher, 7.
Masses, attempts at educational improvement of, 33–37.

380 INDEX

Material equipment of the schools before the war, 200.
Mecklenburg Declaration of Independence, 41.
Memorial of citizens of Fayetteville, 135; of the Central North Carolina Teachers' Association, 297, 298; of the State Teachers' Association, 305, 306.
Mental defectives, school for, 366.
Merrimon, A. S., 254, 257.
Methods of education, discussed, 125-29.
Methods of teaching, in academies, 58, 59, 60; in "old field" schools, 152.
Military governments supersede State Governments, 226.
Mixed-school question, 231, 232, 234, 253.
Monasteries, suppression of, by Henry VIII and Edward VI, 15.
Moonlight schools, 365, and note.
Moral defectives, school for, 366.
Mordecai, Jacob, 59.
Morse's *Geography*, 198.
Moseley, Edward, library of, 9, 10.
Murphey, Archibald D., 59, 69, 82, 368; report of, and plan for schools, 70-74.
McAden, Rev. Hugh, early teacher, 38.
McCorkle, Rev. Samuel C., and Zion Parnassus, 40.
McIver, Alexander, 251, 254.
McIver, Charles D., 321, 322, 331, 333, 334, 335, 336, 342, 368.
McPheeters, Rev. Dr., 58.
McQueen, Hugh, bill by, 115, 134, 135.

Nash, Abner, 45.
National Teachers' Association in 1865, 213.
Needs of the present school system, 368-74.
Negroes, tax on, for schools proposed, 35; in Constitutional Convention of 1868, 227; during Reconstruction, 238; provisions for education of, 265; schools for, aided by Peabody Board, 281, 282, 284, 285, 286, 287; normal schools for, 312; normal instruction of, 323, 352, 353; agricultural and mechanical college for, 353; supervision of elementary schools of, 360.
Newbern, private school, in, 36; school chartered in, 37.
Newbern Spectator, 145.
New England Freedmen's Relief Association, 242.
News and Observer, 361, note.
New York National Freedmen's Relief Association, 242, 243.
Noisy schools, 203.
Normal College, 171, 172, 173.
Normal schools, 257; established, in 1877, 261, 262; work of, 300-02; established in, 1881, 312; for negroes, 339, 353.
Normal school work, beginnings of, 171-73; 184, note; 258, 259, 321; at Trinity College, 302.
North Carolina Day, 338, 361, and note.
North Carolina Education, 354, 362, 363.
North Carolina Educational Association, 103.
North Carolina Educational Journal, 364, note.
North Carolina High School Bulletin, 363.
North Carolina Journal of Education, establishment of, 177, 178, 187, 364, note.
North Carolina, law of 1715, 23, 30; of 1755, 25, 26, 29, 30; of 1760, 26, 27; of 1762, 26, 28, 30, and note; of 1764, 27; of 1777, 28; influence of its *antebellum* schools, 63, 64; constitutional provisions for schools, 64.
North Carolina Reader, 188.
North Carolina Teacher, 364, note.
North Carolina Teachers' Assembly, 362, 363.

INDEX

North Carolina Teachers' Association, 302.

"Old Blue-Back" speller, 194, 195.
"Old Field," article by, criticizing the policy of the Legislature, 133.
"Old field" schools, description of, 150, 151, 152; jealous of the public-school system, 150; teachers in, 150, 151; curriculum of, 151, 152; methods of teaching in, 152.
Olney's *Geography*, 198.
One-teacher schools, 369.
Orange County Sunday-School Union, petition from, 81.
Outside educational agencies during Reconstruction, 242, 243.
Oxford Mercury, 159.

"Pædophilus," letter by, 119, 120.
Pattillo, Rev. Henry, library of, 12, 45, 46.
Peabody Board, work of, 215, 242, 253; opposed to mixed schools, 254, 255; 261, 262, 301, 302, 341.
Peabody Fund, 48; work of, 271–92; creation of, 272; States aided by, 276; amounts distributed from, in the South, 277; towns aided by, in North Carolina, 279, 280, 281, 282, 284, 285, 286, 287, 288; results of, 289–92.
Peabody, George, 271, 273.
Peabody Normal College, 48, 289.
Peabody Rural Supervision Fund, 360.
Peabody School of Education, 352.
Peabody Trustees, 272; plan of, 272, 273, 274.
Pegram, William H., 303, note.
Pensions, for teachers, 365, note.
Perquimans Precinct Court, records of, 19, 20, 21.
Pestalozzi, 73.

Physical equipment of academies, 56.
Pinewoods Teachers' Institute, 259.
Poe, Clarence, quoted, 324, 326, 327, 330, 334.
Pollock, Mrs. Louise, 303, note.
Pollock, Miss Susie, 303, note.
Pool, Stephen D., 260, 364, note.
Poor, duties of overseers of, 16, 17; authority transferred to overseers of, 28; plan for the education of, 73–74; education of, proposed, 79–80.
Poor-law and apprenticeship system, 12, 14–31.
Poplar Tent Academy, 41.
Population of North Carolina, 2, 32, 116, 129.
Presbyterian General Assembly, 243.
Presbyterians, influence of, 32, 38–40.
Present needs of the schools, 368–74.
Present school system, 345–67.
Presidential plan of Reconstruction, 220, 226.
Primers, used before the war, 195.
Princeton College, influence of, 11, 32, 38, 58.
Printing-press, first in the colony, 32.
Program of educational convention in 1874, 258.
Progress of education in 1858, 178; between 1885 and 1900, 315–28.
Protestant Episcopal Church, 243.
Providence Academy, 41.
Prussian school system, admired by Wiley, 189.
Public education, beginnings of, 138–57.

Qualifications of teachers before the war, 200.
Quakers, interest in education, 6, 38. *See* Friends.

INDEX

Queen's College, first institution chartered by the State, 40, 41.
Queen's Museum, 40, 41.

Race riots, 324.
Rainsford, Rev. Giles, missionary, 7, 9.
Raleigh Mutual Aid Society, 365, note.
Raleigh Register, 80, 118, 119, 145.
Raleigh Sentinel, 227.
Raleigh Standard, 184.
Raleigh Star, 134, 144.
Reading books used before the war, 196.
"Rebel question," 226.
Rebellion, Bacon's, 1.
Recent educational progress, 349–52.
Reconstruction, beginnings of, 212–37; congressional plan of, 213, 220, 225, 227; presidential plan of, 220, 226; benefits of, 267, 268; education during, 238–70; overthrow of, 261; evils of, 266, 267; influence of, on education, 263, 269.
Reed, Rev. James, sermon on education by, 36.
Reform Legislature of 1870, 316; composition of, 249.
Reid, James, 251.
Religious dissensions, unfavorable to educational growth, 2, 3.
Rigsbee *vs.* the town of Durham, 319.
Riots, in Wilmington, 324.
Royal rule, education under, 32–42.
Ruffner, Henry, 299, note.
Rural elementary education, progress in, 340, 341.
Rural high schools, 340, 354–59.
Rural libraries, 337.
Rural secondary education, 354–59.
Rural schools, agents for, 359, 360.
Rutherfordton Gazette, 145.

Salaries of teachers, 370, 371; in academies, 56–58.
Salary of state superintendent reduced, 249.
Salisbury high school, 40.
Scarborough, John C., 261, 304, 305, note, 310, note.
Schism Act, 5, 12, 37, 41.
Schoolbooks recommended by Wiley, 194.
School fund proposed, 69, 79, 81.
School funds, influence of, 85; purposes of, 85–86; in other States, 88; poorly managed, 98, 99, 100, 101.
Schoolhouses, 56.
Schoolmasters, scarcity of, 32; occupation of, scorned, 128.
School population, 371.
School statistics (1857), 174, 175; (1858), 179, 180; (1860), 181; (1869), 241, 242; (1870), 245; (1872), 251, 252; (1873), 255, 256; (1874), 260; (1884), 313, 314, 315; (1914), 350–52; 163, 164, 165, 168, 303, 304.
School system, introduction of, in 1839, 146, 147.
School taxes, authority for, 262.
School Teacher, 364, note.
Science Hall and Clio's Nursery, 39, 40, 45.
Scotch and Scotch-Irish, influence of, 11; immigration of, 37, 38.
Sears, Rev. B., 253, 254, 262; made general agent of the Peabody Fund, 273; 277, 279.
Separate schools, discussion of, 228, 229, 231.
Shepp, Edwin S., 364, note.
Sickles, General David E., 226.
Silent schools, 203.
Simmons, W. G., 257.
Slater Fund, 353, 360.
Slaves, increase of, 129.
Smith Academy, 46.
Social and economic conditions, 129–32.
Society for the Propagation of the

INDEX

Gospel in Foreign Parts, 6–10, 36.
Soldiers' Memorial Society of Boston, 242.
Southern Educator, 364, note.
Southern Education Board, 331, 336, 341.
Southern education, loose statements concerning, 212–14.
Southern Index, 173, note.
Southern South, quoted from, 216.
Southern Weekly Post, 160.
"Spelling-bees," 195.
Spelling-books, before the war, 194, 195.
State Association of County Superintendents, 339, 363.
State Church, 3. *See* English Church, Established Church.
State Literary Fund, 338, 339.
State Literary and Historical Association, 338.
State Normal and Industrial College, 322, 336, 352.
State School for the Blind, 365.
State School for the Deaf, 365.
State superintendent of public instruction, office abolished, 189, 190, 223, 224.
State Teachers' Association, 166, 180; memorial of, 305.
Stevens, Thaddeus, 218, 226.
Stonewall Jackson Training School, 366.
Sugar Creek Presbyterian Church, 40, 41.
Sumner, Charles, 283.
Sunday-School Union of Orange County, petition of, 81.
Superintendent, provision for office of, 156; duties of, 156; office of, abolished, 189, 190, 223, 224.
Supervision, lack of, before the war, 155.
Supervisors, of rural elementary schools, 341.
Supreme court decisions, 246, 249, 316–19.
Surplus revenue, 93, 94, 95, 96, 97, 136.

Tate, Rev. James, 39.
Tate's Academy, 39.
Taxation, fear of, 65; beginnings of, local, 97; hostility to, 113; authority for, 262; for school purposes, 308.
Taylor, Rev. Ebenezer, missionary, 9.
Teacher-training, 352, 353.
Teachers' institutes, first in the State, 184, and note; held in 1872, 252; in 1874, 258, 259.
Teachers' Reading Circle, work of, 341.
Teachers, scarcity of, 2, 3, 245; required to be licensed by Lord Bishop of London, 4, 5; in academies, salaries of, 56–58; movement to organize association of, 119, 120; description of, 126, 127; exempted from certain duties, 148; in the "old field" schools, 150, 151; comparison of salaries of, 170, note; 180, note; 370, 371; aided by, the Peabody Fund, 282, 284, 286, 287; present condition of, 369.
Teaching, methods of, in academies, 58, 59.
Term, present length of school, 369.
Textbooks before the war, 193–200; lack of uniformity of, 193; distributed through the Peabody Board, 245, 257, 277, 278; in Virginia, 194, note.
The American Universal Geography (Morse), 198.
"The Educational Duties of the Hour," 213.
The North Carolina Institute of Education formed, 120.
Thyatira Circulating Library, 11.
Tomato Club work, 360, 262.
Tomlinson, J. F., 364, note.
Tomlinson, Thomas, private school of, 36; assistance solicited for, 36.

INDEX

Toon, Thomas F., 330, 333.
Tourgée, Albion W., 227.
Transportation of pupils, 370.
Trinity College, 173; normal school work at after the war, 302; School of Education of, 352.
Tuition, in academies, 56, 57.
Tutorial instruction, for the well-to-do, 12.

Uniformity of textbooks, lack of, before the war, 193; urged by Wiley, 193.
Union Institute, 171, 172.
Union County, educational conditions in, in 1857, 205, 206.
University of North Carolina, chartered, 64, 65.
University of Nashville, 48.
University School of Education, 352.
Urmstone, Rev. John, missionary, 8.

Vance, Governor, 104, 184, 297, 298, 300, 302.
Vaughan, George, offer of, to aid education of Indians, 35.
Vestry Act, of 1701, 3; of 1715, 3; of 1764, 27, 28; of 1777, 28.
Virginia, educational conditions in, in 1857, 154; influence of, on North Carolina, 16, 18, 29; law of, 1743, 17, 19, 24; of 1705, 24; of 1748, 24, 29; Literary Fund of, 69, note; plan for education in, in 1817, 75; textbooks in, 194, note.
Vogell, Rev. H. C., 279.

Walker, John M., report of, 70.

Walker, N. W., 354, note; quoted, 258, 359, 363.
Wallis, Rev. James, 41.
Warren, E. J., 249.
Washington College, 48.
Welker, Rev. G. W., 232, 251.
Wentworth, educational rally at, 334, 335.
Western Carolinian, 78, 80.
Western North Carolina Journal of Education, 364, note.
Wiley, Calvin H., first superintendent of public instruction, 63, 101, 102, 104, 146, 148, 150, 155, 159, 223, 246, 257, 277, 368; appointed superintendent, 156; educational revival under, 158 *ff.*; early work for the schools, 161 *ff.*; school reports of, 163 *ff.*; difficulties confronting, 165 *ff.*; educational philosophy of, 187; value of his reports, 187; advocated the education of the freedmen, 188; textbooks by, 188; proposed for superintendent in 1872 and 1876, 190; general agent of the American Bible Society, 190.
Wilkes County, first educational meeting in, 207–09.
Winwright, James, will of, 47, 48.
Wise, Governor of Virginia, 154, 155.
Woman's Betterment Association, 336.
Women teachers, scarcity of, 165.
Worth, Jonathan, 226.
Wright, Robert H., 363.

Yancey, Bartlett, 82.

Zion, Parnassus, 40.